Corporate Policy and Governance

Management: Mastering Complexity
Volume 2

Fredmund Malik

Corporate Policy and Governance

How Organizations Self-Organize

Translated from German by Jutta Scherer,
JS textworks (Munich, Germany)

Campus Verlag
Frankfurt/New York

The original edition was published in 2008 by Campus Verlag with the title *Unternehmens-politik und Corporate Governance. Wie Organisationen sich selbst organisieren.*
All rights reserved.

ISBN 978-3-593-39545-6

Cover design: Hißmann, Heilmann, Hamburg
Typesetting: Publikations Atelier, Dreieich
Illustrations: Alex van de Hoef, Dreieich
Printing: Druckhaus "Thomas Müntzer", Bad Langensalza
Printed in Germany

This book is also available as an E-Book
www.campus.de

For Hans Ulrich,
who gave me the freedom and the courage
to think beyond limits

Contents

What This Is All About

There are many ways to systematically solve problems – but only one way to systematically avoid them: the cybernetic way. The design of a system to avoid problems must begin with the permanent realities at the core of all beings and things – their *function*. At the same time, it needs to integrate today's perception of the problem if it is to be understood at all. This is why I gave this book a title relevant to most top managers' world view: *Corporate Policy and Governance*. Only a few such managers, however, will be familiar with its content: the constants of how complex systems work – how *general systems policy* and its *Master Controls* can be used to organize organizations in such a way that whatever needs to be organized in them will organize itself.

Every organization, and indeed every human being, senses the effects of the profound change we have been undergoing ever since the age of complexity dawned. Almost everybody senses that rapid change is increasingly part of everyday life. Many people today – in particular those carrying great responsibility – find they can only fulfill their tasks at the expense of their personal lives. Hardly anybody would doubt that we need new foundations for management that are better suited to meet the new challenges than those still in use.

With this volume of my series *Management: Mastering Complexity*, I am presenting the key element of what general management needs in this age of complexity: the chief prerequisite for the organizations of the future, organizations that will work autodynamically. However, the concept will only unfold its elementary power, as it were, in conjunction with both the entire book series and the *Malik Management System*. Only when all other parts of the system work together can it achieve its maximum impact. This is why I start by explaining the concept and the logic of the series on the following pages.

Everything to be said about the subject of this book is much easier to express (and even easier to implement) in models than to put in succinct words without exceeding the scope of a book. Some of the paragraphs may therefore seem superfluous to one reader while another will find them to be precisely what he needs to understand the subject matter well. That is the price of rigorous management writing: it needs to use a language suited for everybody yet sometimes requires newly invented terms.

The questions as to what exactly needs to be done in corporate policy and governance can only be answered individually for each organization. With this book, I am making available a fully equipped *toolbox*, so to speak, along with the *operating instructions for each of the tools*, so that top managers will be able to perform the necessary *craftsmanship* in their organizations.

Directions regarding this volume and the entire series are given before Part I. That part then describes the key premises to be observed in order to master complexity. It also contains a *roadmap* for developing a corporate policy as I understand it. The roadmap explains how the remaining three parts of the book are structured. Part II explains the concept of a *Master Control* in complex systems: what it is, how it works and what it is needed for. The modules of *Master Control* will be presented in Part III. In Part IV, I will address top executives in charge of developing a corporate policy, explaining what needs to be done in order to achieve the system behavior required and what *Master Controls* managers need to apply to themselves. The appendix provides some concise information on the *Malik Management System*.

At this point I want to thank Maria Pruckner for her invaluable help in structuring and formulating this manuscript. As a student of Heinz von Foerster and an experienced management practitioner, and with her profound knowledge about the cybernetics of complex systems, she has helped me to better sort out my own thoughts and their cybernetics. The interaction of speech and thinking is one of her specialties. There is hardly anything that could be more important for an author and his readers.

Further, my thanks go to the members of the Board of Directors and the Group Management Board at Malik Management, in particular to Elisabeth Roth, Walter Krieg, and Peter Stadelmann for relieving me of some of my management tasks while I was writing this book.

It is a principle of mine not to publish any of my books until their content has proven valid in years of cooperation with hundreds of managers

– including clients as well as colleagues in various top management bodies – and after both critical discussions and field tests have been passed. I owe my sincerest thanks to all of them.

Concept and Logic of the Series
Management: Mastering Complexity

This series of six books has a modular structure. The first book, *Management. The Essence of the Craft,* provides the basis and gives an overview of the series's overall concept, as well as of my approach to *right and good management.* The remaining volumes elaborate on the topics of each individual chapter.

In other words, each of the volumes deals with a subject matter en bloc. Each can be read independently of the others, and in any order. Readers of one individual volume may, however, find it helpful to have a look at the introductory volume *The Essence of the Craft* in order to be able to position an individual topic within the overall context, according to the graph shown in figure 1.

A key concept for this series of books is my "Basic Model of Right and Good Management", frequently referred to as the "Management Wheel" due to its shape. In my book *Managing Performing Living* it is described in detail[1]. The statements I made in that book are a prerequisite for fully understanding the contents of the series *Management: Mastering Complexity.*

Foundations

The basis for all my books and papers is *Strategie des Managements komplexer Systeme* ["Strategy of the Management of Complex Systems"][2], a

---

1 *Führen Leisten Leben* was first published in 2000; the English translation *Managing Performing Living* followed in 2003. A revised and expanded edition of the German version was published in late 2006. All at Campus, Frankfurt/New York.

2 *Strategy of the Management of Complex Systems,* 10th edition, Berne/Stuttgart/Vienna, 2008.

considerably expanded version of my habilitation treatise. This, in turn, is based on the books *Systemmethodik Teil 1 und Teil 2* ["Systems Methodology – Basic Principles of a Method for Researching and Designing Complex Socio-Technological Systems"][3], the joint PhD thesis by Peter Gomez, Karl-Heinz Oeller, and myself. These books cover the theoretical principles of cybernetics and systems science, which represent the cornerstones of all my thinking with regard to management topics.

Figure 1: Concept of the book series Management: Mastering Complexity

---

3 Gomez, Peter; Malik, Fredmund; Oeller, Karl-Heinz: *Systemmethodik – Grundlagen einer Methodik zur Erforschung und Gestaltung komplexer soziotechnischer Systeme*, Band 1 u. 2, Bern 1975.

Connections

For the present volume on *Corporate Policy and Governance,* I have expanded figure 1 to make the connections between the six books more transparent. Figure 2 shows how the subject matters of all six books overlap, which corresponds with the systemic relations between the individual topics. Together they form a whole: an inseparable system for the integrated management of a complex societal institution – the General Management System I have developed, and tested in practice, over the past 30 years.

In the inner circle, we have the summary volume *Management. The Essence of the Craft.* It is embedded in the second volume, *Corporate Policy and Governance.* The latter, in turn, is embedded in four outer circles: the volumes on strategy, structure, culture, and executives. All are connected to each other in the manner illustrated in figure 2.

Possibilities and Limits

The systemic relations between the individual volumes come up against the limits of descripteveness of complex systems – with consequences for both the content and design of the individual volumes. The subject matters of the books stretch to the limits not only of language but also of conceptual comprehension.

While complex systems are relatively quick and easy to demonstrate and even easier to experience in certain ways, they are almost impossible to describe. The medium of language, and thus this book, is not really suitable for describing, capturing, and communicating the complexity of interconnected systems. This is one reason why maps and nautical charts were invented. With complex systems, the everyday maxim "easier said than done" is quickly reversed to "easier shown and done than said…"

What possibilities do we have, then, despite the limitations of language and books, to make complex systems halfway comprehensible and transparent?

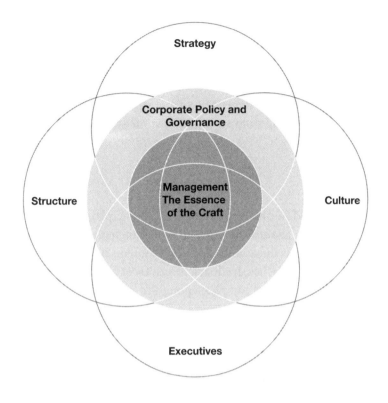

Figure 2: Systemic relations between the volumes of the series Management: Mastering Complexity

Redundancy

As the six volumes describe one system with its subsystems, repetitions are inevitable, and indeed intended.

The first reason why redundancies are inevitable is that the subject matters, while clearly distinguishable, are also inseparable, which is an important but rarely mentioned aspect of systemic thinking. They form one whole and must therefore be understood with regard to their interrelations.

Secondly, redundancy is intended because it is an indispensable tool to ensure certainty of communication and understanding. Thus, according to communication theory, redundancy is by no means superfluous. Not always are these two kinds of redundancy clearly distinguished. Functional redundancy facilitates orientation and comprehension by the reader.

Here, redundancy is not simply repetition but dealing with the same subject matters from different perspectives. One of the reasons why this is necessary is that the interrelations between subsystems are mutual but not symmetrical. For instance, the relation from strategy to structure is not of the same kind as the one from structure to strategy.

Graphs

As has been pointed out before, descriptions and explanations of complex systems are pushing against the limits of what language is capable to communicate. Language is linear and thus, for all intents and purposes, unsuitable for describing branches, feedback loops, recursions, and other nonlinear concepts. It is also not complex enough to reflect the real complexity of systems.

In order to describe the non-linearity and complexity of systems without resorting to mathematics, the only means that a book has to offer besides textual redundancy is illustrations. But even illustrations can be highly inappropriate for complex systems. Firstly, there is only a two-dimensional surface – the book page – to depict multi-dimensional systems. Secondly, the depictions in a book are static while systems are dynamic by nature.

For representing the systemically constitutive phenomena of complex systems, such as their being embedded, interconnected, and dynamic, the book is basically an outdated medium. More adequate means of depiction include hypertext, hyperlinks, and the whole browser technology which is making ever more rapid advances.

The subject matter of this second volume, *Corporate Policy and Governance,* more than any other book of the series, requires the use of system models and corresponding illustrations to explain complex systems, and the modern techniques mentioned above would be much better suited for that.

Exploring Things on the Web

The dynamics of a cybernetic system are best explored in dialog-type interaction. To overcome the limitations of the book medium, interested readers may want to visit the website www.malik.ch to explore the *Malik Management System*, better understand its workings, and use it in practice. This website offers the easiest possible access to the management of complex systems.

What Readers Need to Understand in Order to Understand this Book

With the book series *Management: Mastering Complexity* I am publicizing my management theory and my management system for the age of complexity. In retrospect, historians will probably date its beginning, as well as the associated emergence of a new society, to the early 21st century, knowing that epochal transformations can hardly be pinned to a fixed date.

It is a fact, though, that as far back as in the late 1940s, at the legendary Josiah Macy Conference, a new science emerged in response to the issue of complexity: the science of cybernetics. The focus of interest for related research is complexity. With his book *Cybernetics and Management*, published in 1959, the British top manager Stafford Beer laid the groundwork for management cybernetics because the core problem in management is complexity. We later cooperated closely. In 1968, my academic teacher and mentor at St. Gallen University, Prof. Hans Ulrich, took the next decisive step when writing his *Systems-Oriented Management Theory*. Together with my friend and colleague Walter Krieg, he presented the *St. Gallen Management Model* in 1972. Hence, ever since my time as a university student, my thinking has been challenged and influenced by thought leaders far ahead of their time. I was privileged enough to work with several of them, research and develop things with them, experiment and discuss with them. My doctoral thesis deals with the *methodology* used to research and design complex systems, and the title of my habilitation treatise of 1978 translates as *Strategy for the Management of Complex Systems*.

Against this historical and scientific background, the purpose of *Management: Mastering Complexity* is to enable the men and women of our New Society to survey and take advantage of the output of the relatively quiet yet enormously fruitful development work that has been going on over the past approximately 60 years. In this book series, the most essential things about complexity, management, and cybernetics will be pointed out in clear and comprehensible language. It is intended as a contribution to support the viability of the New Society, the functioning of its institutions, and the safe orientation of people in a world driven by complexity.

The change that the 21st century brings will be more dramatic than most people can imagine. The conditions for fundamental restructuring are in place. Although this may appear to be a paradox, its main cause is the enormous worldwide success of the kind of Western management practiced to date. This conventional kind of management has been so successful that it is no longer able to understand and control the systems it has generated, as they have become too complex. It is analogous to the protagonist of the famous ballad by Goethe, the *Sorcerer's Apprentice*, who was unable to control the spirits he had called. The complex systems of the 21st century cannot be managed with 20th century thinking – because this is what has called them forth.

Success Programming Its Own Failure

Never in history has a period of success been permanent. It is inherent in every success that it will systematically overtake itself because it generates the conditions of its own failure. This is one of the many paradoxes of complex systems.

Few people are capable of recognizing previous success as a cause of current problems. Few are capable of understanding that new solutions are required because the previously successful methods, owing to their very success, tend to lose impact or even become counterproductive, further exacerbating the difficulties they bring with them.

Whenever difficulties arise in a period of success, most people try addressing them by doing "more of the same". This well-known, well-researched human behavior in complex situations is typical. It is also very wrong.

When Thinking Fails to Grow With Practice...

History has shown that periods like this keep demanding new ways of thinking, new methods and systems. Drawing on previous practices has seldom been successful; in most cases, radically new concepts were called for.

Today, we are facing the conditions for radical change *on a global scale*. The Western world's practices have been such breakthrough successes that they have spread all over the world. Hence, all over the world there is a challenge to create a new order of systems of organizations, the nature of which cannot be predicted in advance.

The two successful concepts of the West are *market* and *management*. Wherever they have been applied so far they have caused the forces of free markets to be unleashed, and all available resources to be used ever more efficiently by management.

The impact of free markets is still being maximized by the elimination of boundaries and of national regulation. The impact of management is being maximized by computers and MBA programs. Unless they are fundamentally changed, both of these success methods will be hard pressed to survive the conditions they have created. A synthesis of both methods can lead to a sweeping success. However, this success will set clear limits for managing it, for simultaneously with the synthesis of market and management a process of gigantic complexification has set in, characterized by a progressive intertwining of an ever greater number of systems. As a result of this side effect, the functionality of societies and their institutions is being pushed to its limits. They become inefficient, which threatens to overstrain society as a whole.

When entire systems keep getting more and more inefficient, clear signals are exhibited. These include:

- more and more input being required to obtain less and less output,
- former liberties leading to excesses, and
- previously decreased regulation returning as exponential degrees of bureaucracy.

In other words, the system gets under pressure from its own coercions. What used to be success turns into its opposite and becomes a liability. All the systems of our society are becoming increasingly unstable because the market and management-focused success methods that have been practiced are now generating systemic risks and potential collapses. What used to be healthy growth turns into cancerous tumors.

Problems and Systems

It is in the nature of problems resulting from success that they cannot be solved with the same methods which led to that success. It is also in their nature that the success methods in practice turn into a problem and, over time, into the underlying problem. A main reason for that is that these methods are based on the knowledge of the 20th, in part even the 19th century. This knowledge stems from a world where the main issues to be dealt with were substance and force or, to put it differently, matter and energy. It was a world consisting of simple systems. They may have been *complicated* but – another presumed paradox – they were not particularly *complex*.

The texture of the age of complexity is different: as the name implies it is an unprecedented complexity which was brought about by the success of the approaches so far used. That is the common denominator of today's societies and their institutions.

Different as commercial enterprises, hospitals, universities, and administrative agencies are, what they all have in common is that they are complex, dynamic, non-linear, probabilistic, networked systems. Their respective environments – complex systems themselves – form an interlaced and interwoven, dynamic, non-linear system ecology. Healthcare, educational, and social systems, utility, energy, transportation, and logistic systems, the field of media and information, the field of information and communication systems, the global financial system, legal and tax systems – to mention just a few – form a network of complex systems which are essentially fuzzy, opaque, and absolutely inscrutable to conventional reason.

Complex systems have their own laws, qualities, and behavioral patterns which are fundamentally different from those of simple systems. Consequently, the focus of management in and of a complex system must be very different from that of the management of a simple system: it must work with the inherent laws of the particular complex system in itself. These laws are what enable us to correctly predict the mode and behavior of a system, at least in its fundamental orientation, and control it accordingly.

For most organizations, operating in the highly complex system ecology of the age of complexity requires a radical redesign of the way they are managed, as well as of their strategies, processes, and structures. However, society and its institutions are presently not equipped to comprehend the natural conditions created by complexity.

Old and New Sources

Managers intuitively feel that they need to adopt new ways and approaches, although few are able to explain why. Their search for suitable solutions is tedious experimentation and groping around, because they still lack the necessary theories, models, and concepts for dealing with today's dimensions of complexity.

Successfully mastering this much complexity requires a fundamental reorientation, starting with the basic model of management. This fundamental change of perspective is comparable to the Copernican transition from the geocentric to the heliocentric view of the universe. On the one hand, it requires radically new concepts of management; on the other, taking into account fundamentally new insights about information, systems, and their complexity.

The knowledge required for this reorientation cannot be found where people have been looking for it. It is derived neither from economic science nor from the classical natural sciences. They were the sources of the old solutions – those that are now outdated. The insights about complex system, which will be indispensable in the future, can be derived from systems, bio-, and neurosciences, as well as from evolution theory. Why is that so? Just imagine what it would be like if living organisms were organized in the same manner as our present social organizations. They would not function, they would not be viable. However, as biological systems are amazingly viable and versatile, we need to use them as a reference in designing man-made organizations and complex systems. We can and must learn from them.

Cybernetics as a Source of Relevant Insight

It is not enough, however, to simply draw upon the analogies between organisms and organizations, because while organisms are organizations, organizations are not organisms. Insights from the bio- and neurosciences cannot (or can only very rarely) be transferred directly to societal organizations.

Reliable help can only be found where there are regularities that biological and man-made systems have in common. These regularities have been researched and revealed in the context of cybernetic studies. This is how, among other things, computers and modern medical technology, regulation and control systems in cars and airplanes, modern security systems, and satellite navigation were developed. In the entire field of technology and in several other disciplines cybernetics has been used for many years. Wherever that is the case, there have been demonstrable and obviously break-through achievements.

Cybernetics is the science of structuring, controlling, and regulating complex systems by means of information and communication. Related skills are crucial for society and its institutions' ability to function in today's complex world, and generally necessary for the management task as such.

Few things are more important for man in the age of complexity. It is not so much different attributes or qualities that distinguish him from the man of previous centuries, but his fundamentally different knowledge and, even more, what he does not know, as well as the conditions in which he needs to act and decide. This is precisely where the insights from cybernetics can be of invaluable use.

Two Leaps of Evolution

There is no doubt that cybernetics works well in technological systems. The management of complex organizations, however, includes much more than technical applications. To achieve the same kind of breakthroughs in management as have been achieved in technology, based on the insights from cybernetics, two evolutionary leaps must be taken simultaneously:

- The first is applying cybernetics to much more complex systems than there are in technology, namely to living and social systems which, in relation to the former, can be referred to as *hypercomplex*.
- The second is applying cybernetics to the *results* achieved with the first step, or in other words, to systematize cybernetics *itself*.

In principle, complex systems are inscrutable and incalculable. Due to their complexity they cannot be analyzed or understood, which is why they cannot be organized and controlled in detail. For particularly complex systems, as those entailed by an organized society, this is all the more valid. Cybernetics with its questions and search routines shows us how to successfully deal with such systems, master their complexity, and even take advantage of them. This is difficult to imagine as long as you assume that man, and in particular a manager, is in complete control of the functioning of systems. It only becomes plausible when you apply one of the most fundamental insights of cybernetics: that complex systems organize themselves, and they do so in accordance with the natural laws defined by cybernetics. Man can either come to terms with them, or otherwise be dominated by them just like he is dominated by any other force of nature.

The second evolutionary leap is a logical consequence of the first: since in principle we cannot know enough to control, regulate, organize and develop a system, we need to make sure it will do all these things by itself – as intelligently as nature is able to. Hence, cybernetic management is the application of cybernetics to management, and the decisive step towards a systematic use of all the "self-concepts" and "self-skills" (as I call them) provided by nature. It is the step from regulating to self-regulating, from organizing to self-organizing, from structuring to self-structuring, from coordinating to self-coordinating, from developing to self-developing – or, in other words, to evolution. In this context, and particular when talking about corporate policy, I also use the term *Master Control*.

Taking Advantage of Complexity

Today's societies and their institutions are systems which restructure themselves, permanently and unpredictably. They are systems of a particular type. They are characterized by the fact that they are a result of human action but not a result of human intent and purpose, in that these systems are more complex than man could ever plan and design them to be. They generate themselves, and that is the main reason why man will not readily accomplish what he wants and expects. Heinz von Foerster has referred to this circumstance in a manner now legendary when he used the metaphor of "trivial" and "non-trivial machines".

The two evolutionary leaps mentioned above, which are responses to the hypercomplexity of our self-originating systems and to the self-capabilities of systems, are comparable to the historic transition from the flat-earth to the spherical-earth theory in terms of their dimensions and consequences. They have very far-reaching effects.

Cybernetic management does not simply take away the fear of complexity and its consequence, the urge to reduce it. On the contrary, by applying cybernetics to management it becomes possible to take advantage of the properties of complexity and its perpetual self-generation. This is done by creating simple and often ingenuous solutions which enable organizations and society as a whole, to function better and more independently.

All major achievements and advancements result from the increase and better use of complexity, not its reduction. For instance, Ancient Rome drew its superiority from the greater complexity of its traffic routes and from the expertise in orchestrating complex armies. Gothic builders knew better than Romanic ones how to deal with complexity. Global business is facilitated by the complexity of modern communication technology, which is exponentially higher than the technology of the 20th century.

Cybernetic management and the deliberate, systematic use of complexity also help dissolve most of the contradictions and paradoxes that exist in traditional management thinking. Seemingly irreconcilable opposites can effortlessly be integrated by using this way of thinking. Systems managed and regulated by cybernetic principles are able to overcome the paradoxes of simplicity versus complexity, of freedom versus order, of variety versus unity, of autonomy versus centrality, of community versus the individual, of free economy versus control of excesses, of reason versus intuition. Reductionist either-or thinking is replaced or supplemented by systemic as-well-as thinking.

Right Management Is Cybernetic Management

Sixty years of research into complexity and cybernetic phenomena are not that easy to summarize, even more difficult to prepare for a broad audience, and equally difficult to communicate in a credible manner. One could almost say that only those who have experienced and done it themselves may feel reasonably certain. With such certainty, and looking back at my 40 years of research, 30 years heading a business organization, and over 20 years as an entrepreneur, I can say this much: cybernetics – and only cybernetics – helps us recognize what right and what wrong management is under complex conditions. It shows what kind of overall management system complex institutions in complex environments need in order to function, and what subsystems they need to have. It provides insight on what the components of that management system should be, and how these – such as corporate policy, strategy, structure, and culture – should be designed so an organization will be able to deal with complexity. Cybernetic management shows us how, in the age of complexity, power and money need to be replaced by information and knowledge.

Understanding the regularities of complex systems is the key *knowledge* of the age of complexity. The key *skill* will be to use these insights gained from cybernetics. Both together provide the fundamental prerequisite for managing and mastering complexity in a system-compatible way. It is naturally required for the functionality of societal institutions, and for the ability of individuals to cope with life.

Mastering and taking advantage of complexity is the purpose of my management system. Only by keeping this purpose in mind, can my management models be studied, evaluated and applied correctly. Where exactly they differ from the management theories of the 20th century is described in the different volumes of the book series *Management: Mastering Complexity*. The 21st century manager does not need any different qualities. What he needs are different skills, another view of the world, other insights, and another way of acting.

Part I

From Organization
to Self-Organization

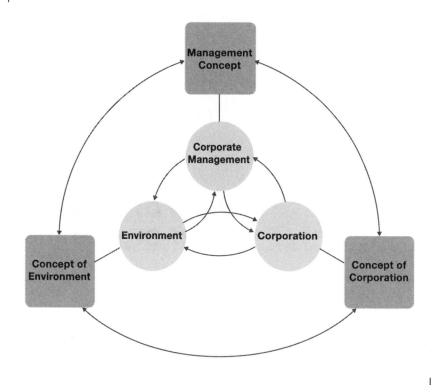

Chapter 1

Manifesto for Corporate ᴿEvolution

This book is a program for ᴿevolutionizing top management. Its main focus has to be on top managers, as only they are in a position to take the decisions needed in due time.

Radical changes are managed at the top – or not at all. In the latter case, they simply happen. There is no choice, no option to say yes or no. The only option we have is to carry through this ᴿEvolution, well or badly, to be proactive and precipitate it or to be passive and let it happen – in which case we will probably be on the losing end.

The ᴿEvolutionary Transformation

The reason for ᴿEvolution is simple. Both the world of business and society at large are going through one of the most fundamental transformations that ever occurred in history. What is currently happening is not simply change. It is change of a new logical dimension, a meta- and mega-change. About one-third of the managers I work with are aware of this but do not see a solution. Another third sense the change, but feel uncertain and are unable to pinpoint it. The final third turn a blind eye, believing in today's world as the only possible one.

The ᴿEvolution will not leave any of today's organizations unscathed, be it commercial enterprises, universities, hospitals, or government. This must be the a basic assumption for top managers. I have been discussing this with top executives for years. They force themselves to accept this premise, in order not to run the risk of underestimating the change ahead. Many organizations will go down, either because they are unable to accomplish the transition or because they are no longer needed. Almost everything will have to be given a new order and many new organizations will emerge, with new purposes and tasks.

Forecasts are useless, but certain outlines are already discernible. One thing that is quite certain is that we are in the midst of the emergence of a new society, which can most accurately be referred to as the *society of complexity* – in a transition from the information to the knowledge society, from the society of organizations to the society of complex systems. Companies will no longer essentially be engines of force intensification but of intelligence intensification; rather than economic money machines they will be information and communication systems. Steering, regulating, and organizing become self-steering, self-regulating, and self-organizing. Predominant terms will be *complexity, system,* and *cybernetics*.

Categorical Change – Change of Categories

I prefer the term *categorical change* to the well-worn "paradigm change", which has become useless for anything save banalities. What is happening is nothing less than a *revolution of the fundamental categories* in which society and economy have to be perceived in order to understand them – comparable to the Copernican transition from the geocentric to the heliocentric concept of the world, but encompassing many more dimensions.

Few of today's categories for understanding the economy, organizations, and management will remain useful; they will no longer be able to guide people's actions in any reliable way. That is true even for the world and for what we call *reality*, as the sciences teach us ever more spectacularly – in particular the bio- and neurosciences, but lately also physics again.

These sciences and their results are visible and they shape public awareness. By contrast, the sciences truly relevant for top executives in societal institutions have not had that much influence to date, although they are already bringing permanent changes to our lives: specifically the sciences of complexity, cybernetics, bionics, and the systems sciences. From a logical perspective, these sciences rank even "higher" because they will bring a change of categories, thus revolutionizing traditional sciences as well.

Quite certainly, in retrospect historians will speak of an epochal change and of a profound break in thinking, when they attempt to categorize the epoch we live in. And the crucial effects will have been brought about by executives' actions and by the workings of societal institutions.

Will the Company Survive?

In parts of the business sector, enterprises of the current type will continue to exist. But even they will have to restructure radically and redesign their management from scratch.

In the New Society there will be many top managers who will be functioning as the nervous systems and brains, as it were, but "below" them there will not necessarily be companies in the current sense because everything can be sourced from outside. It will not even be necessary to buy resources because it will suffice to control them; it will be possible to source, re- and outsource, to form alliances and other forms of cooperation, create networks, dissolve them, configure and reconfigure them. A substantial share of the smartest top management bodies will confine themselves to "composing and directing" while the "orchestra" will keep changing, as is common in the world of music.

From Money to Knowledge:
Will There Still Be Shareholder Meetings?

While we might continue to pay with money, the complex world will not be driven by it. It will be driven by knowledge, even though economists and analysts will try to uphold the monetary illusion for quite a while. For instance, the knowledge of how to set up successful business deals in China is several times more important than the money required to invest there, since without such knowledge investments will be lost faster than they are placed. Conversely, those who know how it is done will always be able to raise the necessary funds.

Taking this into account, what kinds of rights should be conceded, for instance, to shareholder meetings largely populated by investors, who – apart from their money – usually have little to contribute to the knowledge and intelligence required for the business, or to the functionality of its complex systems? Let them have generous dividends, let them enjoy handsome share price gains – but why should they have a part in electing the supervisory board, the group of people that is responsible for directing and supervising the company's fate? So will there be two general meetings, one for investors and one for the owners of knowledge? Imagine, say, three dozen companies cooperating in constantly changing network structures, which jointly establish an integrated management of the entire problem-solving process, from the identification of the customer's problem to its solution. How is our present form of corporate governance supposed to work in such a structure? Instead of corporate governance we will need systems governance. But how will it have to work when the performance networks of a global society will be systems continually reconfiguring themselves?

From Knowledge to Insight: Mundus Novus

Even knowledge is not enough. What we need is perspective, insight, and comprehension. After all, knowledge is nothing but a resource. Only its *application*, comprehending and understanding how complex systems work, lets us take the decisive step towards *exploiting* complexity – utilizing it to persist in a new dimension of global competition and to succeed in a new business environment. To create and apply knowledge and transform it into benefits, we also need knowledge – but of another kind: rather than *knowledge of the subject matter* we need *system knowledge*.

Most of the ingredients of the New Society are in place for everyone to see, even if not everyone can understand them. Hence, a better comparison than Copernicus, although less known, is Amerigo Vespucci, the Florentine explorer after whom America was named. Amerigo realized that it was a *New World*, while Columbus, who had discovered the new territory, never until his death understood what he had accomplished. He kept on thinking he had landed in India, and so, regardless of his discovery, he tragically remained a citizen of the Old World. Amerigo Vespucci was the first citizen of the New World because he had understood the significance of the newly discovered territory. Stefan Zweig has left us an impressive account of these events.

As discussions regularly show, seasoned top executives are well able to conjecture how the existing components will reconfigure themselves to form systems of systems. But even they find it difficult to recognize the parts as elements of a new whole, because they still lack the categorization system, the grid, the coordinates of the new dimensions that one would need for true understanding. Hence, many are only able to see a number of puzzle pieces – but they have yet to develop an idea of the image that these pieces will form.

With this book, I am providing the categorization system required for safe navigation, for the reconstruction of societal institutions, and for corporate ᴿEvolution. The remaining volumes of the series will describe the thinking devices and tools required.

Right Corporate Policy is Systems Policy

The most accurate title for this book would be *General Systems Policy*. Yet this title would not immediately be associated with the management of business organizations, with corporate policy and governance. It can therefore be an ultimate goal for this book but not the way to get there.

The double title *Corporate Policy and Governance* is a concession to the way these issues are still perceived in the world of business. While this book takes account of those perceptions, it goes much further in that I talk about the general management tasks in *all* institutions, although with a focus on business organizations. As far as language is concerned, I will use the terms largely common in the business world. It will, however, be clear from the context that (and how) the respective content can be applied to other than commercial institutions.

The book should really be entitled *General Systems Policy* because it deals with the shaping and directing of all organizations – including business ones – at the top level, corresponding to the nature of complex *systems*. This requires more than the usual understanding of policy, referring to specific subject matters. It requires a systems policy taking into account the universal laws of a special kind – the cybernetic kind – which apply to any complex system.

From the entirety of the management system I have developed, I will only select the modules by which every organization directs, regulates, and organizes itself, starting from the top and going all the way down to the peripheral units. Thus, the terms comprised in the book title relate to my new concept only to the extent that they address its application to a certain subject area – the top management of companies, organizations, and institutions[4].

Management in the Age of Complexity

Important as it may be, the economic dimension alone does not suffice for the management of a company, and even less for other kinds of societal institutions. Hence, the issues raised in this book go beyond the prevalent one-dimensional, economics-centered way of looking at things, as well as the associated neo-liberal perspective with its exclusive focus on profit optimization. The book addresses the following questions:

- What is a functioning system?
- How can it be made to work, and maintained that way?
- What are the regularities underlying its functioning?
- How do systems need to be regulated so that they can basically expand without limits?
- How can systems be regulated so as to make them regulate and organize themselves?

The answers to these questions can be found in the laws of complex systems. They have been investigated and described in both cybernetics and systems sciences. They apply in a *double* sense: for all productive social systems that need to be managed and for all systems needed to manage them (i.e., their management systems).

Cybernetics as the *science of functioning* provides new solutions to many fundamental issues and unsolved problems of management, solutions that are more effective than traditional concepts. For some questions it provides the very first answers. Hence, the insights from cybernetics are what my understanding of general management and the *Malik Management System* is based on.[5]

---

4 Although my concept is universally valid, I am using business enterprises as an example here, even though general systems policy also works for all other organizations of society according to this principle, only with a different terminology.
5 Several coincidences during my university study made me recognize this early on,

Among other things, a cybernetic consideration of the issues of corporate policy and governance will provide the following:

- new answers to questions of influence, power, and leadership at the top,
- new solutions for a professional way to deal with and take advantage of complexity,
- new opportunities for and requirements of the regulation, control, direction, and development of companies,
- new possibilities for the organization of companies,
- new solutions for change management,
- new possibilities and requirements for information and communication,
- in general, new approaches to questions of the overall functionality and viability of any institution.

Furthermore, my perception of right and good management, as outlined in *Management. The Essence of the Craft* and in *Managing Performing Living*, has new consequences for the abilities, ways of thinking, and skills required both from the professional manager and from management as a profession. Above all, this concerns the continuous education of an ever greater number of people with general management tasks. In the 21st century they face unprecedented challenges. This calls for different concepts, models, methods, and tools than have been customary so far – of the kind that I am presenting in this book series, each as a separate module, in the overall context of the entire *Malik Management System*.

Systemic Corporate Policy

As has been mentioned at the beginning, this book is a part of the series by which I present my management system in its entirety. Hence, *corporate policy* and *corporate governance* are not to be viewed as an isolated topic – neither in this series nor in the context of my management system. They are architectural elements of my *overall system* for general management.

---

and my academic teacher in St. Gallen, Hans Ulrich, reassured me when, while discussing a working paper on a chapter of my habilitation theses, he once said en passant: "Malik, you are on the right track, but don't run too far ahead too fast ..."

As such, the subjects of *corporate policy* and *governance* in several important respects assume a different meaning than they would if they were considered separately, that is, independently of the overall context of management, as is still fairly common today.

In my management system, *corporate policy* and *corporate governance* are part of a greater whole. Their function and their design result from the interaction with all other parts of the overall system. On the one hand, they are only systemic modules within a greater configuration, just as atoms are modules of molecules and molecules are modules of more comprehensive structures. On the other hand, the modules of *corporate or systems policy* are what turns systems into effective systems.

It is fairly comparable to the way a computer needs an operating system so that individual software programs running on it can function properly. Hence, *corporate policy* and its "little sister", *corporate governance*, have particular and absolutely crucial significance. Whatever goes wrong here cannot be corrected in any other part of an organization. Whatever is regulated correctly here will not have to be dealt with anywhere else, because it will enable the system to function.

Systems Logic and Subject-Related Issues

If this book was a monograph, or a textbook or specialist book, I would have structured it differently. As one component in an overall system, however, this book has to fulfill its function in the context of my management system. To this end, I need to lift *corporate policy* to a *higher* logical level than is presently common in expert discussion. In my management system, *corporate policy* and *corporate governance* are not addressed at the subject-specific level but at the *subordinate* level of system *regulation*. Corporate policy and governance are the existential and constitutive *controls* required for an organization to work. They are the architectural and functional principles which rank similarly to the articles of a constitution, and which I refer to as *Master Controls*.

This overriding perspective of system regulation is necessary because statements referring to concrete subject matters at companies can hardly be generalized, or if they are, they quickly become *outdated* because they are overtaken by reality. Consequently, books about corporate policy tend to become irrelevant within a short period if they focus on the subject level. Attempts to generalize statements at the subject level, in order to make them permanently valid, will usually render them *devoid of meaning*. At this level, statements of true political significance – that is to say, fundamental, general, and permanent stipulations – are hardly possible.

By contrast, at a *higher* level – from the perspective of system regulation and direction – we encounter an *invariant* logic; that is to say, rules, basic principles and organizing principles which we could actually refer to as "eternal truths" because they have two critical qualities: they have significance with regard to *content* and they are *universally* valid. Hence, their effectiveness results from providing orientation above and beyond the specific issues at hand. Using them as a point of reference, it is possible to define in advance how specific issues are to be dealt with. They are superordinate to specific issues. It is a question of knowing how to avoid problems from the start, or how to solve them thoroughly enough to prevent them from reappearing.

Effective Master Controls

The effectiveness of superordinate system regulations, in the sense of system or corporate policy, is powerfully demonstrated using a few examples. For instance, a principle often violated in company acquisitions is the system rule to *never buy a company unless you will be able to manage it with your own people within 12 months*. The proven failure rate for mergers & acquisitions of over two-thirds could be reduced to less than one-third, if this system-political rule was strictly observed.

Another example is the principle permanently disregarded in innovation management: *separate the new from the existing business!* This rule helps avoid most of the typical difficulties and failures occurring in innovation efforts.

Rules like these not only exist in corporate management but in practically all areas, such as sports or games. Modern game theory, which was awarded the Nobel Prize for economics, is the scientific approach to dealing with such rules. It exceeds the realm of economic issues by far and also originates from cybernetics. In chess, apart from the well-known rules of the game there is also a set of principles not everybody is familiar with, such as: *keep your knights in the center.* Or, to put it more generally: *try to strengthen your position with every move.*

Principles of this kind – we call them heuristics – are part of the well-guarded know-how of every chess pro, and they allow him to keep his calm in situations where anyone with a lesser knowledge would long have lost his bearings. Heuristics gain relevance when any other type of decision has become impossible due to the immense complexity of the game. In a detailed study of the decision routines of humans and computers in chess, the Russian grand master and former world champion M. M. Botvinnik has dealt with principles of this kind. They are the *principles of succeeding and winning in hypercomplex situations.*

Issue Policy vs. Systems Policy

While the subject level and the system-related management level are related to each other, they are entirely different in nature. In natural systems and in corporate management practice, they overlap or are often interlinked to an extent where it is difficult to tell them apart. In order to do so, one needs to develop an eye, even a sense for their interaction, and have access to the right models and methods to differentiate them and put them into a sensible order. Part of that is dealt with in this book.

At the two levels – the subject-matter and the systems level – we face *different* core problems in the management of business organizations. The key issue at the *subject level* is how to make *profit.* At the *system* level, the key issue is how to maintain a business system for an unlimited amount of time. *Doing business* and *staying in business* are two entirely different sets of skills and targets. At the system level we have the phenomena of *shaping, directing,* and *regulating complexity.* Regulating, direction, sorting out, and shaping are different forms of the same thing: of *dealing with complexity.* Hence, the subject level and the system-related directional level rest on two different *knowledge bases.*

The *subject level* is all about markets, products, technologies, personnel, and finances. It is about growth, revenues, costs, and profits. These are the familiar categories of managers' business environment. The foundation of the subject level is the economic sciences, in particular business economics, as well as technical disciplines and natural sciences.

At the *directional level*, however, it is not the growth targets for each business line that are of primary concern. The central topic here is the *principles* for *regulating* growth as such, or the way in which the company grows. Typical questions are, for instance, whether growth is healthy or unhealthy, stable or unstable, and how much growth the company can take without getting out of control.

In other words, at the level of direction-setting and regulation, as opposed to the subject level, the central theme is *functioning sustainably*. It is all about the company's basic ability to operate, about issues of stability and flexibility, of conservation and renewal, of adaptation, evolution, and the ability to develop further. The foundation for the directional level is cybernetics, the science of regulating and functioning (as has been mentioned before). Closely linked to it are its sister disciplines, system theory and bionics.

So the subject level is about *operating the business,* the directional level is about *shaping a system* for the operating of businesses, and about the shaping of *systems for entire business systems.* For instance, the global success of McDonald's is not owed to hamburgers but to the *system* that McDonald's has chosen for the way it works. The company's general managers are really *system architects* and *system designers*, which in the complexity-driven society will be the central tasks of top and general management, in particular of CEOs. Another case in point is Microsoft, whose success stems from the company's general management rather than its product, while DaimlerChrysler was not able to master, at the top management level, the complexity of a major merger.

Corporate Policy, Systems Policy, Governance

What has been discussed so far leads us back to the question posed at the beginning, whether this book should better be called *Corporate Policy* or *Systems Policy.* An alluring thought would be the argument that the term *corporate policy* in the traditional sense should be restricted to the subject level. However, I have decided to keep using the term *corporate policy* when relating to the tasks of systems policy. It is actually quite appropriate as far as it relates to corporate policy as an element of system regulation. The important point is that, demonstrably, corporate policy can have the substance it often lacks in practice due its non-binding nature – the very substance that brings about high-performance systems.

The ideal term for the corporate policy module in the *Malik Management System*, however, would have been *corporate governance* – and, in more general terms, *systems or institutional governance* – because it entails the crucial radical of cybernetics. The word *cybernetics* comes from the Greek *kybernetes*, meaning *helmsman,* which in English changed into *governor* and *governance* over time. Even the original definition of corporate governance by the Cadbury Committees fits my own thoughts: *Corporate Governance is the system by which companies are run.* However, the current perception of corporate governance has diverged so much from this line that the term, used as a synonym for system-oriented corporate policy, would cause more confusion than it could provide clarity.

Today, *corporate governance* is associated with a travesty of corporate management, characterized by the scandals and white-collar crime of the past 15 years rather than by a comprehensive understanding of complex systems. In truth, this has resulted in an extremely questionably practice of misled corporate government, as I have pointed out and argued in my book *Wirksame Unternehmensaufsicht – Corporate Governance in Umbruchzeiten* ["Effective Supervision of Companies – Corporate Governance in Times of Change"] which was published in early 1997. When the third edition came out in 2002, there was already plenty of evidence for the flawed logic underlying shareholder-value-based corporate governance. The developments in the financial markets that went on from the beginning of 2000 until the end of 2002 had revealed the false doctrines for what they were, although by far not everybody knew how to interpret them correctly. For the third edition of the book, published in 2002, I have revisited these recent experiences and, after adding numerous amendments, published everything under another title: *Die Neue Corporate Governance* ["The New Corporate Governance"].

Remaining Blind for System-Immanent Natural Forces

So far, the development of the concept of corporate governance has been a pathetic history of missed chances, in many different respects. What is more, it exemplifies a set of circumstances in which something fundamental is lacking: the consideration of how complex systems function and operate. It is a history of an enormous confusion of terms, and of the massive mismanagement of companies, resulting from fundamental misperceptions of the nature and purpose of companies as complex systems.

Corporate governance, as it is understood today, has little to do with corporate management's basic task – corporate policy. It does fulfill its required function with regard to financial markets, financial analysts, and financial media. As such, it needs to be given proper attention here. However, when looking at it from the perspective of management (in the proper sense of the word) and in particular when management is oriented by complexity, today's concept of corporate governance is slanted towards the financial side of things and excessively focused on legal aspects; also, it is aimed towards the wrong purpose – shareholder value – and altogether overregulated.

The *corporate governance codes* in use today regulate *too much* yet at the same time *too little*. They give *too many wrong recommendations* and *not enough right ones*. The perspective of corporate management, the actual issue of controlling and directing, is largely overlooked or blocked out. On the contrary: the way *corporate governance codes* are handled leads to an increasing strangulation of top-level management bodies, and as a logical consequence of this, they are getting further and further removed from their entrepreneurial task. Members of management bodies nowadays have less and less time to look after the company's welfare, as they have to make sure they comply with legal provisions, pamper the financial media, serve the short-term interests of investors (which are often harmful to business) and protect themselves against liability claims. In the real economy there is a clear tendency toward embracing formal governance rules, and a clear decrease of things like entrepreneurial farsightedness, courage, the willingness to take on risks, and imagination.

It is due to this one-sided perception of *corporate governance* that the term could not be used as the sole title for this book, although by virtue of its etymology and meaning it would actually be the correct term. It is hard to say whether it will ever assume its real meaning. So far, there are no signs of it – on the contrary: the half-hearted attempts to reform it are once again leading in the wrong direction, aiming at a revival of the so-called stakeholder approach. Apparently the "reformers" are not aware that it was the *failure* of the stakeholder approach which led to the emergence of the shareholder concept – which does not work, either.

The issues being addressed with attempted reforms – such as corporate social responsibility or corporate citizenship – are very legitimate, since they are neglected and even systematically violated by the shareholder approach. The solutions proposed, however, are of absolutely no use. It is necessary to strike another path which I will outline in this book.

The fact that a business organization is not only an economic profit engine but also a social, political and moral institution was also pointed out by the doyen of management theory, Peter F. Drucker, in his early essays from 1946 onward. This fact is just as topical today as it was then. Entrepreneurs and seasoned managers have always been aware of it and acted accordingly, as otherwise their ventures would not have worked out. However, system-immanent facts like these do not lend themselves to economic theorizing remote from reality. Therefore, the above-mentioned pseudo-reforms of corporate governance are bound to lead in the wrong direction.

This book is meant for all those in charge of corporate policy and corporate governance in their organizations, its purpose being to provide guidance on setting up system-compatible organizing principles and dynamic regulation systems.

Chapter 2

Work Plan for Cybernetic Corporate Policy

In this prelude chapter, I will sketch out the work plan – the roadmap – for setting up a corporate policy in the sense described above.

In part II, there will be three chapters explaining the basics, which need to be given some space here so that the new categories of *Master Control* in the complexity-driven society will be comprehensible. What they comprise is, firstly, the constants ensuring safe orientation in the midst of *categorical change*; secondly, the *Master Controls* to be created by means of cybernetics corporate policy; thirdly, the use of models for capturing and exploiting complexity.

In part II, three chapters will describe the structure and contents of the three core elements of policy: the *concept of corporation,* the *concept of environment,* and the *management concept.*

Part IV deals with the new tasks which the top-level organs of companies need to perform if they want to understand, shape, and govern their companies as complex, self-organizing systems.

The more difficult issues will be dealt with more frequently than well-informed readers may appreciate, but from a different angle every time. My long-standing cooperation with top-level executives and my experiences from hundreds of training sessions and workshops with top-notch managers have taught me that it usually does not suffice to say things once.

Roadmap to a Cybernetic Corporate Policy

The function of corporate policy becomes most obvious when considering the work plan to set up a policy, or in other words, the work plan that is required for making decisions which are to shape and direct the company. This work plan – or roadmap – can provide readers with some support in deciding whether they wish to, ought to, or even have to concern himself with the book any further.

What needs to be done, and why, when the issues are corporate policy and corporate governance? How is it to be done, and by what means? Who has to do it? This roadmap is independent of the line of business and the size of a company, or whether a corporate policy is to be set up in one shot or in an iterative and evolutionary process. It is usually a mixture of both. In any case, what we need is a concept, a structure, a work plan, in order to ensure that the policy will be one coherent whole, and open to further development without losing coherency. This book provides the concept and the necessary content.

Corporate policy, understood correctly, is the company's *Master Control system*. The question is: "What are the decisions and principles by which entire organizations (of any kind and size) can be shaped and steered in such a way that they will function well, even in complex circumstances and – as complexity will be the outstanding feature of 21st-century societies – that complexity will be the secret of their success rather than their problem?"

What needs to be done and why?

The "why" can be answered easily: because top management needs to work from the assumption that we are in the midst of a profound societal transformation, in the course of which not many things will remain the same. Overestimating change involves less risk – underestimating it can be fatal. My suggestion is to proceed on the basis that we are witnessing the emergence of a New Society. Its chief characteristic will be complexity.

There are *three* basic questions to be answered, which will lead us through the whole book:

1. What should the corporation do?
2. Where should the corporation compete?
3. How should the corporation function?

The first question refers to the corporation and its activities, the second refers to its business environment and the third to its management; that is to say, to the management system which puts the company into a steady state, a so-called dynamic equilibrium, with its environment – irrespective of the changes that occur.

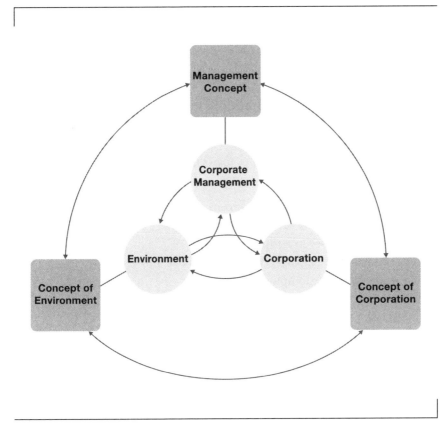

Figure 3: Basic system of corporate policy

The output of the work plan is three well-matched, integrated concepts for

- the corporation,
- its environment,
- its management.

They are the chapters of an all-encompassing, wholistic corporate policy and – joined up to it – a corporate governance guiding the thoughts and actions of the company's managers. (Dear reader: please indulge my preference for "wholistic" – when addressing concepts that refer to *the whole* – over the common spelling "holistic", which has awkward philosophical overtones in German). They correspond to the three chapters in part III of this book. Together, these three concepts form the company's *Master Control system* which is the basis and guideline for all further decisions.

Figure 3 shows the basic model by which the corporate policy is orientated. It is a navigation aid for this whole book.

Institution and Concept of Corporation: What Should the Institution Do?

The concept of corporation defines the organization's activities. Questions to be answered include the following:

- What is the purpose of the organization?
- Should it be primarily profit-oriented or is there another, society-related purpose? Is there even a third purpose?
- What function should stakeholder groups be allowed?
- What are the ethical implications?
- What is the business mission of the company and, if applicable, of its divisions?
- What are the factors that drive performance?
- What are the most important functions – such as research and development, marketing, finance, etc. – for which a set of principles has to be determined?
- Are there any special issues to be regulated, such as branding, quality policy, pricing, and the like?

Environment and Concept of Environment: Where Does the Institution Have to Function?

Every organization is strongly influenced by its business environment. Right management must be geared from the outside to the inside, not the other way round, and based on a specific logic: the *in-out-in logic*. Typical questions are:

- What does the organization need to pay attention to in its environment?
- What, and for what reasons, are the most important influencing factors – such as customers, investors, employees, and others?
- What geographical regions are important to the institution?
- What societal, political, social factors influence it?
- What long-term trends and tendencies need to be taken into account?
- What theories and methods must lead the way in order to arrive at a concept of the environment that is suitable for navigation?

Corporate Management and Management Concept: How Should the Institution Function?

Every organization needs a management system. It is defined in the management concept. Key questions include these:

- Based on what principles should the organization be managed?
- What management system does it need in order to function?
- What principles should be applied to the most important parts of the management system – the organization's strategy, structure, culture, and executives, as well as its entire staff?
- How should the different groups of staff be trained in order to manage in a professional way?
- What management tools, methods, and aids are required?
- What information and communication principles have to be observed?
- What principles have to be observed with regard to accountability and ethics?

How to Do It All, and by What Means?

The two most important means of regulating a complex organization are *models* and *rules*. Their significance for management has little to do with traditional management concepts. The function of models is similar to that of a navigation system in a car or airplane. The function of rules and principles is to enable the institution to organize itself. Under complex conditions, any other form of control is ineffective.

Who Has to Do It?

It is up to the institution's top-level organs to design and implement a corporate policy. Depending on the size and human resources available, the preparatory work has to be done by the chief executive himself and/or a small team. It depends on the structure and size of the organization how these decision and commitment processes should be designed. Hence, well-functioning top-level organs use information rather than force.

Master Control – Using Natural Forces in the System

The roadmap described here, with its work plan for an effective corporate policy for self-organization, reveals the kind of dedication required from top managers even when applying management cybernetics. Before we get to that, the chapters following the roadmap will introduce readers to the kind of work that the nature of complex system performs on its own, if assessed and used correctly.

It is followed by a depiction of the contributions that top managers need to make within the framework of corporate policy, in order to allow their organizations to work in a self-organizing manner.

Orientation in the General Management Context

Figure 3 shows the basic system to be controlled. Figure 4 below shows the *Master Controls* which top management works with to shape, control and develop the overall system made up of the institution and its environment.

The outer circle represents the institution's environment, followed by the *Master Controls* of corporate policy and, embedded in them, corporate governance. On the inside, embedded in corporate governance and in essence supported by it, we find the sub-controls – strategy, structure, and culture – as well as the executives shaping and using all the different controls. These controls in their different dimensions, which will be discussed, as well as the dimension of time, together bring about the evolution of the system.

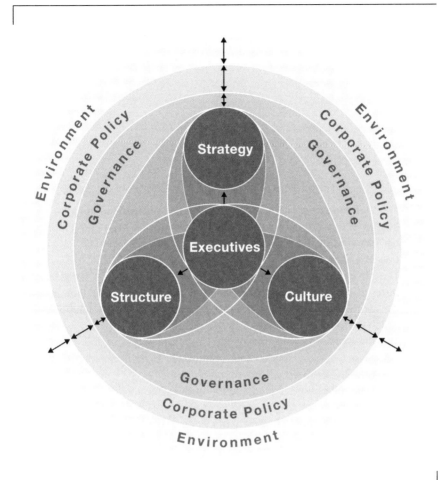

Figure 4: Master Controls of top management

Chapter 3

Hypotheses

1. Although the complex systems of the 21st century resulted from the successes of the 20th century's mindset and methods, they can no longer be managed by these because the systems have become far too complex at a global level.
2. The 21st century has already brought with it a more radical change to the deep structures than can be seen at the surface. It is not just a paradigm change that is taking place but a change of the categories in which we perceive paradigms as such.
3. The categorical dimensions of the new conception of the world are complexity, system, functioning, control, *self-organization*, information, non-linearity, knowledge, and cognition
4. Global societies are transforming themselves into *societies of complexity* – in steps by which they change from a society of individuals to a society of organizations to a society of systems – of complex systems. Because of their complexity they have intrinsic dynamics that call for fundamentally different management than previously
5. Knowledge has become more important than time or energy, information more important than money, the ability of companies to self-organize purposefully more important than power
6. The knowledge that is relevant for the working of this society comes from the sciences of complexity: cybernetics, systems theory, and bionics. It is by the application of this knowledge that we achieve the relevant cognition.
7. The crucial challenge to be mastered in order to work successfully in the 21st century is complexity. The most important skill is the ability to master and make use of complexity. The most important function to achieve that skill is cybernetic management. The most important means of achieving it is cybernetic corporate policy. The most important prerequisite for it is conditions for self-organization that exploit the intrinsic dynamics of complex systems and enable people to manage themselves.

8. The most important effect of corporate policy of this kind is as a Master Control for self-organizing, self-regulating, self-directing complex systems.

9. Depending on the organization, the center of complexity and starting point for Master Controls is the customer, the client, the patient, the student, the voter – in short, anyone who needs the organization's services and who pays for them in some way. An organization cannot be successful unless it provides the recipients of its services with effective solutions for mastering complexity.

10. The era of arbitrariness of and in management is over: cybernetics is establishing the laws and standards that are scientifically imperative for effective management in the age of complexity. Along with it, what is also coming to an end is the era of randomness-based opportunism, as has been found in management consulting services of all categories.

11. There will only be two groups of people left: firstly, there will be those who only perceive the old in the new, no longer being able to understand enough, because they have ignored the past decades' findings about the world, reality, systems, and information. Secondly, there will be those who recognize the new for what it is and make use of it, because they have been watching this development closely and grasped its meaning long before its impacts could be felt.

12. The social institutions of today will undergo an [R]Evolution or disappear altogether, because they have become unmanageable and no longer fulfill their purposes. Difficulties with financing are merely a symptom of their malfunction: Its cause is the lack of right management – management that is suitable for dealing with complexity.

13. While government policy will continue to be important in the new global society, in its present-day form it will increasingly be a source of disruption, hindrance, and restraint. Today's political parties no longer serve any purposes because the ability of social systems to function does not depend on any party colors or ideology. There is no right or left, only right or wrong.

14. The key ability for human beings in the society of complexity is mastering professional management and self-management. It will have the same significance for social survival, as well as for the viability of any society and its ability to evolve, as reading and writing have had for the transition from illiterate bond slave to politically mature citizen. Solid cybernetic management will be the functioning and cultural ability of the society of complexity.

Chapter 4

Terminology

In addition to the term definitions provided in the first volume of this series, the following notes are important for readers of this book.

Control

When I use the term *control* in this book I refer to the (self-) directing and (self-) regulating approaches which, when applied to a system, help achieve the appropriate and thus desirable skills and behaviors of that system. Hence, *control* refers to conditions that exist, or have been created, to enable the mastering and using of complexity, the functioning of systems, and thus a strong resistance to errors. This means that *control* is much more than having a system under control. The system is much more than "under control": it is controlled and regulated in such a way that it will fulfill its intended purpose, eliminate or compensate possible disturbances, and be able to keep evolving.

General Management

This is the generic term describing those functions of shaping, steering and developing an organization that can be *generalized* because they are independent of the kind, size, line of business, and legal form of an institution. General management is the sum of all functions that an institution needs in order to operate.

The antithesis of general management is *special management*, a term I occasionally use despite its being rather uncommon. To give some examples, special management includes the typical functional areas of traditional companies, such as production, marketing, finance, human resources, and the like. They cannot be generalized because in this case, every institution has different tasks to fulfill.

Also, general management is *not* identical to top management. Top management only refers to the general management at the top level of an organization; in addition, it also requires its own special management tasks to be performed.

General management is required at all levels of a complex institution, in all matters where the same (generalizeable) tasks and functions have to be fulfilled.

Information

The term *information* is not to be understood in its every-day meaning; rather, it refers to the signals, data, and news that depict differences, and which trigger still more differences or bring about changes. By this definition, information includes, above all, decisions, distinctions, and new insights.

Information is the third basic element of nature, besides matter and energy, which has to be considered in order to understand states and events in systems, and in particular the way they work. In that sense, it was one of the most important and first discoveries in cybernetics.

Complexification

This is the process by which complexity increases, resulting from the natural behavior of systems and their interaction.

Complexity

This is perhaps the most fundamental characteristic of reality. Complexity results from a multiplicity of possible differences and distinctions. Where these differences come from, and what their causes are, is not that important for verifying complexity as such, but it will be important when dealing with complexity in the sense of managing it.

The *consequences* of complexity are inscrutability, incalculability, non-analyzability, non-predictability, permanent change, dependency on history, but also all the superior qualities found in biological and social systems, such as versatility, ability to learn, flexibility, responsiveness, the ability to evolve, creativity, and identity. These consequences of complexity make management difficult; on the other hand, however, they are what makes it successful if they are handled in the right way.

The *measure* of complexity is *variety.* The term denominates the number of possible *distinguishable states* a system can have or develop based on its configuration.

Cybernetics

This is the science of (self-) control and (self-) regulation in complex systems by means of information and communication. Its primary focus is on the nature of auto-dynamics of complex systems.

Cybernetic Management or Management Cybernetics

This is the application of cybernetics to complex systems of society, that is, its use for the management of all kinds of organizations. Management cybernetics means mastering and exploiting complexity by influencing a complex system through information.

Malik Management System

This is the name of the entire cybernetic managements system I have developed (including all its subsystems, management models, and their systemic and contents) aimed at assessing, shaping, controlling, regulating and developing organizations, companies, and institutions of any kind depending on their nature and complexity.

Master Control(s)

These are the most fundamental regulations taking effect in an entire system down to its periphery, irrespective of their source – be it laws of nature, structural conditions, or man-made stipulations in the sense of regulating principles. The most important Master Controls are decisions and principles that bring about the cybernetic *self*-capabilities of a system, which are self-regulation, self-organization, self-direction, and self-control.

Self-organization

Self-organization in a cybernetic sense and as a management concept is the ability of complex systems to function and fulfill their purpose without any need for external interventions. The purpose of each system can be system-internal or external. Self-organization depends on the structure of the system and on the information that it processes and generates.

An important distinction to be made is between the self-organization of complex systems in their entirety, and the self-organization of persons in the sense of personal working methods.

Controlling, Regulating, Directing

These are approaches to effecting changes in complex systems by means of information, which, in cybernetics, have proven to enable complex systems to function.

System

A *system* is a conjunction of different parts connected by mechanical, energetic, or information links, generating functions that differ from those generated by its individual parts. Systems are never only objects, organizations, or organisms in themselves, but always *in conjunction* with the relevant environment.

System, Model, Concept

A *system* is the section of the world that is, or should be, interesting to us from the perspective of a certain purpose, and of the functionality defined by that purpose.

A *model* is the depiction or image of what we know about the configuration of systems – including the blank spaces of our not-knowing, the "white spots on the map".

A *concept* is what we want to observe and do, based on the model of a system.

Having systems, being a system

Quite frequently we find that executives have an aversion against the term "system". Some associate it with rigidity, schematism, and bureaucracy. The problem solves itself when we distinguish between the meanings of "*having* systems" and "*being* a system". Any experienced manager will be prepared to accept that companies need systems to function – while taking care that these systems will not become too bureaucratic. Many top managers also know that an organization and its environment together *form* a system. Consequently, this is the point where we need to ask what kind of system we are dealing with.

Systemic, Content, Form

Three *dimensions* are important in my management theory: Systemic, content, and form. The first two are constitutive, the third can be varied.

Systemic refers to the *logical* structure or architecture of a management system or management model. The systemic must describe the structural logic of a functioning system, and thus of a cybernetic system, because the cybernetics of a system defines its function and vice versa.

Once the systemic are right, the rightness of management depends on the *content*. As terms ("the words in the boxes") are not identical to content ("what the words mean"), a mere congruence of terms does not necessarily mean that the content is identical as well.

The *form* in the sense of graphic depiction can be varied, as long as this will not change the systemic or logic.

System methodology

This is the set of methods and technologies for investigating, designing, steering, and developing complex socio-technical and productive systems.[6]

Top management

This refers to three things: corporate bodies, persons, and functions at the top level of organizations. Their definition can differ in detail, depending on the relevant legal system and the organization's internal rules and regulations. As has been mentioned before, top management is not identical to general management. The antonym of top management would be "bottom management", possibly also "layer management" if it refers to different levels between the bottom and the top – in any case, terms that are not in common use.

---

6 System methodology was first developed in: Gomez/Malik/Oeller, *Systemmethodik – Grundlagen einer Methodik zur Erforschung und Gestaltung komplexer soziotechnischer Systeme*, Band 1 u. 2, Berne/Stuttgart, 1975.

Part II:
New Times – New Management

At a management conference, during the coffee break:

A: So how about you? What would you say your management style is like: intuitive, charismatic, pragmatic, or rather systemic?

B: Actually I don't really manage at all, in that sense. I just find ways to deal with the things I cannot change.

A: Ah. So you've come to terms with the fact that everything has gotten too complex and too complicated?!

B: No – I've come to terms with the fact that I might just as well forget everything I used to hear and think about management.

Chapter 1
Constants through Change:
Invariance, Self-Organization, Evolution

Don't fight forces; use them.
Buckminster Fuller, a "20ᵗʰ century Leonardo"

Change is constant. This seeming paradox points to both the problem and the solution for how professional corporate policy needs to be designed. Change alone is chaos. Constancy alone is paralysis. Both together, however, generate a dynamic order for the function of and life in systems.

If, in the flux of constantly changing events, there were no invariance, stability, steady patterns, and structure, effective action would not be possible. This is true for nature as well as for societal institutions. The generation and exploitation of dynamic order is a principle of life laid out by nature itself. It is also the purpose of management, in particular of corporate policy as the regulating function for any institution of a functioning society.

Safe Landmarks at the Top Level

One of the chief prerequisites for top-level management positions is the ability to recognize what remains constant in the midst of change and to steer change by means of constants – that is, by principles and rules. Successful corporate leaders have demonstrated that ability. Looking back at what they have achieved, they will usually comment on the *permanent and fundamental* principles underlying their actions, not the hustle and bustle of everyday business occurrences.[7] The latter are used for illustrative pur-

---

7 Two prime examples of recent years are the writings of Helmut Maucher and Wendelin Wiedking, two former CEOs and long-standing corporate leaders – the former at Nestlé, the latter at Porsche. See also the articles by Heinrich von Pierer, Bernd Pischetsrieder, and Michael Hilti in: Krieg, Walter/Galler, Klaus/Stadelmann, Peter (eds.), *Richtiges und gutes Management: vom System zur Praxis*,

poses at best. Their main interest focuses on reliable orientation criteria which in the turmoil of events have provided safe pointers for right decisions.

Successful top managers reflect on those rules which have helped them cope with uncertainty and time pressure. They talk about the principles that enabled them to maintain their aplomb even when relevant information was hard to get at, and when even the sharpest intellect was not enough to assess all possible influences and consequences. In short, they talk about the principles that helped them cope with *complexity*. In doing so, they differentiate between rules that strangulate and rules that liberate.

The greater the external changes they had to cope with as architects, commanders and conductors of their organizations, or which they themselves brought on as innovators, the more important they found the constant in change. Without exception, the constants for the best of the successful corporate leaders include five things:

- the customer,
- six control parameters,
- awareness of the permanent risk,
- awareness of the limited time available,
- responsibility for continuation after they leave.

Greater Performance through Indirect Control

Undisputed masters in top management regulate things not only at the top management level, but also at the "top thinking level". It is the essence of their top management task. *They make the right decisions by applying the right principles – at those points where information is lacking.* They replace the information that is missing by the insight inherent in permanent truths. This is the method of indirect control, as opposed to direct influence.

Of course, successful top managers are also well-versed in using direct methods, such as instructing, directing, and commanding; however, contrary to managers with no experience in dealing with complexity, the successful leaders use direct methods specifically to bring to bear the indirectly working forces in the system.

Bern/Stuttgart/Wien 2004. Also, Warren C. Buffett, the legendary CEO of Berkshire Hathaway, has published exemplary statements on this subject.

They use basic principles, rules, and organizing principles as powerful regulators, wherever direct methods fail because things are getting too complex to keep track. In fact, such regulators are not one out of many but *the only* tool to cope with extreme complexity. Above all, however, indirect controls are the levers for exploiting complexity. Using these approaches, well-versed top managers achieve better system performance, greater problem-solving ability, and more success.

Indirect system control through general rules and provisions increases the controlling influence far beyond the boundaries of what the human mind and personal presence can cope with. The indirect way of controlling through rules literally enables a system to expand without limits, to spread and grow in the same way as natural systems do, by way of evolution as can be observed in concrete examples.

The same systemic form of managing through suitable regulating systems is possible not only by natural but also by social systems – based on the same principles. They only take more abstract forms here, and are therefore not as easy to recognize at first sight. Recognizing them is made difficult by the natural limitations to the human brain. This is one of the least-understood regularities of complex systems. However, it is obvious that principles and rules of this indirect kind, and thus of the kind prevalent in all complex systems, have to be a central theme of corporate policy and governance.

At the Center of Systemic Natural Forces

With the regulations of every corporate or systems policy that follow the laws of complex systems – which means they are based on applied cybernetics – we are advancing toward the essence of the nature of complex systems: the insights on the *innermost laws of their regulation.*

These system-immanent laws contain the most important information that can exist about any system: the information on how it functions. Knowing it is having access to the greatest non-violent impact on a system, and to the deepest insight, perception, and comprehension. Rather than from human power, it results from the way that complex systems work. Mahatma Gandhi's non-violent liberation of India from the British colonial power is one historic example, and even Sun Tzu ranked the indirect approach highest among the list of effective approaches.

Power in the sense of effectiveness – not in the sense of violence – is not inherent in persons as such, nor is it in their positions. It only shows in persons who understand the laws for regulating complexity, and who put them into effect through a system of rules and principles. Whatever they may be like as individuals, charismatic or rather nondescript, their effectiveness results from the principles and regulations of the system they shape.

The effect that any person can have can only reach as far as it is visible and audible. The effect of a system, and a corresponding set of regulations, however, is potentially unlimited. If it is a complex system capable of self-organization – and even small companies form complex systems in conjunction with their environments – it will use more information and intelligence than even the smartest architect can ever have access to.

Insights about nature and the function of systems have been among the best-guarded secrets of all times.

In the ancient cultures, the owners of such secrets were usually the priest castes, only rarely the rulers themselves. As sovereigns, they would receive from the priests just the information they needed in the immediate situation – if only for reasons of self-protection. The passing on of insights about self-organizing phenomena has always been subject to magical rituals, relicts of which are still to be found in modern-day societies.

Universality through Universal Principles

The most important insight from cybernetics is that successful regulation in and of systems will follow the same logic always and everywhere. It happens irrespective of the diversity of applications, cultures, and manifestations of systems, both in animate and inanimate nature.

The ever-effective functioning patterns of complex systems can be found in all areas of life, and in what appear to be countless manifestations. Recognizing what they have in common is the art that can be learnt from cybernetics. It distills the essence of generally effective phenomena – the laws of the innermost function of systems. Hence, the bandwidth of applications is enormous.

Control and regulation in the cybernetic sense can be found, for instance, in a simple water faucet as well as in the evolution of nature, in grammar as well as in modern market and legal systems. For instance, genetics are largely about the investigation of regulation mechanisms in biology, and jurisprudence – an entirely different field – is about dealing with one of society's most important regulation systems. In the absence of rules there is chaos and the rule of force. Wherever there is order there must be regulation, otherwise there will be disorder. Regulation relates to all orders and all processes. If you know the laws underlying them you can apply them anywhere.

How to get Your Own Way

Anyone with a *general* knowledge of cybernetic regulation will master regulation as such. He will thus be able to get any kind of system to both "high altitudes" and "long distances".

Cybernetics does not provide any of the popular, but usually counterproductive, "sure" formulas for concrete, factual work in management. Instead, it offers answers to the central question of *how to get your own way*, as one of the great pioneers of cybernetics, W. Ross Ashby, put it.[8] It is one of the best mottos for designing a system-compatible corporate policy.

Once you have understood how complex systems by nature control and regulate *themselves,* using the effect of information – that is to say, once you know the backgrounds of *Master Controls* in corporate policy, or the cybernetic laws of nature – you will have understood it for any conceivable application, for this regulation logic is *invariant.* Once you have truly understood it you will have more than *information* and more than *knowledge.* You will then possess the deepest insight.

Insight into the phenomena of *Master Controls* will not only enable you to see the world with different eyes. It will also provide you with a new understanding of what happens in a systemically interconnected world, which is impenetrable to the traditional way of thinking due to its complexity. Strictly speaking, the world can only be understood by understanding its systems.

---

8 Ashby, Ross W., *An Introduction to Cybernetics,* London 1956, 5th edition 1970, p. 243.

The general cybernetic laws[9] are universally valid. They apply to anything dependent on information. Hence, they are valid not only for business organizations but for *any* kind of institution, no matter what its purpose and what area or industry it operates in, for any kind of life and living being, and for the systems of inanimate nature. The cybernetic laws of nature are universal principles which provide reliable orientation and security particularly when circumstances are complex.

When Cybernetics Is Ignored

No organization whatsoever could exist without regulation and self-regulation. It would have never come into being, as every institution is created and maintained through regulation and self-regulation. Whoever ignores this fact ignores the actual situation of a system.

For instance, anyone with cybernetic system knowledge was able to realize early on that the Daimler Chrysler merger was unlikely to succeed for complexity reasons – or if it did, it would be under extremely favorable conditions of the kind one should never rely on – and that the most probable result would eventually be a costly separation. It was the topic of a presentation I gave at the company's training center in spring 1999, addressing the roughly 100 managers – half of them Americans, the other half Germans – who were to implement the merger. Many of them were in a contemplative mood because they had an uneasy feeling about what lay ahead of them. By contrast, the members of top management, who were also present, were not very amenable to these considerations. The category of complexity was beyond their thinking.

The foreseeable dangers were also, from the beginning on, discussed at my public management training courses which were often attended by

---

9 It would lead us too far here to explain the cybernetic laws in the narrower sense in sufficient detail. On the other hand, a brief overview carries the risk of numerous critical misunderstandings, from linguistic on to interpretative barriers. In my books *Systemmethodik* and my habilitation treatise *Strategie des Managements komplexer Systeme* they are dealt with at length. A poignant overview of the meaning of cybernetics as a theory of corporate management is provided by Michael Mirow, "Wie praktisch ist eine gute Theorie?", in: Krieg, Walter/Galler, Klaus/Stadelmann, Peter (eds.), *Richtiges und gutes Management: vom System zur Praxis*, Berne/Stuttgart/Vienna, 2004.

Daimler managers. The damage that ultimately occured, in the order of magnitude of almost a hundred billion Euros, could have been avoided by paying attention to the cybernetics of this case, and it could have even been turned into a success if the laws of complex systems had been taken into account.

At least in theory, an interesting question arises with regard to the responsibility of consultants and supervisory bodies: Should not people in these functions know more about cybernetics and complex systems? It looks as though it was an utter lack of knowledge about the nature and manageability of complexity that made people recommend and approve of the merger, defend it with faulty arguments, and ultimately hesitate too long when a new and better corporate policy decision was called for.

It would certainly be wrong to seek the causes of failure at the subject level of the individual case, or at least to seek them *only* there. Questions of manageability, controllability, coping with complexity, and maneuverability of such a situation are much more helpful in explaining this situation than are model policy, technology, cost, prices, and marketing.

What Managers Sense But Have Yet to Use Better

For many managers, the everyday experience with the market's self-organization leads to a peculiar *ambivalence*: on the one hand, they clearly recognize the superior ability of free markets to unleash enormous powers of performance, coordinate them, establish coherence, and create new things by way of competition as a mode of discovery. Hence they are perfectly familiar with the principles of freedom, self-responsibility, and use of local intelligence and information. On the other hand, many of them hesitate to establish comparable rules in their own organizations, in the form of a constitution and a policy, to turn their companies into similarly high-performing systems.

The main reason, in my opinion, is that most managers in the course of their education have had little or no opportunity to study *complex, self-organizing systems*, that is to say, to learn about *cybernetic system theory*. The university courses that today's executives have attended lack the common element of the *theory of complex systems*. In other words, managers are taught almost nothing about the very field in which they will pursue their profession, and about the very "object" that they will have to manage, applying the very perspective on the problem that makes their profession necessary: the mastering of complexity.

Knowledge about complex systems makes it infinitely easier for top managers to *integrate* their subject-specific knowledge, their experience, and their personal competence at the point of their central task: the overall management of their companies as networked, complex systems, using cybernetic laws for structuring and steering.

There are a few study disciplines where relevant knowledge about these things is taught. Law students are taught some knowledge about regulation, and students of some technical disciplines learn about control engineering. However, seeing the *common element* in the different disciplines and projecting it onto the problem at hand – corporate management – requires an integrating context, which I have established with my management system and its basis, the *theory of the management of complex systems*.[10]

Accidental Experiments for Self-Organization

While cybernetic principles are certainly applied in organizations where modern management is practiced – otherwise they would not be able to function, due to their complexity – this is usually done in a random, uncoordinated and intuitive manner. The approaches used have no systemic foundation in the relevant basic laws of control. Moreover, systemic-cybernetic principles keep getting thwarted with diametrically opposed, reductionist-mechanistic solution approaches, to the point where they lose their effect.

Varieties of complexity-compatible solutions, such as decentralization, divisionalization, business unit organization, or management by objectives and self-control, empowerment, and enablement, remain largely uncoordinated experiments. They are somewhat accidental manifestations of the same cybernetic principle, attempting – although in a piecemeal approach

---

10 By integrating relevant disciplines, such as jurisprudence, mass psychology, and cybernetics, Constantin Malik in his book *Ahead of Change,* Frankfurt/New York, 2010, arrives at further-reaching solution concepts, by showing that an anticipatory legislation is possible at the control level of systems, and where it has to focus to be able to prevent crises.

– to bring this principle into effect. The constant aim is to organize an institution in such a way that it can organize itself, or in other words, to organize the setting free of forces without losing overall control.

If all this is done in a targeted, systematic manner and grounded in theory, the effect will multiply rapidly. What these experiments have in common is that they create scope and *liberties* for establishing local responsibilities and accountability, so that the general corporate policy rules can intelligently be applied to the particular situation.

In this context, freedom is usually perceived as either a motivational factor or a superior philosophical and political *value*. And indeed, it can be both these things. Above all, however, freedom is an *organizing principle*, a *cybernetic* organizing principle which releases the self-steering forces of a system while enabling their optimal use through regulating principles.

The reason that freedom will turn into a superior *value* in the narrower sense – for instance, in the sense of liberalism – is that this organizing principle has a very high regulative effect on the systems organized, and is therefore considered a good worth protecting and maintaining. Self-organizing and -regulating systems, or societies, are therefore more powerful than those organized in a collectivist manner, because they are able to mobilize and utilize more intelligence, information and knowledge than any other type of system. The substance of these principles, which Friedrich von Hayek has recognized as being clearly cybernetic, was familiar to the earlier philosophers of the true (Anglo-Saxon) liberalism, and a central element of their concept of society. However, it was only modern cybernetics that revealed their true nature and recognized them as being universally valid for all kinds of systems.

Master Control, Cybernetics, and Governance

Master Control by way of corporate policy is fundamentally different from the traditional perceptions on this subject, which are purely economics-centered. *Master Control* is more than corporate policy in the sense generally known. It is comprehensive systems policy which triggers the evolutionary leap from regulation to *self*-regulation, and from organization to *self*-organization, by making use of forces intrinsic to the system.

Directing (or controlling) and regulating are only different words for the same thing: *managing*. Both have the same basic meaning: *establishing order where otherwise there would be none* and *providing direction (or control) where it is lacking*. Regulation is achieved with rules. System-compatible regulation always follows the same cybernetic logic.

It is not without reason that the name *cybernetics*, the science of the functioning of complex systems and their regularities, stems from the Greek *kybernetes*, which translates as *helmsman*. There is no helmsman that steers his ship using his own physical strength – quite the contrary. A helmsman will always take advantage of the forces provided by the waters and the weather by correctly assessing their power, adapting to them, and taking advantage of them for his purposes. Cybernetics is the *science of control and self-control, of regulation and self-regulation of all complex systems in animate and inanimate nature by means of information and communication*. Norbert Wiener, the mathematician and founder of modern cybernetics, in his original definition spoke of *Cybernetics – or Control and Communication in the Animal and the Machine*, which should make it clearer why I refer to a corporate policy in this sense as *Master Control*. In the course of this book, and of the entire series, it will become evident that cybernetics will be the key science in the age of complexity.

The words *gubernator* in ancient Latin, as well as *governor* and *governance* in English were also derived from the Greek *kybernetes*. *Governance* in the sense of corporate policy, properly understood and based on cybernetics, is the *opposite* of rigid financial control, for which the term has unfortunately gained currency. In a cybernetic sense, *governance* means *organizing a system in such a way that it can organize and regulate itself as far as possible*.

Strength by Exploiting Complexity

Wars are not won by combat strength as such, but by *making use of* combat strength through proper *control*; they are lost when this is done wrongly or not done at all. Vietnam and Iraq are cases in point. They also prove that the metaphor of David and Goliath holds true to this day. In the age of complexity, it will have even more significance than it had in times of brute force. Judging an army by its combat strength, as is customary, has little sense as long as its cybernetics are not known – that is, its systems of information, direction, and control.

It is not combat strength that matters but strength of complexity, as it might be called – the ability of a system to regulate and direct itself. That is universally valid. If you have no command of foreign languages you will have a hard time getting by in foreign countries. If you do speak foreign languages the world will be open to you because you will have access to more variety, and therefore more regulating power in a complex environment. A company that manages product range extensions more expertly than its competitors will be able to offer its customers more variety, thus having access to a bigger market and better growth opportunities.

Regulating better always means *using more variety*, more opportunities, a greater range of options. The more effective a system's self-regulation, the better its performance will be. *Increasing* its regulating capacity will give it wings, often carrying its performance and success potential beyond all previous limits. Performance increases of this kind can be achieved in management by viewing corporate policy not as a set of subject-related rules but as overriding *systems policy*, as I have pointed out in the introductory chapter. The key prerequisite for this is that the problem-solving insights of cybernetics are considered and applied. It leads to solutions which get the highest performance, the greatest viability, the best function out of a system without burning it out.

Out of Control–A Synonym for "Problem"

As long as it works, the self-regulation of complex systems will not be apparent to the layman. Because this is so, many do not even realize that something is *under control*. Most people believe this to be a normal state, a matter of course, so why should it attract attention? However, they will realize at once – often unpleasantly and painfully – when something is *out of control*. When regulation does not work, or does so poorly, there is *a problem*. Only then will it become apparent that without the regulation described by cybernetics, there is basically only dead matter, of not much more use than an arm hanging down limply, paralyzed after a stroke.

Every accident that prevents us from using a hand or bending a knee provides a drastic example of what it is like to be *out of control*, if only in part. The dysfunctions of the nervous system and brain reveal the whole tragic of regulation problems, as the neuronal system with its *Master Controls,* which are located in the brain, is the organism's primary control system.

Other examples include plane crashes due to malfunctions in their regulation systems, or car crashes due to regulation failures including, of course, those of the driver – for he is part of the system. A bomb threat at an airport, though "merely" an information and irrespective of whether it is true, will stop all traffic; the collapse of an ecological system indicates the collapse of its regulation.

Whenever there are difficulties, the reason will usually be insufficient regulating capacity. Problems like these will eventually manifest in the categories of matter and energy, and in business, in the category of money. They can, however, be understood and solved only in categories of information, regulation, and control. Monetary costs will only arise if regulation fails.

Subject-Related Issue or System Problem?
Understanding Systems Better

The regulating knowledge needed for the *Master Controls* of a system-compatible corporate policy is *knowledge of a higher order.* If, however, all thinking stops at the subject level of the operation of a system, one will inevitably get caught in the details of subject-related issues and fail to get access to the system-related ones.

Familiarity with cybernetic, so-called *emergent* system characteristics, such as stability, adaptability, manoeuvrability, cohesion, dynamics, interconnectedness, information and communication – to name just a few – enables one to arrive at an assessment of complex systems that is often diametrically opposed to what is achievable by merely appraising things at the object level.

The MIT professor Jay Forrester[11], one of the pioneers of modern simulation methods, was quite to the point when he spoke of *counterintuitive behavior* vis-à-vis complex systems, which he was able to observe repeatedly when conducting his simulation studies. What he meant was that sys-

---

11 Forrester, Jay, *Industrial Dynamics*, Cambridge Mass., 1969.

tems will usually behave very differently from what is expected after even the most careful conventional analysis.

Assuming yet another perspective, the groundbreaking studies by Bamberg-based psychologist Dietrich Dörner[12] prove that man, with his natural physiological and mental set-up, is not particularly capable of skillfully dealing with complexity. We gather our life experience, both as generations and as individuals, in the context of *simple* systems. Our activity as managers, however, takes place in the context of *extremely complex* systems for which there is next to no education available to date.[13]

As might be expected, sociology plays a major role in understanding man within the complexity of his system ecology. True masterpieces, in terms of both language and content, have been delivered by the St. Gallen-based sociologist Peter Gross with his writings about the multi-option society – a paradigmatic term referring to the society of complexity – as well as with his latest book about the return of religion, *Jenseits der Erlösung* ["Beyond Salvation"]. With these, he has made one of the most important contributions to man's orientation in a situation of hypercomplexity.[14]

With a sound knowledge about cybernetics and complexity, it would have been possible not only to correctly judge the DaimlerChrysler case early on, but also to see that the United States' Iraq strategy was doomed to fail. For this viewpoint, which I have taken from the very start, I was criticized very harshly by some people over a period of two years – until the turn of events became my strongest advocate. The line of dissent and the degree of incomprehension were similar to what I encountered years ago, in response to my publications about the non-viability of the New Economy idea. Or to my timely warning against the instabilities inherent in the financial markets, which then became visible in the years 2000 to 2003. Or to my wake-up call addressing the foreseeable difficulties with the shareholder approach and a corporate governance concept that was based on it and centered around financial and short-term goals only. Re-

---

12 Dörner, Dietrich, *Logik des Misslingens. Strategisches Denken in komplexen Situationen*, Reinbek 1989, 2004, as well as the very insightful study entitled "Hitlers Handeln", in: Krieg, Walter/Galler, Klaus/Stadelmann, Peter (eds.), *Richtiges und gutes Management: vom System zur Praxis*, Berne/Stuttgart/Vienna, 2004.

13 Those interested can obtain information about such education, leading to the degree of Master of Management®, at my institute.

14 Gross, Peter, *Die Multioptionsgesellschaft*, Frankfurt, 1994 and *Jenseits der Erlösung*, Bielefeld, 2007, as well as many other writings.

sentment of this kind – both emotionally understandable but unjustified on factual and subject-related grounds – is the result if systems issues are mistaken for problems relating to specific matters.

Collapse or Evolution

Regulating *is* managing and managing *is* regulating. Regulating means *mastering and exploiting complexity* for a continually better function of systems.

Complexity is variety, or more precisely, the number of possibilities that latently exist or could arise in a system. Seemingly simple systems can quickly grow to a complexity of astronomical proportions. The influences of markets and technologies – in particular information technology which, for its part, is based on cybernetics – have caused society's complexity to grow at a speed and degree that exceeds anything previously experienced. Globalization and an ever more rapid increase of knowledge are among the most obvious effects.

Compared to that, the dissemination of cybernetic knowledge and its use for the management of organizations has grotesquely fallen short. It is all the more absurd as, due to the advances made in cybernetics, this knowledge is more easily obtainable than ever before. In many areas of technology and science, it is systematically used, in part with spectacular success, and is basically open to anyone. Nevertheless, explicit knowledge about systems and regulation, as well as its systematic application, are still unknown to large parts of society.

Owing to the boom in MBA programs that came with globalization, there has even been an increasing trend in the opposite direction – departing from a wholistic, system-focused way of thinking. In the context of a corporate governance driven by shareholder-value thinking and financial capitalism, what has been taught is a mechanistic way of thinking, amounting to little more than a reductionist focus on financial figures and deriving its powerful status – which has lately been declining – from the *illusion* of outstanding progressiveness.

At the same time, any profound analysis using the tools of complexity research, cybernetics, and systems sciences will reveal an increasing number of systems displaying ever clearer symptoms of instability. There are countless signs of being *out of control*. In many areas, the explosion of complexity has led to a potential for collapse that might be irreversible.

We are faced with systems that nobody understands, and where nobody knows what kinds of effects can be triggered by interventions. The central problem of the 21st century will be unmanageable systems. That is not the opinion of illiterates and laymen but of the very experts for such systems. Cases in point are the international financial markets, of which the most notable experts say that they have become too complex to understand and that the so-called system risks have become incalculable. Further examples include international terror, the drug scene, radicalization, fundamentalism, and the internet. The greater the knowledge people have about a certain system, the more likely it is they will arrive at the same diagnosis. The poorer a person's knowledge is, the more naïvely he will believe in the alleged functioning of societal institutions, hoping that "someone" will surely understand and have everything under control.

More and more problems of society as a whole, as well as political problems, belong in this category of potentially unmanageable systems. With the prevalent reductionist approaches, aimed at repairing errors and curing symptoms – and incurring gigantic cost in the process – these potentially unmanageable systems are artificially perpetuated and thus made more and more unstable. For their necessary reprogramming we need *Master Controls*, based on a profound knowledge of the innermost laws of regulation of complex systems.

When Systems Are Embedded in Systems

The 20th century was characterized by the world of *organizations*. When Peter F. Drucker first called attention to the *"Society of Organizations"* in the late fifties, the idea was radically new. Although many people have yet to understand this, we have in fact outgrown the society of organizations. We now live in a world of *systems* or, more precisely, of systems *embedded in systems*. Few have realized earlier and more clearly than Peter F. Drucker himself that we were heading that way, a fact that he pointed out as early as in 1957 in his book *Landmarks of Tomorrow,* and which he reemphasized one year before his death in his preface to my honorary publication.[15]

---

15 Krieg, Walter/Galler, Klaus/Stadelmann, Peter (eds.), *Richtiges und gutes Management: vom System zur Praxis*, Berne/Stuttgart/Vienna, 2004.

What looks like, or is described as, an organization in the traditional sense – such as a company, a clinic, or a university – is really a system of systems. Many are too complex to be overlooked and understood in their entirety by any of the people involved, so long as they apply the usual mindsets and ways of thinking, so they cannot be effectively controlled with direct mechanisms. The fact that there are certain zones of direct control within such organizations only nourishes the illusion that the whole system can be kept under control this way. Depicted conventionally, however, these organizations cannot be seen in their true nature. It is as though one would depict man as a mere skeleton.

Virtually every organization today is embedded in a system context much too comprehensive to be overseen by one individual. Its function depends on this context much more than on the details of the institution itself. Organizations, for their part, are embedded in a much greater matrix of systems – almost like atoms are. Their configuration and their means of embedding can be manifest in two different forms:

- firstly, as systems which nobody has planned, and
- secondly, as systems with deliberately designed *Master Controls*.

The following paragraphs provide a few examples which should help give a sense of the two types of systems.

Two Kinds of Systems – Two Kinds of Management

I have touched on the subject of system control before, but not in the detail corresponding to its significance. Some more information is required.

Phenomena are commonly classified as either artificial or natural ones – that is, those made by man and those emerging without human intervention. In the former case we are dealing with *construction*, in the latter with *evolution*.

Systems of the first kind are the result of *human intention*, and accordingly, of *purposeful human action*. These systems do not do anything by themselves, except that they can break down without human intervention.

The second kind of systems, the natural ones, come into being *without* any human action being involved, much less *human intention* or planning.

They evolve on their own, due to their very nature, and what happens in them also happens by itself. Mankind has developed in this manner.

So far so good. But difficulties arise from the fact that man interferes with these natural systems – and he no longer does this as an ecological part of those systems, as animals and plants may in their own ways, but based on intellect and reason, two characteristics that distinguish man from the systems of nature. As we know today, human intellect and reason are not equipped well enough to interfere with complex systems without involving the risk of unintended side effects and follow-on damages.

The archetype of artificial systems is the *machine*; of natural systems it is the *organism*. Both types of systems, the *mechanistic* and the *evolutionary* type, are associated with certain philosophical mindsets and corresponding behaviors which have shaped, directed, and also misguided European intellectual history and, along with it, political history. These mindsets are linked to the best intellectual achievements, but also with a mire of misconceptions, confusion of ideas, and errors.

Two basic types of thinking, however, ought to be known to managers, which is why I will single them out here. *Artificial systems*, or machines, result from a way of thinking which is referred to as *mechanistic*. As is appropriate for the prototype of these systems, mechanistic thinking is how machines are designed, planned, and built. The point is that mechanistic thinking extends to the last detail, because the construction of a machine requires it in order to function. These days, mechanistic thinking is often seen in a bad light, which is wrong. After all, it is this type of thinking to which we owe the great achievements of technology, as well as the emergence of civilization – though not of culture.[16]

The negative aspect of mechanistic thinking is something else: the fact that it is generalized to an unacceptable degree and applied to entirely different areas where it is bound to be ineffective, even detrimental. The un-

---

16 For those who specialize in the subject: Mechanistic thinking used to be referred to as "constructivist" thinking, which today would lead to misunderstandings, what with the philosophy of constructivism. Philosophical constructivism addresses the fact that the perception of reality is actually not an objective representation provided by the sense organs but a construction of the human brain. In my book *Strategie des Managements komplexer Systeme* I use the term "contructivist-technomorph thinking" rather than "mechanistic thinking" because it was in use even before philosophical constructivism, as proven by Friedrich von Hayek's writings.

disputed achievements of mechanistic thinking in the field of technology lead people to apply it to natural, evolutionary systems and in particular to social and commercial organizations. When this happens, the method of *construction* has turned into the issuing of very specific and purposeful instructions, directives, and *orders*. Evolutionary systems, however – and social systems belong in this category – do not obey orders or directives. So the tried and tested methods which are effective for mechanistic systems do not work there. For instance, we cannot order anybody to trust us or love us; we cannot force a child to go to sleep, or command a negotiation partner to conclude a contract. That is obvious to anyone as long as it refers to their familiar environment.

It is equally obvious, though, that we are not forced to remain passive in such situations – we can always resort to the method of *cultivation*. That is to say, we can create conditions in which the odds are good that the desired behavior or condition will materialize on its own or can be accomplished indirectly. We create these conditions directly. Their effect is an indirect one. When we – directly – create favorable conditions we have no guarantee of their indirect effect, but we certainly increase the chances.

To the rationalist mind, this approach does not appear to be particularly efficient, which is why it prefers to produce the desired effects in a direct manner. Since that is objectively impossible, however, there is no choice but to take the indirect path. The reason why it is impossible lies in the immense complexity of evolutionary (including social) systems, which results from their inevitable momentum.

What appears to be a weakness at first, however, quickly turns into an enormous *opportunity* when we are neither hesitant nor reluctant but appreciate the nature of complex systems and, out of this higher insight, readily accept that the indirect way is the *only* way to deal with complexity. Once we have accepted that, we can dedicate all our strength to developing better and better, increasingly effective indirect methods. We can become *masters of the indirect approach*. Just like a jiu-jitsu master uses the strength of his opponent, we use other people's strengths by *directing* them the right way without having to muster any of our own strength or energy. What matters in this context is not the material world but the informational one; not the 20th century categories but those of the 21st century: intelligence, information, knowledge, and insight.

All at once, complex systems cease to be stubborn adversaries we have to force or command to do something, and turn into partners helping us to accomplish more and greater things. We no longer struggle but *dance with the system*, as Heinz von Foerster used to say.

When Systems Arise Unintentionally

Mechanistic systems can only develop as far as their *constructors* can think. In other words, they are limited by their creators' abilities and knowledge. By contrast, evolutionary systems are not restrained by any kind of constructor or his plans. They can grow, unfold, and develop as far as their *inner programs* permit – basically without limits, for programs are information. Once it is there, information can be replicated infinitely, as happens with the genetic code. Here lies the secret of life and its potential for expansion, which is basically limitless.

Life, intelligence, information, and order – in the sense beyond everyday perception – may even be conceivable without matter and energy. We have no way of knowing. Perhaps they exist through a kind of communication which is not necessarily tied to matter and energy. It is these questions and things that are categorically different and new in the emerging society of complexity.

So are the principles and possibilities for management in the age of complexity, provided we find the right *programs* – programs which free organizations from the restraints of the human mind and of current management, and spur their evolution.

Admittedly, not everything evolving in this sense is truly useful. We need an additional *distinction*: between *self-organization for success* and *self-organization for failure*. Not every kind of self-organization is necessarily desirable.

There are social systems whose evolution is guided by bad programs. Their self-organization has a detrimental and destructive effect, and ultimately leads to a collapse. In a manner of speaking, they have an inbuilt program or *logic of failure*, as Dietrich Dörner calls it. There are other social systems which do the opposite: their evolution program guides them to ever greater performance. These systems carry a *logic of success* in them – a very to-the-point phrase coined by Maria Pruckner.

Even though systems cannot be perceived in the way objects can, anyone can "see" that many of the social systems we have today are evolving, all on their own, to form enormous, agglomerated, interconnected structures which nobody has planned or designed that way – rather, they are "simply happening to us". Examples include:

- the healthcare system,
- the educational system,
- global business,
- global transport systems,
- our social systems in the Western world,
- the global financial systems
- national tax systems,
- market economy, and
- the Internet.

These are systems of a special kind. While they *result from human action*, they do *not result from human intention*[17], such as an overall design, a plan, or a certain construction concept. Having arisen from the actions of millions of people who do not know each other – actually cannot know each other – they have long evolved beyond the scope of rational planning. If they conform to planned interventions, they hardly ever do so without unintended side effects.

Some of these systems work well and fulfill their purposes. Others stagger out of one failed reform and into the next. Some have internal run-up programs, some run-down ones.

Due to the hypercomplexity of such systems, it is virtually impossible to understand, analyze, or mentally penetrate them in any *traditional* sense. With the *thinking devices* of cybernetics and systems theory, however, it is possible to understand the laws governing their function, and to establish for them a *constitution* and a *policy* which ensure they will work adequately.[18] The market economy, democracy, and federalism are cases in point wherever they work well.

Measured against the amount of public dissatisfaction, the European Union, for instance, a system of gigantic complexity, works much less

---

17 A phrase coined by the Scottish philosopher Adam Ferguson, a representative of the School of Common Sense.

18 Main contributions in this field include the philosophy of Hans Albert. See, e.g., his essay *Freiheit und Ordnung*, in particular his remarks on "Europe and the taming of sovereignty", Tübingen, 1986, as well as his essays listed in the References section of this book.

poorly than is often maintained. There is no doubt, however, that it could work several times better if cybernetics were explicitly applied.

One of the most intriguing and well-functioning systems in this context is Switzerland (as a non-Swiss native I believe I can say this without being suspected of chauvinism). The cybernetics of Switzerland is nearly unknown abroad, and even many Swiss people – including numerous intellectuals – are not really aware of it. According to conventional political theories, Switzerland should not even be able to function, which might be an indicator of possible flaws of these theories. Among other things, Switzerland is a fantastic object of study in terms of the wide variety of ways to design a Federalist system, compared to Austria or Germany, for instance; this variety, in turn, gives rise to different degrees of self-organization and self-control. A particularly interesting element in this context is the cybernetics of the Swiss tax system, and it is not without reason that its success does not find much favor among other countries.

Systematic Self-Organization, Systemic Evolution

The second type of hypercomplex systems are those that were built around a deliberately and carefully designed core of regulation, in such a way that they can grow and unfold in an orderly manner.[19] Due to this enormous functional capability, even these systems can quickly become impenetrable for the individual. However, with every expansion of the system, the laws that safeguard their functionality are carried to their finest capillaries, so to speak. They grow with the system – for instance, an enterprise – just like the nervous system grows with an organism. As a result, the same functionalities are present and active, both at the periphery or basis and at the highest level of regulation, or the center.

This is perhaps the best example for how *Master Controls* work: they are *regulators for entire system configurations* which in principle are able to expand at random. For a graphical depiction, the only appropriate

---

19 See Haken, Hermann, "Synergetik: Von der Laser-Metaphorik zum Selbstorganisationskonzept im Management", in: Krieg, Walter/Galler, Klaus/Stadelmann Peter (Hrsg.), *Richtiges und gutes Management: vom System zur Praxis*, Berne/Stuttgart/Vienna, 2005.

means is network diagrams. Traditional organization charts are not only unsuitable but also misleading. Basically and essentially, Master Controls are *programs* for generating functional system worlds with the potential for top performance.

Examples of this type of systems include the following:

- Alliances, franchise and license systems that work, such as those of the McDonald's variety.
- Companies like Aldi and Lidl and other large retail chains.
- The StarAlliance around Lufthansa, which not only includes the most renowned airlines but also hundreds of other companies without whom the alliance would not be viable.
- The Nestlé group – an outstanding example of a system that works well.
- Well-functioning systems have also emerged in global tourism, in the form of hotel chains and clusters, based on a variety of providers and producers across the whole economic problem-solving chain.
- An area where new system configurations continuously emerge is the automotive industry. This gets to a point where OEMs themselves no longer manufacture cars but confine themselves to defining specifications and brands, while everything else is done by cooperating networks which keep reconfiguring themselves. They may be the first prototypes of systems where there is a *corporate management* but not necessarily a *corporation*. They might even be the dominant kind of systems in the age of complexity.
- While this is going on in the industrial sector, other sectors are already leading the way. Large media companies belong to the new kind of systems, or are well on the way there. Key characteristics of these systems are even more apparent in symphony orchestras, and perhaps most evident in organizations whose output is noticed and often admired worldwide, while hardly anyone knows how that was accomplished: examples include the big festivals in the cultural and entertainment business, or major events of any kind – from the Love Parades on to major cycle races, the Formula-1 business, and the greatest showpiece of all, the Olympics, including everything associated with it, from sports organizations on to the sponsoring scene and the global communications machinery. These are systems which come to life temporarily, comprising over a billion people at the peak of their function, and which fade away afterwards.

- Law firms and consultancies also belong to this type of systems. By industry standards they may be small, but as knowledge organizations they are often exponentially more complex than macroscopic large systems. Frequently, successful private banks also belong to this category of systems. The *Master Controls* in this case include the partnership agreements.
- The global insurance industry works in accordance with intricate systems of this kind, unknown to the general public and largely ignored by the media.
- Depending on the country, there can be very interesting system and network structures in the field of cooperatives, which, in their often rather silent way are enormously successful - although, according to what is taught in business administration textbooks and MBA courses, they should not even be able to function.
- Last but not least, a prime example of an organization clearly working by rules – although somewhat sensitive because it is regularly misunderstood – is the Catholic Church. This also includes Catholic orders, of which the Benedictine order has the most well-known rules. The Church's activities may not please many people. However, even its adversaries have to acknowledge that it has existed for approximately 2,000 years, surviving a number of crises, and that in fact it may be considered to be the only truly global organization. Management experts ought to be interested in the reasons for that, at least as an object of study, no matter how they personally feel about the Church's policy.

The second type of systems, those that have systematically been organized in a system-compatible way, include highly successful companies who have deliberately and systematically opted for a system approach, and for using cybernetics as their Master Controls – and who have done it early enough to be able to ascribe their often grand successes to that fact. They are systematically organized in a systemic way, rather than systematically organized in an unsystemic way, like so many others.

- One example is the Liechtenstein-based company *Hilti*, whose worldwide success in fastening technology has been based on a system approach since the early 1960s.
- Another case in point is *Würth* in Germany, which explicitly attributes its impressive rise – from smallest beginnings to world market leadership and a headcount of over 30,000 within five decades – to their cy-

bernetic management system.[20] The Würth example proves that even very small companies need to establish the right *Master Controls* from the start in order to evolve successfully.

That does not necessarily mean, however, that these systems will also function in the future. They could degenerate, decay, or die of "immune deficiency". It could happen that a new generation of managers is no longer able to recognize the basic principles of previous success, and believe they can do much better. Firms like these can easily reach complexity limits, the overcoming of which requires *new* regulators whose implementation may or may not be successful.

If they fail, however, the reason for their demise will be that they allowed their regulating principles or *Master Controls* – the "eternal truths" of proper function – to degenerate. If they continue to be successful or their success even multiplies, then that will also be owed to their regulation intelligence – their ability not only to cope with increasing complexity but to use it actively and offensively.

The wealth of systems in society fully reflects the abundance of natural systems. When we look beyond their differences we will see the similarities. The principles of function are the same in both cases; they are universal and invariant. It is always a question of complexity and its regulation, of control and communication, of systemic-cybernetic regularities.

Neither Biologism nor Social Darwinism

One of the recurring organization patterns of institutions which have worked well over long periods of time and through many eras of crises is the cell structure. Systems like this can basically expand freely as long as their fundamental rules are effective, because their Master Controls grow along with them, as pointed out before.[21]

The basic principle always is to use the cybernetic principles of natural evolution without falling into the trap of primitive biologism or even Social Darwinism. There is a considerable danger of gross misunderstandings, platitudinous analogies, and outright nonsense. Among other things,

---

20 Venohr, Bernd, *Growing Like Würth. The Secret of Global Success*, Frankfurt/ New York, 2006.
21 In volume 4 of this series, the cell structure will be one of the main topics.

bionics is sometimes misused when amateurs attempt to get attention by pointing to behavioral principles from nature and deriving ambiguous recommendations for corporate management. Companies are not packs of wolves or lions, nor do they resemble colonies of ants or bees. There are similarities but also clear differences between biological and socio-cultural evolution.[22] Biologistic approaches are wrong because complex social systems are not based on biogenetic rules part of them is based on rules that have been passed on through culture, and some have been set deliberately. Socio-cultural evolution is therefore much faster and reaches much further than biological evolution does. Both do have the same problem-solving logic, which is success-controlled trial and error – an optimal approach under hypercomplex conditions, as the bionics expert Ingo Rechenberg has demonstrated.[23]

The *logic* of evolution is not tied to certain materials and biological processes but can be manifest in different types of systems and at various degrees of effectiveness. It is independent of the biosphere because it is a common method of exploring, solving problems, and identifying opportunities, as the philosopher Karl Popper has shown.[24]

Evolution is not the struggle between the stronger and the weaker, nor is it a struggle for existence, as common clichés would have it. Contrary to widespread opinion it is a rather unbloody affair. Evolution is a competition among systems for an ever better use of energy and, above all, of complexity. It is a competition among regulating systems, be they biological, nervous, technical, social, or managerial ones. Evolution is not so

22 Blüchel Kurt G./Malik Fredmund (Eds.), *Faszination Bionik. Intelligenz der Schöpfung*, Munich, 2006. See also the proceedings (DVD) of the 1st and 2nd International Bionic Congress for Top Management, entitled *Der Quantensprung im Top-Management: Mit Kybernetik, Systemik und Bio-Logik die Zukunft sichern*, Interlaken, March 2006, as well as *Strategie der Evolution: Phantastische Lösungspotenziale für komplexe Probleme*, Interlaken, March 2007, Malik Management, and in particular Friedrich von Hayek and his criticism of sociobiology in: *Law, Legislation and Liberty*, Vol. 3, London 1979, pp. 153 et seq. Rupert Riedl has depicted both the biological and the socio-cultural evolution in his book *Strukturen der Komplexität* as well as, in simple words, in his essay *Der Verlust der Morphologie* which was posthumously published by his daughter.
23 Ingo Rechenberg describes the logic and methodology of evolution strategy in: *Evolutionsstrategie '94*, Stuttgart, 1994.
24 Popper, Karl R., *Objective Knowledge. An Evolutionary Approach*, Oxford 1972, and perhaps most impressively in: *A World of Propensities*, Bristol, 1990.

much a struggle *against* something as it is a struggle *for* something: the superior solution to a problem. Whoever has the better regulating system, the more effective Master Controls, and the more successful policy, will be a winner in the competition for the use of information, knowledge, and insight.

Chapter 2

Prototypes of System and Self-Organization

What needed to be pointed out in the previous chapter, but in relevant literature often vanishes in a metaphysical-esoteric haze, will be illustrated in this chapter in the simplest way possible, using one prototype for system and one for self-organization.

System Prototype: Water

The phrase *"The whole is more than the sum of its parts"* is generally considered a good approximation to the meaning of *system*. Another, perhaps more elucidating way of putting it is *"The whole is something different from the sum of its parts"*. But even this phrase is not entirely to the point, as the meaning of *sum* remains quite cryptic.

The best and simplest example of a system is *water*. As everyone knows, its components are two oxygen atoms and one hydrogen atom. When they combine they form water. None of the atoms has even one of the properties of water: none is wet or liquid, none vaporizes at 100 degrees Celsius, and none freezes at zero degrees. Conversely, water has none of the properties of its atoms.

We can analyze water by focusing on its properties as a system, or in such a way as to destroy these properties. When we break down water into its components we will find interesting things – but the system will be gone. By contrast, if we combine them – or better even, let them combine – the system will be there.

Thus, two of the most important aspects of systems can be viewed at the level of elementary chemistry: the concurrence of known parts and the formation of something new. In system and bio sciences we speak of *emer-*

gence. Konrad Lorenz, the famous Austrian behavioral scientist and Nobel laureate, also used to speak of *fulguration*.[25] *Risk*, for instance, is a typical emergent phenomenon. Another thing that can be demonstrated using this water example is the relationship between synthesis and analysis. Above all, what becomes evident is that there are different kinds of analysis: one that is reductionist, and destructive for the system, and one that is wholistic and maintaining the system.

Note that I said the water example is the best of all *simple* examples. Readers should keep this in mind because this book is about *complex systems*. There are more system aspects than can effectively be illustrated on this basis. One of the phenomena which the "water chemistry" example cannot explain is the way systems are historically conditioned – their historicity – which plays a crucial role in dealing with complex systems. The emergence of water from its components can infinitely be repeated, which obviously contains a history of its own – but one that comprises the same elements and follows the same course over and over again. The histories of social systems, however, are always unique, non-recurrent, and non-repeatable.

Also, water is one of the systems that can be reduced to its components. It can be broken down into its atoms. This is precisely what reductionism is based on, as well as the corresponding concept of science and of the universe. However, only very few systems can be reduced to their components in this way. Just like apple sauce cannot be turned into apples again, complex systems cannot be set back to their former conditions and configurations.

Among other things, the decomposition of a system also depends on what we consider to be its components. For instance, we know that 2 plus 2 makes 4 and we rely on this to apply at all times. It does not – only under arithmetic conditions. Two drops of water plus two drops of water do not make *four* drops of water but a *small puddle* – and we cannot turn that puddle into the drops it originally consisted of.[26]

---

25 Lorenz, Konrad, *Behind the Mirror. A Search for a Natural History of Human Knowledge.* New York/London, 1977.

26 I was fortunate enough to learn this little water puddle example from the great Karl Popper himself, at the very beginning of my university studies, in the context of the question as to when and to what extent mathematics could be applied to reality. It was one of those coincidences which early alerted me to some of the traps of what is called "scientific", and to the difference between academia and true science.

While we are at it, let me demonstrate something else: In school we learn to answer questions of the above type, such as *"How much is 5 plus 5?"*, and we readily answer them. Another type of question, however, is hardly ever asked: *"How many ways are there to get 10 as a result?"* That is the type of question that is crucial for understanding complexity, systems, society, politics, business, as well as entrepreneurship and management.

Asking this kind of question turns the perspective by 180 degrees – in terms of category – from the input of systems to their output. Instead of *"What kind of output do we get when we have this input?"* we now have *"How does the system arrive at a certain desired and required output?"* It is one of the key elements of control in the cybernetic sense.

For systemic thinking we need both types of questions: not only either-or questions but also those of the "as well as" type. It is the latter kind which leads us into the world of synthesis, synergy, integration, syntegration, creativity, communication, and self-capabilities. They may all have to do with the function of the right hemisphere of the brain, as is often maintained. Above all, however, they have to do with another way of seeing things and of asking questions.

Self-Organization Prototype: Traffic Circle

Self-organization is easy to recognize in natural systems – it just happens. But what about self-organization in artificial systems? Does it exist at all? The simplest example for that is a traffic circle (or roundabout). I have been using this example since the early 1980s in my training courses on *System-Oriented Management*. It helps to illustrate both the main features of self-organization and the solutions, which are often surprisingly simple.

There are three ways to regulate an intersection:

The first is the traffic police which, while regulating according to the specific situation, represents a solution with many disadvantages: policemen need to be replaced because they get tired and may get inattentive; they must be protected from water, cold, exhaust fumes, and other inconveniences – and above all, they are only able to regulate simple intersections because complex ones push the limits of their perception and mental processing capability.

The second means of regulation is the traffic light. It regulates reliably and tirelessly, but also mechanistically, stubbornly and not adjustable to the situation. Just why drivers should stop at a red light in the middle of the night, even though there is no other car in sight, is a question that frequently taxes people's patience. Moreover, even the control program of a traffic light will be overstrained once the complexity of the intersection exceeds a certain level.

The third means of regulation is perfect self-organization and -regulation of the traffic through a traffic circle, with the clear rule that vehicles approaching the circle give way to those on it. As a simple work of construction, it is applicable to almost any complex intersection; it is also low-cost, robust, and reliable because, instead of regulating, it enables traffic participants to regulate and organize the traffic flow themselves, using their own intelligence and knowledge, as well as their current observation and information to help themselves, and a clear rule to resolve potential conflict.

In a general manner of speaking, the key is to *organize a system so that it can organize itself*. What does this mean for our traffic circle example? The *system* is the *whole traffic situation* – with practically any intersection pattern – which is organized by a *structure* – the *traffic circle installation* – in such a way that traffic participants of a constantly changing, unpredictable number and type will be able to organize and regulate themselves, irrespective of such factors as the manning of the police force, the weather, the availability of electrical power, etc. Remember that the traffic circle is the *simplest* example. This book is about much more complex systems and the respective solutions for self-organization will require much more effort; on the other hand, they will also accomplish much more in a similarly elegant way.

As for the traffic circle, by the way, my first encounter dates back to the early 1960s when I was taking driving lessons. I was quite surprised when it disappeared shortly after that because everyone thought traffic lights were a superior solution. It was probably understandable and typical of a time when all hopes were placed in technology and – just think of IT – even common sense was entrusted to it. Hence I find it hardly surprising that traffic circles are getting popular again.

Chapter 3
Master Control through Corporate Policy

> Effective executives don't make many decisions.
> They solve generic problems through policy.
> *Peter F. Drucker, who discovered both the significance of*
> *management and its description*

So how do we establish in our corporations and other societal institutions the kind of quality and self-organization that was described in the previous chapter using the simple examples of water and traffic circles? This is clearly a question of corporate policy, in the sense of systems policy by Master Control. A corresponding corporate policy for the era of complexity will produce three kinds of results:

1. business success in complex environments,
2. the institution's ability to function,
3. the power of control of management.

To achieve these three, corporate policy must be *right* and *effective*. This may seem trivial, if considered superficially or taken out of context. However, it is a fact that a policy can be *wrong* or it can be right but *ineffective*. Once its effects start to show, it is usually too late for corrective measures. There are more than enough examples for this.[27]

The fact that about two-thirds of all mergers and acquisitions fail is doubtless down to poor corporate policy, as is the fact that for roughly two decades now the U.S. automotive industry has been dropping behind the Japanese and European competition. Flawed growth strategies, as in the case of DaimlerChrysler, and policies oriented at short-term profits, thus impairing a company's chances at investment and innovation, are further examples of misdirected corporate policy.

---

27 Just think of the veritable or almost-disasters of the New Economy era, the megalomaniac period in the late 1990s, which is all too easily disregarded and forgotten. Examples include Credit Suisse, Zurich Group, Allianz, Deutsche Telekom, to name just a few.

Right and effective policy, conforming to the nature of complex systems, is the *most important* tool of top-level corporate management. Few things distinguish a competent from an incompetent top management team as clearly as its ability to make the right corporate policy decisions and put them into effect.

What Corporate Policy Is

As a management tool, corporate policy is still not fully understood. Many managers are skeptical of it for several reasons which partly conflict with each other. One is that a policy entails a long-term commitment, which many dread and tend to avoid. Another reason is the converse point that policies are often noncommittal and meaningless. A third reason for executives' skepticism results from the fact that written-down policies often have little in common with reality; a fourth is that they tend to quickly become obsolete as they are overtaken by real-life changes. All these reasons carry some weight – at the same time, they are exactly what helps distinguish good from bad policy.

Another reason why corporate policy is barely understood is that lately it has been eclipsed by the corporate governance debate. The subject of corporate governance seemed sufficiently concrete and hands-on, it was in line with the zeitgeist and appeared to represent an advance in corporate management. By now, a growing number of executives have realized that the current understanding of corporate governance is the result of a misguided development.[28]

A milestone for a better understanding of corporate policy was the book[29] written by my academic mentor Hans Ulrich who, together with my colleague Walter Krieg, developed the St. Gallen Management Model[30]. It initiated a change in the foundations of management – from the business-administration view to cybernetics and systems science.

---

28 Wiedeking, Wendelin, *Anders ist besser*, Munich, 2006. See also: Malik, Fredmund: *Die Neue Corporate Governance. Richtiges Top-Management/Wirksame Unternehmensaufsicht*, Frankfurt am Main, 1997, 3rd edition 2002.
29 Ulrich, Hans, *Unternehmungspolitik*, Berne/Stuttgart, 1978.
30 Ulrich, Hans/Krieg, Walter, *Das St. Galler Management-Modell*, 1972; published again in: Ulrich, Hans, *Unternehmungspolitik*, Berne/Stuttgart/Vienna, 2001.

According to Ulrich, corporate policy is *"the entirety of all basic deci-sions that are to stipulate, over the longer term, the baselines of everything that is going to happen in a company in the future"*.[31]

It is still the most succinct and useful definition that exists. As you can see, the term corporate governance is not actually used here, as in Ulrich's time the separation between corporate policy and corporate governance did not exist. What today is considered corporate governance, and in need of regulation, used to be (and still is) a matter of course in well-managed companies, something that does not need to be specifically regulated. This is one of the reasons why I consider corporate governance to be a part of corporate policy, not vice versa.

While Ulrich's definition of corporate policy is based on its content, the term is also used in other meanings. Corporate policy can also stand for the *documentation* of policy decisions, or the system by which basic deci-sions are brought about, or in other words: the pertinent opinion- and decision-making processes. This latter use of the policy term is relatively rare in the business world; it is common in government politics, where the original meaning of "policy" was the fundamental constitution or frame of civil government in a state or kingdom.

The Core of Functioning

Considering the aforesaid, when we speak of corporate policy we get to the *core of the function* of a corporation. Policy means mastering com-plexity through the use of guidelines and regulations. In an institution, these are the general purposes, values, rules, and overriding goals. They are the result of normative decisions.

Decisions are normative when they are *primal, general,* and *timeless.* Corporate policy decisions are primal because they *cannot be derived from other sources.* They are general because they *refer to all elements and ac-tivities* in an organization. They are timeless because they *are valid until they need to be changed* – which, again, can only be done by way of policy decisions. Hence, in highly complex systems this is the origin of indirect steering which – if done the right way – grows with the system.

---

31 Ulrich, Hans, *Unternehmungspolitik*, Berne/Stuttgart, p. 11.

Good corporate policy rules enable a number of employees – an unlimited number in principle – to coordinate themselves, organize themselves, and render their contributions in line with the company purpose, independently and according to the particular situation. This is where the crucial regulation effect for complex circumstances lies.

The more effective corporate policy is as a Master Control, the fewer follow-on decisions need to be taken. They actually *take themselves* based on their stipulation and regulation, and precisely where they are relevant at the time. The information contained in the corporate policy rules results in *anticipatory* regulation and coordination. As a consequence, a system controlled in this way will largely be able to regulate and organize itself. Organizations lacking these capabilities, or with employees who lack the training required for dealing with and applying corporate policy rules, will usually not be able to function.

Information as such, important as it may be, is not enough. Only rules, for both right management and right corporate policy, enable people to produce true information – that is, select relevant information from the data glut.

Misconceived Pragmatism

The opposite of corporate policy decisions, in the sense of *Master Controls,* is *ad-hoc decisions.* Instead of whole classes of events and situations being governed in their entirety by well-thought-out general principles, each case is analyzed and decided on by itself. Ad-hoc decisions are made to suit the demands of the moment; that is, in each particular case that occurs they are taken as fresh decisions in their own right, which also means they are taken in isolation from previous decisions, frequently even contradicting them.

An approach of this kind can, at best, work only when circumstances are very simple. Once matters get even slightly complex, top management will find that the practice of ad-hoc decision-making takes up too much of its time and resources; it is impossible to imagine that hypercomplex systems could be controlled that way. Managers acting in this way generally justify what they do as *pragmatism.* They like to see themselves as particularly down-to-earth, "practical practitioners". They are generally also proud of making quick decisions. *"Better to take a wrong decision than to take none at all,"* they will say, dismissing questions of general principle as merely "theoretical".

This is a fundamentally wrong understanding of pragmatism. The practice of such pseudo-pragmatic ad-hoc decision-making implies, that the action taken does not have any discernible logic or continuity and therefore no baseline. Any kind of alignment is impossible. As a consequence, the action taken cannot take on any sort of order, which means that a system cannot develop – let alone one that functions on its own.

Nobody can accumulate any experience because each case is newly regulated. Independent action is impossible because there are no reliable guidelines or principles; nor are there any criteria for judging right and wrong, good and bad, permissible and not permissible. As a consequence, there will be no learning, – neither at the individual level nor at the level of the organization – because there is no certainty as to what kind of behavior will be rewarded and what will be sanctioned. Under this kind of pseudo-pragmatic management, it is almost impossible to work without being overcome by anxiety. It leads to the kind of dismal situations which Franz Kafka so masterfully described in his novel *The Trial*.

This approach is anything else but pragmatic or even practical – it is *confused* and *confusing*. By working like this, managers lose not only effectiveness and efficiency but also credibility and authority. Even worse, they are forced to compensate for self-generated deficiencies by using power, authority, and directives, because their actions are inappropriate, aimless, opportunistic and arbitrary. Where their decisions affect people, they are often unfair as well or they are perceived that way.

With this misconceived pragmatism, resulting from a lack of knowledge about the nature of complex systems, what people end up with is over-regulated systems where a lack of control is replaced by excessive supervision. This way of acting may be referred to as management, but is has nothing to do with professional management. What looks like or is made out to be pragmatism is simply bustling, hectic activity. It is people like these – basically failures – who shape the public image of managers, because they attract plenty of attention and are therefore often described by the media as the epitome of the manager. In truth, they are a caricature of right management.

All those who steer their organizations with system-compatible policies are much more effective; however, due to their cultivated and quiet way of understanding, avoiding, and solving problems, they are much too low-key to get the attention that they deserve and so miss the opportunity to set the right example.

Examples of Complexity-Compatible Corporate Policy

The function of a good policy is always the same. Its names and forms can be very different, depending on the organization. A few examples help to illustrate this point:

- The *Master Controls* for states are constitutional laws. For governments, it is government programs and regulatory frameworks. Political parties have statutes, manifestos, and party platforms.
- World religions are regulated by their dogmas and creeds. Within Catholicism, for instance, the Rule of St. Benedict is known to a broader public. Ever since the 6th century it has been the basis for the order's functioning.
- In business, corporate policy has many different names, including business mission, charter, business policy, or corporate principles.
- A master in the use of right and good corporate policy was Alfred P. Sloan, the long-time CEO and President of General Motors.[32] It was not without reason that Peter F. Drucker called him the "true professional". In his 36 years heading the company, General Motors became the best and most profitable corporation of its time. Far-sighted policy decisions almost invariably provide a basis for long-term success, irrespective of coming and going fashion trends in the still-immature discipline of management. Coca Cola, Shell, and Nestlé are cases in point.
- Since the beginning of the 1990s, Porsche has been providing an example of the enormous impact of a clever policy, and at BMW the founda-

---

32 Sloan, Alfred P., *My Years with General Motors*, 1964, 1999. Alfred Sloan's particular significance is due to the fact that he was, although not the inventor, the first systematic user of the corporate policy tool. To my knowledge, he is the only top manager so far to have reflected more on *functioning management* than on his own biography after retiring from his posts. His book may be even more instructive today than it was in his day. Among other things, it contains a chapter on "policy creation".

tion for success was laid even 20 years earlier with a policy whose main features are still in place.

- As I have mentioned before, the American large-scale entrepreneur Warren Buffett stands out for his clear principles: they can be found in his shareholder letters and are accessible to anyone on the internet. Unperturbed by the New Economy confusion and the stock market hysteria, they have been guiding the development of Berkshire Hathaway.
- A particular effective way of studying the effects of good corporate policy – though one that is rarely possible for the general public – is to look at successful family-owned enterprises. Particularly in difficult times their policy principles have proved their worth and the most effective decisions have been taken with foresight.
- Examples from an entirely different area are the principles and policies of warfare. In World War II, General George C. Marshall led the U.S. Army based on well-thought-out, clear principles. It is not without reason that the then British Prime Minister, Winston Churchill, called him the "Organizer of Victory". The publicly visible leaders of the troops were the field commanders, Generals Eisenhower and Montgomery. They got all the media attention. Marshall, however, was the master mind and *Master Control* in the background, hardly known to the public at the time.
- The Chinese general and military strategist Sun Tzu[33] laid down his remarkably enduring principles of the art of war as early as around 400 before Christ. Current Chinese thinking, too, strikes one as being based on long-standing principles – a trait hardly compatible with the short-term orientation of the Western world. Another outstanding example is the principles of warfare laid down by Carl von Clausewitz[34] some 200 years ago. They are still valid today because he managed to find exactly those kinds of principles which are not affected by change, even technological change. That is precisely the purpose of a policy.

---

33 Clavell, James, *The Art of War Sun Tzu*, 1983.
34 Clausewitz, Carl von, *Kriegstheorie und Kriegsgeschichte: On War*, translated from German by J.J. Graham in 1873/19098 (incomplete version) and by O.J. Matthijs Jolles in 1943; edited and provided with an introduction by Anatol Rappaport in 1968 (Viking Penguin); translated and edited by Michael Howard and Peter Paret in 1984 (Princeton Universtiy Press).

So regulation systems of the type we call corporate policy today are nothing new. Long-term successful organizations have always been directed by policies.

What is *new* is that, due to global complexification in the age of complexity, we have no choice but to manage societal institutions using applied cybernetics; that is to say, manage them by *policies*, or in other words, by *Master Controls*.

Another point that is *new* is that, thanks to cybernetics, we now know more about system regulation. What used to be trial and error can now be accomplished straightaway and purposefully by means of this knowledge.

Most importantly, though, it is *new* that for the age of complexity we need new *content*. Principles alone do not suffice. They need to be the *right* principles for the given degree of complexity.

More of my considerations regarding functional principles which have proven their worth in the course of history can be found in my book *Strategie des Managements komplexer Systeme*[35]; some of the most important ones are covered in the last section of this book.

True Leadership and "Great Man Fantasies"

Master Control by corporate policy leads to a new understanding of leadership and opens the most effective, though largely ignored path to true leadership. My previous publications on leadership, in particular my criticism of the current perceptions of leadership, are often misunderstood. I have never denied that there is leadership – but it does not originate where most people expect and search for it: in a person's individual characteristics. True leadership is a result of the right corporate policy.

In today's sensationalist media, the headlines are full of *"great men"*, *"leaders"*, *"bosses"* and *"industry captains"*. It all has little to do with the reality of decision-making at the top of the company.

---

35 Malik, Fredmund, *Strategie des Managements komplexer Systeme – Ein Beitrag zur Management-Kybernetik evolutionärer Systeme*, Berne/Stuttgart, 1984, 9th edition 2006.

These "great man fantasies" lead people to look for leadership in *personal* characteristics of *individuals* – an assumption that clearly does not hold, as the biographies of relevant persons show. This does not mean that there is no such thing as people with a special talent for leadership, or even charisma. The problem with such people is that historically they have left behind more destruction than blessings – which, unfortunately, is something that is generally impossible to anticipate.

True, effective, *and* positive leadership is not based on personalities but on the *right policies*. Only the right policy will produce leadership, while the wrong policy will produce mis-leadership. It is obvious in national politics, as numerous examples from history and the present have demonstrated. The same is true for business.

Right corporate policy provides a basis for leadership in *two ways:* firstly, as leadership of the *company* in its lines of business, in the sense of market, quality, and cost leadership; secondly, as leadership of *people*, also based on the right policy. True leaders never rely on their personal qualities – even if they do have them. Their leadership is based on the fundamental decisions that they take for their organizations, and which prove to be right for them and their people. It is not because someone is a leader that he pursues the right policy – rather, because he pursues the right policy he will be perceived as a leader.

Corporate Policy and Solid System Work

Among other things, leadership depends on the ability to recognize connections and think about the big picture. *Thinking conceptually, in a structured way, linking and combining things* – that is typical of people who are perceived to be leaders and who act in the way that is associated with leadership. Some have the natural gift of structured, "panoramic" thinking. Up to a certain degree, however, this way of thinking can also be learnt. Key tools for that have originated from cybernetic research findings on the functioning of the brain and the function of models, as will be shown at a later point in this book.

Right Policy is Simple

Questions of corporate policy are complex, as otherwise we would not need corporate policy. The answers, however, can be quite simple. In particular the *best* policies are remarkably simple.

Regulating systems only gets complicated when their master regulation fails; that is, when universal principles no longer hold true. Only then is it necessary to regulate in greater detail; and more so if there are mistakes in the general logic of situation and action. Complexity cannot be countered with complicatedness.

Hence, managers' intuitive demand for simplicity is soundly based. They want simple solutions for their problems, simple systems, structures, and processes. To the extent that this demand is directed against *complicated* solutions, it is entirely justified. But there are *two* sides to simplicity.

Experienced managers distinguish between *right* and *wrong* simplicity. They know that there are solutions which are so simple that they *cannot* work. For instance, half a piano keyboard may be "simpler" than the whole but it does not allow one to play Beethoven. Therefore, the maxim of experienced managers is: *As simple as possible – but no simpler than that.* Cybernetics helps to provide clarity here. The question is: "What is the *simplest* regulation that can generate *sufficient complexity* to allow the system to function?"[36]

The internet, for instance, is a relatively simple system from a technical point of view, but the complexity it creates and drives is enormous. In nature, the principle of "complexity through simplicity" is ubiquitous, too, as we will see in one of the following chapters. As a general rule, it is never about "simplicity" as such, but also about "simplicity *generating complexity*". Consequently, the best corporate policies consist in a set of very simple and few rules, providing the system with the points of reference it needs to be steered into the intended direction and to generate the necessary complexity.

What this means in practice is that yout need to ask the right questions. Only then is it possible to recognize and comprehend the relevant problems – those that will generally arise and need to be tackled in the right

---

36 Gomez, Peter, „Die Kunst der optimalen Vereinfachung im Management", in: Krieg, Walter/Galler, Klaus/Stadelmann, Peter (eds.), *Richtiges und gutes Management: vom System zur Praxis*, Berne/Stuttgart/Vienna, 2004.

way – , ultimately arriving at the right answers which help everyone in the organization to solve their local tasks and problems independently and correctly. This is anything but easy. Once the right solution methods have been found, however, almost any management question is easy to solve – particularly the great ones. What I am saying here is diametrically opposed to what we usually find in current management literature, where everything can be regulated with just a few simple concepts. In view of the highly complex and thus highly sensitive management practice, there is nothing to justify such naïve simplification. That includes what most media say about management. In most cases, the intellectual level of such publications is an offense to the intelligence, experience, and responsibility of executives; it also falls short of the exigencies of their tasks. There is absolutely no discernible reason why the management of an organization should require less brains, education, or experience than, for instance, the tasks of a computer whiz, an attorney, an automotive engineer, an architect, or a cardiac surgeon.

Policy Is Self-Composed and Brief

Truly competent managers, the truly genuine leaders, write the policies for their organizations themselves. The results are clear, unambiguous, brief – and sometimes linguistic masterpieces. They need neither teams nor consultants for that.

In its totality, the corporate policy for a global group might require a certain volume of documentation. A single policy, however, such as a branding or human resources policy, rarely comprises more than one or perhaps two pages; often it is just a half page or less. Anyone producing more pages should review them critically, in particular checking whether they have descended into a degree of detail inappropriate for the policy level.

Alfred Sloan in 1928 needed only a quarter of a page to formulate – based on previous comprehensive studies, of course – his *Europe Policy*, which provided the basis for the most critical decisions on GM's internationalization. It remained valid until well into the 1960s. In Sloan's book about his time at General Motors, we find many more examples of his impressive ability to steer the company with concise, to-the-point, expressive policy statements, which explains much of his success with General

Motors at the time. Marshall and Churchill, too, were masters of formulating policies, and an unsurpassed example of succinctness is the Ten Commandments.

Master Controls must be universally valid rules, but the *thinking process* that generates them must oscillate between the universal and the specific, the general and the detailed. It is the only way to accomplish truly good principles. Again and again, the general must be tested against the detail and the detail must be tested for its significance to the general. This mental oscillation process distinguishes accomplished corporate politicians from two other types of managers: nitpickers and high-flyers.

In my work as a consultant I have been dealing with corporate policies for decades, and I had plenty of chances to observe the enormous differences between concise, succinct statements and epic treatises on basically the same issues. There are few other areas where professional leadership quality is as evident as in the formulation of policies.

Mind you, when someone writes corporate policy himself that does not necessarily mean he will manage autocratically. People often confuse the result – the policy – with the way to get there – the thinking process. In most cases the formulation of a policy is preceded by a comprehensive opinion- and will-forming process which, due to the importance of the issues to be resolved, needs to encompass what – depending on the organization – may be quite a number of people, their knowledge and their power of judgment.

Therefore, such processes tend to be tedious and time-consuming. Cybernetics has generated one of the most significant improvements in this area: the so-called *Syntegration* method. Based on the Team Syntegrity theory[37], it is a mathematically optimized communication process for using the knowledge of the largest possible number of people in the shortest possible time. In the standard case, which can be varied in many ways, it will be 42 people and three-and-a-half days. The number of people can be

---

37 Beer, Stafford, *Beyond Dispute. The Invention of Team Syntegrity*, Chichester, 1994; and for a brief overview: Pfiffner, Martin, „Der genetische Code wirksamer Kommunikation. Vom Workshop zur Syntegration", in: Krieg, Walter/Galler, Klaus/Stadelmann, Peter (eds.), *Richtiges und gutes Management: vom System zur Praxis*, Berne/Stuttgart/Vienna, 2004.

increased to around 100, which is usually enough even for the largest organizations.

Noncommittal Nature, Overregulation, Openness, Universal Validity

Inevitably, every policy will *firstly* be positioned somewhere between the extremes of noncommittal nature and overregulation. If a policy is too general it will not get implemented in real life because how it applies to a particular case is not clear. If it is too concrete it will also lose effectiveness, or have the wrong effect, because for many cases it will not be right; so they will either remain unregulated or be regulated the wrong way. Both problems are easy to avoid, as we will soon see.

Secondly, every policy will be positioned somewhere between openness and universality. The stipulations that are *not* defined are just as important as those that are defined. The opposite of openness is universality, which describes stipulations that could refer to all organizations or situations, or at least very many of a similar type.

Noncommittal Nature

Statements are useless if they contain no information. In logic they are referred to as empty statements. To recognize empty phrases reliably, there is a simple test question:

> Is the logical opposite of a statement
> a conceivable alternative for the institution?

If the answer is no, the statement is devoid of content. A large proportion of institution-specific documents are full of empty statements, and quite tellingly this also includes numerous corporate governance codes.

For instance, the sentence *"We shall take a targeted approach"* is devoid of content, as is easy to see if we ask the test question. For the logical alternative would be: *"We shall take a random approach"* – something that in most situations no one in his right mind would consider doing. It depends on the individual case how the statement would have to be modified to make sense. A similar example is the much-used phrase: *"Appropriate measures should be taken."* Statements like these are out of place in a policy. Aloys Gälweiler, the best strategic thinker by far in the German-speaking region, has put down some interesting and amusing thoughts on this subject.[38]

Overregulation

For the second problem, overregulation, criteria are not as precise. The best protection from excessive regulation is power of judgment, experience, and sound management skills at senior management levels. Experienced managers tend towards broader policies rather than overprescriptive ones. The urge to overregulate is noticeable primarily in junior executives or inexperienced staff, as well as in consultants still lacking practical experience with the effects of overregulation.

In principle, corporate policy decisions
must have the largest possible scope of validity.

It is the *general clause* method, which is familiar to people with legal training. Once a general clause has been found it can be trimmed back if necessary. The starting point for corporate policy regulations, however, must be the search for a general clause; that is, the regulation with the largest-possible scope of validity.

Openness

Something to be differentiated from inapplicability is a policy's *openness*. Policy decisions sometimes also regulate what should not be regulated. The principle here should be

Restriction to the necessary and sufficient minimum

Due to the complexity of the institution-environment system, a good pol-

---

38 Gälweiler, Aloys, *Strategische Unternehmensführung*, Frankfurt/New York 1990, 3rd edition 2005, p. 95 et seq.

icy must and should leave many things open; that is to say, *deliberately* leave them unregulated, as a kind of "white spot on the landscape".

"Necessary and sufficient" is a principle of formal logic and mathematics governing the layout of axiom systems, which makes it a policy principle in itself. It means that *all* those questions should be regulated without which a policy would not have its intended effect, or in other words: all that are necessary because otherwise the purpose would be missed. It also means that nothing more should be regulated, *only* the things serving that purpose. Openness in this sense is a source of flexibility, adaptability, creativity, leaning, and evolution, for it is also a manifestation of experience and wisdom.

Universality

The universality of statements is often confused with their applicability or inapplicability.

> As has been pointed out, statements are inapplicable if they are devoid of content. Universal statements are those with the most powerful content, as they are not only applicable but also can be applied to any conceivable case.

This is most evident in statements referring to laws of nature. The physical law of gravitation is universally valid; otherwise it would not be a law of nature. The same is true for the cybernetic laws of functioning.

Managers are often skeptical of corporate policy statements that could apply to any organization. The issue is quickly clarified, however, when the subject level is separated from the system level; that is, the level of the business from the level of functioning, as is required for the purpose of corporate policy, as I have outlined above. On the subject level, companies need to differentiate as far as possible. It would be strategically wrong if BMW had the same product strategy as Audi. In terms of functioning, however, the same regularities apply to all systems – namely, the cybernetic principles of complexity, regulation, control, and communication. For these reasons, my management theory and system are universally valid. This becomes evident when right management is distinguished from wrong, and good from bad, as I have explained at length in *Managing Performing Living*. That is why I chose "Right and Good Management" as a motto for my approach.

Ethics and Morality

Ethics and morality are indispensable dimensions for business enterprises, as for all societal institutions. However, corporate policy is much less a question of ethics and morality than is generally assumed. People are much too quick to associate the two terms with corporate policy, almost reflexively, and to bring them up in related discussions.

It was certainly right for a broader ethics debate to be sparked by the intolerable deficiencies and limitations of corporate governance, for without ethics there is no functioning management. However, people often fail to see that it is primarily the facts and subject matters associated with the *functioning of systems* that need to be established. Ethics and morality follow from them.

In my management system, while ethics are partly a prerequisite for action, they are much more its consequence. Ethics are primarily relevant for *two* corporate policy decisions: first, for the decision on *purpose and mission* of the institution, second, for the decision on the *management system* itself, due to its effect on the way we deal with people. Overriding principles for my management system are *professionalism, performance, effectiveness*, and *responsibility*, and I consider them to be ethical principles in this context.

A *third* aspect of ethics lies in *every* person himself, because only he can decide whether he will observe the rules that permit the system to function.

Management – and I repeat again – must be viewed as both a function and a profession. Management must be *right* and *good* in terms of content, so that people can explore and exploit their performance potential without fear. Only then can they experience a sense of purpose in what they do. Clever systems policy provides a sound foothold, permitting people to find the kind of fearlessness that fully brings their intelligence and competence to bear. Only then can they and their customers feel they are treated correctly, both ethically and morally.

So for corporate policy, in the sense of *Master Control* as a central element of my management system, the key point is: corporate policy must primarily be *right*. That means it must comprise the right decisions in terms of *content*, as well as rules that are *right* for people, and thus for the functioning of the organization. This demand is not as self-evident as it may seem. On the contrary, it is extremely difficult to fulfill. The false doctrine of shareholder value illustrates the fundamental importance of having a corporate policy that is right; it is also an example of how the misconception of a subject matter will inevitably lead to ethical and moral problems. The difficulty of setting up the right policy is one of the reasons why managers tend to remain noncommittal in these questions. The result is mere lip service instead of effective policy; in exchange for that, however, managers do not risk being held accountable for leading their companies in the wrong direction.

It is wrong, for instance, to prioritize shareholder value over customer value. I have publicized the rationale long ago; the most important arguments can are contained in this book. Wrong statements abound in corporate policies, referring to questions such as profit, growth and size, innovation, change, employee motivation, team work, and leadership. I will come back to the related arguments at a later point.

While corporate policy cannot do without ethics and morality, these dimensions of value are the consequence, though not the origins, of right and good corporate policy. As soon as the question is modified, so as no longer to refer to management in general but to the *particular* kind of management that I call *right* and *good* management, it becomes evident that most of the relevant topics of corporate policy are not of the ethical/moral kind but questions relating to the proper and reliable functioning of an organization under complex conditions, which, when solved, lead to an ethically and morally desirable corporate culture seen inwardly and outwardly.

Functioning management – that is, *right* management – is not a question of arbitrariness and subjectivity. In management, the functioning of organizations is a factual and systems matter outranking everything else, just as the proper functioning of the human organism does in medicine. Just what a healthy knee joint ought to look like follows from the logic of nature, not from ethics. Likewise, the growth rate required for a company is not a question of ethics but results from the logic of competition.

Normative management, and thus corporate policy, creates and maintains norms for the desirable degree of morality and ethics. However, the word "normative" in the context of right and good management means, above all, a standard for right and good functioning, which also includes the definition of the institution's purpose and business activity.[39] It is there-

---

39 See also: Malik, Fredmund, *Die Neue Corporate Governance*, Frankfurt am Main, 1997, 3rd edition 2002.

fore indispensable for right and good management to have a corporate policy that is right in content and compatible with systems, complexity, and human beings. To fulfill this requirement, the right models for general management are needed. They are a subject of this book.

What Should Be Regulated?

The *Master Control* tool of corporate policy helps to answer the *three* questions I have pointed out in the roadmap chapter:

1. WHAT the institution should be doing (the business):
2. WHERE the institution has to function (the environment), and
3. HOW the institution needs to function (corporate management).

These three questions correspond to the underlying structure of the system "institution". Of course they also correspond to the structure of any other kind of societal institution, considered in their entirety. A wholistic understanding of institutions is indispensable because otherwise we cannot understand and regulate their function. All other questions follow from that: how the three areas should be structured for the purposes of corporate policy, what sections a corporate policy should comprise, and how deep the regulation by corporate policy should go.

In essence, this is where the course is set for what will ultimately be a wrong or right corporate policy. Understanding the institution in this triform way represents a policy decision in itself, and it is anything else but self-evident. Business administration has yet to fully adopt it – which would not matter so much if superficial appearances did not suggest that business economists are particularly skilled in managing companies.

Chapter 4

Navigating in Complexity – Models for Overview, Insight, and Perspective

> A model is a reflection of whatever is the case, which is
> explicitly made available for experimentation.
> *Stafford Beer, founder of management cybernetics*

In the first chapter I had explained why complexity and cybernetics are crucial for coping with and exploiting the change going on in the 21st century. This provides the context for my views on management. The second and third chapters showed how complex systems are structured and steered by means of *Master Controls* and why this requires a complexity-compatible corporate policy – the key to creating and directing systems of basically any size and complexity. This chapter now contains the one foundation that is still missing: *models* as a means and method of mastering complexity. Models are the primal tool of cybernetics. It was this discipline which realized as early as in the 1940s that without models there is no identifying, no thinking, and no steering.

Brain-Like Models

The larger and the more complex an organization becomes, due to the steering power of its policy, the more important it is to maintain an overview of the growing system and its interconnections at all times. This overview is a prerequisite for being able to steer the system in line with current developments and functional requirements. There is only *one* way to do that: by using models. I am not talking about models in the rather diffuse sense in which the term is commonly understood, and in which it is used in completely ill-defined ways. I am talking about models of a very specific kind: cybernetic models. These models have to fulfill certain functions and meet certain requirements:

1. Cybernetic models in the sense of this book are not analyzers but *organizers and synthesizers* of information and knowledge. They organize them in such a way that they become *relevant to orientation and action*.
2. Cybernetic models are *capable of simulation*.
3. They are not static depictions but *dynamic moving maps*.
4. They capture non-linear connections and are not affected by the restrictions of binary logic. Above all, they are *capable of fuzzy logic*.
5. They are *real-time navigators*.
6. They provide platforms for *shared understanding* and *shared communication*.

In short: *cybernetic models function almost like the human brain*. By using them we use crucial findings from neuro-cybernetics and brain research for the benefit of general management. In view of the current state of progress in brain research, it is actually permissible and necessary to speak of *brain-like processes and tools* in this context. This also involves a veritable revolution in the use of modern information technology.

With all the technological achievements made, so far we have not accomplished much more than automating the quill. We are on the brink of implementing the epoch-making work of Stafford Beer, which began with the mathematically formulated brain model in his seminal paper "Towards the Cybernetic Factory" and culminated in *Brain of the Firm*. This raises quite another question, which Beer – himself not only a cybernetician but also a computer pioneer – raised in 1972[40] : "*...what, given computers, the enterprise is now...?*" As a result, the understanding of IT and of the CEO's tasks will experience a Copernican shift as well: from the T in "IT" to the I. In other words, the question of relevant information is clearly gaining significance vis-à-vis the question of data processing.[41] And while

---

40 Beer, Stafford, *Brain of the Firm*, 2nd edition, p. 16.
41 Beer, Stafford, "Towards the Cybernetic Factory", in: von Foerster, H./Zopf, G. W., *Principlex of Self-Organization*, Oxford 1962, republished in Harnden R./ Leonhard A., *How many Grapes went into the Wine. Stafford Beer on the Art and Science of Holistic Management*, Chichester 1994; as well as Beer, Stafford, *The Brain of the Firm. The Managerial Cybernetics of Organization*, Chichester 1972 and 1994. On the issue of IT, clearly and precisely, Peter F. Drucker et al., in: *Management Challenges for the 21st Century*, New York 1999, p. 87 et seq.

the controllers in our companies are yet to have the necessary technical equipment for that task, the best among them show surprisingly rigor in these things, regardless of points 3 and 4 above.

When working with models, *first,* some of the fundamental systemic-cybernetic questions can usually be clarified which – although actually quite simple – in my experience tend to lead to misunderstandings even among corporate leaders with a knowledge of cybernetics. *Second,* they help substantiate why corporate policy needs to have exactly the structure that I have defined in the roadmap. *Third,* it will become clear how the right kind of models will enable a certain approach to steering complex systems: through real-time control

World ➜ System ➜ Model ➜ Concept

At this point four key terms need to be clarified: *world, system, model,* and *concept.* So far I have assumed these terms to be intuitively understandable. In the context of corporate policy, however, and its function as *Master Control* in a complex system, this is not enough.

Once the terms are clear, everything is easy:

A *system* is that part of the coherences in the *world* which we need to take an interest in, based on a certain *purpose and functionality.*

A *model* is what we *know* about it, including the blank spots of our *nescience* – the "white spots" on the map.

A *concept* is what, based on the model, we want to *observe and do.* At the top management level, concepts under this definition are identical to *corporate policy* for an individual organization or system.

All diagrams in this book show *models* in the sense described here, aside from a few exceptions where graphs are purely illustrative. They are models *of* systems, their complexity and inner cybernetics, and models *for* systems, that is, for designing, regulating, controlling, and developing them – in short: models for *Master Control.*

Remember that policy, among other things, means safely navigating the organization through the world's growing complexity. Consequently, policy is the art of navigating: *knowing where you are; exploring where you might want to head; deciding where you must, ought to, and wish to go.* This ability is required in particular in unknown and constantly changing "waters" – such as global business.

To navigate you need *maps*, such as nautical or topographical maps. They are nothing else but *models* – models of systems too complex to capture them intuitively, to understand them without assistance, or to put them into words comprehensively.

Models have their own hard-luck story. As orientation and navigation aids in the cybernetic sense, models have existed in all cultures. Some of them were very simple, but there have also been highly sophisticated depictions quite compatible with modern-day demands to design – I am thinking of some of the discoveries from ancient Egyptian tombs or temples, the depictions of astronomic constellations and events, or the evermore sophisticated seafarer maps.

With the advances of science and the increasing use of mathematics, models came to be understood in a more and more limited sense: as *mathematic* models. Particularly due to the rather pathetic role that mathematics have often played in economics, models were discredited as mere practical orientation aids, for they gained a reputation of being „*theoretical*" in the sense of *incomprehensible* and *useless for practical purposes*. In the course of the New Economy mania, the term "model" ended up having cult status, although in a largely trivial sense: as "business model". The term would be fitting, were it not largely understood as the exact opposite of cybernetic models, that is, as entirely un-cybernetic, simple linear extrapolations of operating figures.

By contrast, if you understand cybernetics to be the *modeling* of complex systems, you have obtained quite a good degree of insight. It was not without reason that W. Ross Ashby referred to cybernetics, among other things, as the "*science of simplification*"[42], by which he meant the *right* kind of simplification. It is not about simplifying thing in the everyday-understanding kind of way, nor about reducing things to a limited number of aspects or to causal variables. With cybernetic models we focus complex systems on their essence, so that we can understand them without

---

42 Ashby, Ross W. et al., in: *Mechanisms of Intelligence*, p. 142.

simplifying them too much, or simplifying them to the extent that they are no longer of any use. In other words, simplification to the exact degree that safe orientation and regulation in the sense outlined in Chapter 1 – *How to get Your Own Way* – becomes possible.

As a side note, in his book on the history of navigation,[43] Friedrich Wilhelm Pohl vividly describes how man gradually learned to deal with complexity, cope with uncertainty and the unknown, and increasingly make use of it to his own benefit. The epoch-making advances from the wind rose, the compass, the North Pole, and the coordinate system to radar and the satellite system clearly have their equivalents in the management of complex systems. Good literature on the emergence, methodology and technology of navigation provides very enriching knowledge for executives, for whose tasks the usual business administration and MBA skills have long ceased to be sufficient.

As has repeatedly been mentioned, navigating and steering are the tasks of the helmsman, or *kybernetes* in Greek. That also explains why Stafford Beer could say that cybernetics was the science of control and management was its profession, or words to that effect – referring to a certain type of system: the complex system.[44] The ability to deal with complexity, dynamics, change, risk, and lack of information is a prerequisite for discovering new territory. To this end we need the models described in the following sub-chapters.

The Model as a Thinking Tool

We do not have a choice as to whether we wish to use models or not. We all have models in our minds – our so-called *mental* models. They are the *thinking devices* of our brains. These mental models are what our perception, thinking, decisions, and actions are based on – no matter whether it happens consciously or unconsciously.

---

43 Pohl, Friedrich-Wilhelm, *Die Geschichte der Navigation*, Hamburg 2004. A particularly instructive example is the story of the Scottish watchmaker John Harrison, who managed to solve what was one of the greatest problems for seafarers in his time: finding a method to determine the exact longitude of a ship's position at sea. See also: Sobel, Dava/Andrews, William J. H., *Longitude*, London, 1996.
44 see Vol. 1, p. 39.

The structures of the models in our heads give us orientation, for they are our categories for organizing the input coming from our sensory organs. Through our perception the model is permanently updated, *online* and *real-time*.

Consequently, models comprise two kinds of elements: *permanent* elements, such as the basic assumptions and knowledge about our environment, and *rapidly changing*, current elements, or information. The key is that models should not contain any data, because any input is immediately placed in the context of the given categories and previous experiences, and thus turned into information.

Strictly speaking, mental models are not only *internal* models of the outer world, as is often said, but also models about *the self in the outer world*. With their help, while we may not be able to exactly predict the future, we can simulate what it might look like by inwardly imagining a situation involving ourselves as players. We can imagine a range of *possible* futures *for and including ourselves*.

The content of the models in our minds is flexible and can be reconfigured from scratch any time. Certain kinds of input, such as a diagnosis of illness, will not change our previous line of thinking but it will take on another *meaning*. Therefore – and I repeat – a mental model is an *organizer* rather than an *analyzer* of knowledge and information. Gathering and organizing information is crucial. The basic function of models is to regulate the behavior of organisms in their environments, in order to enable their survival and viability. Above all, models are survival navigators – for all kinds of organisms, including the most primitive ones. Their chronologically successive function as thinking devices resulted from the co-evolution of man and his increasingly complex natural and social environment. In this phase of evolution, models turned into thinking devices in the sense of intellect and reason. Their basic function, however, remained unchanged: enabling the organism to master complexity better and better.

Realization and Understanding by Means of Regulation Models

What follows from the above is that the "topographical and nautical maps" of management are systems.

The next step is to determine what should be modeled? For anyone trying to find out how to control a system, the answer has to be *modeling the regulation mechanisms of complex systems*[45]. Cybernetic models do not simply map just "anything". Rather, they focus on something very specific, which we could call the *cybernetics* of the system – just as we speak of the anatomy and physiology of the body, or the physics of the cosmos. (For readers interested in philosophy: The *cybernetics* of the system are what turns *something* into a system.) Hence, the cybernetic model for our purposes in management is a simultaneous depiction of the factual system and its regulation system.

As mentioned before, models are the *only* possibility to capture complex systems and understand them better and better over time – even if it can never be in detail, which it *should not*. One of the most important results of cybernetic research is the insight that for successful and effective regulation, detailed knowledge is *unnecessary and sometimes even a hindrance*. One example is the following image, a "classic" by the bio-cybernetician Frederic Vester, in the German-speaking region a pioneer of the visualization of cybernetics and complex systems. Vester was the first to render the highly abstract findings of cybernetics perceptible to anyone, in particular children, and in such a fascinating way that amazement, curiosity, play, and fun all together form one great experience. What I said at the beginning – about being cybernetics easier to demonstrate than to describe – Frederic Vester has masterfully demonstrated.

Anyone who has never come across figure 5 before, which often appears in Vester's publications, will probably not know at first what it shows. The response is typical: as long as people do not *understand*, they begin to do what is generally taught in formal education: they *analyze*. Now, while we can examine the image ever more precisely with highly scientific methods, it will not help us *understand* it better. More detailed investigation – such as determining the shades of grey – will provide more data for the image, but no insight as to what it shows.

Wrong methods never lead to the right solution. The right method, in this case, is the exact opposite of what is generally understood to be science. If we hold the picture at a greater distance, and look at it with blinking eyes, we will blend out the details – and that is what will finally help us comprehend. We will see not only that it is the portrait of a person, but also, that the person shown is President Abraham Lincoln. Why? Because

---

45 Scientific foundations can be found in *System Methodology*.

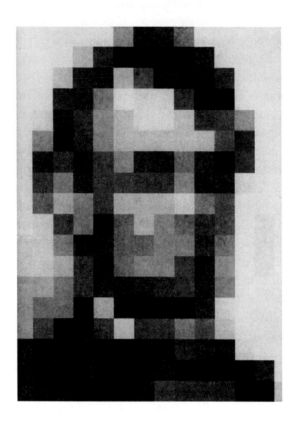

Figure 5: Computer image of Abraham Lincoln

the analysis of the details does not provide any insight regarding the relations *between* the details, or about the *function* of each component of the picture (such as the number of pixels). It is those (inter)relations, however, that we have to recognize in order to *realize*.

Recognizing connections and relations – or systemic wholeness – is the particular *capability of (re)cognition* that characterizes the true general manager, as I said in the previous chapter. It is important not only for corporations. In the midst of complexification in the age of complexity, it is the key skill for the social survival of every person. Whoever lacks insight will not survive socially – and in some cases not even physically.

Knowing What the Talk Is About: The Babylon Syndrome

The purpose of models, as I said, is navigating in uncharted "territory". One of their most important effects is that they help us to know what others are talking about. Models provide the basis for successful management through one *common language* and a *joint understanding* of the system to be managed. In other words, they provide the basis for *effective communication*. It is no coincidence that, as generally known, the definition of cybernetics is "control *and* communication".

I suppose there is hardly a top manager who would not know from first-hand traumatic experience how people can talk past each other in top management meetings, and how tedious it can be for the chairperson of such meetings to keep providing orientation, making connections, and clarifying facts with unending patience. Also, anyone having to give presentations in board meetings will know how incredibly difficult it can be to make oneself understood.[46]

The reason seldom lies in the "stupidity" of those attending, for they are almost always very capable people. *It is the lack of a common vehicle of understanding.* People do not only use different special terminologies; they also use the same words to mean entirely different things without being aware of it. It is almost like planning a joint hike in the mountains for which everyone uses a different map.

The word *management* itself can be understood in so many different meanings within one and the same group, and even after many years, that it is futile to attempt a discussion about management on the premise of mutual understanding. In codetermined companies, the representatives of workers and investors usually have widely differing perceptions anyway. But even within these groups, one person will refer to the management of people, the next to the management of companies, a third to the board members, and a fourth person to the process and function of managing.

Everyone has *their own* model on management, but a *shared* model is usually missing. Consequences are particularly grave in global companies

---

46 Without my own function as member and chair of several top-level corporate bodies, I would not have been able to gain these experiences. From the outside, and with the so-called empirical research that is often performed so purposelessly, it is impossible to achieve this kind of insight.

with management boards of mixed cultural background, or when new people join the organization from the outside.

The same is true for many key terms – that is, not only for management but also for leadership, control, strategy, culture, motivation, and information. It is a particular characteristic of management, and the inevitable result of a lack of training for the management profession. This "Babylon syndrome", as I call it, does not occur in any other profession. Lawyers, engineers, doctors, chemists and such all have learnt clear terminologies in the course of their professional trainings, as well as a common language conducive to understanding. It is a major component of truly professional training.

There is no point in everyone mentally bringing their own private models to a supervisory board meeting. To be suitable for the management of complex systems, models must be explicit, that is, visible to everyone and discussible by everyone. They must be present in the meetings and serve as navigation aids. This is the only way to create a *shared understanding*, *shared knowledge*, and effective communication. Joint models of the institution, its environment, and its management system are the only possible way to solve the orientation and communication problems mentioned above. We could thus speak of *governance by models*, taking effect where the root of the problem lies: at the formation of joint concepts about what is to be managed. The conscious use of models of the kind discussed here can and will revolutionize the work of top-management teams.

Like a Brain: Operations Room – Management GPS

The most [R]Evolutionary solution for that is the so-called *Operations Room®*, or, as I sometimes call it, the *Control* or *Cyber-Room (or Center)*. It is an integral part of the *Malik Management System*.[47] Simply put, it fulfills the function of a control tower at an airport. It is the point where information is organized in a decision-compatible and brain-physiological way, thus pro-

---

47 The concept of the Malik Operations Room is based on the work of Stafford Beer, the management cybernetics pioneer. Until his death in 2003, we cooperated closely. During his lifetime he entered his entire work, including all rights, into our joint foundation, the *"Cwarel Isaf Foundation"*, which was named after Cwarel Isaf near Aberysthwyth in Wales, from 1973 his place of residence in alternation with Toronto.

viding an overview of all aircraft movements at all times. The result is both real-time control of regular flight traffic and a platform for the ad-hoc, situation-specific regulation of exceptional or emergency cases.

The *Operations Room* is comparable to the first analog devices for, say, military operations, space missions, and disaster operations – in other words, wherever hypercomplexity must be managed. The earliest applications of the precursors of the operations room were developed in the military field. A navigation system that everyone is familiar with today also follows the basic principle of the operation room: the GPS system in automobiles.

For successful management of and in complex systems we also need a new kind of map: so-called *Dynamic Moving Maps*. The joint models of the environment, the organization, and its management system, including their sub-models, are – to use the analogy of the former chart tables of military staff – no longer drawn on sheets of paper but depicted on electronic screens. Just like a GPS monitor, they depict the current state of things in the *Operations Room*. The models are animated with information, in a way that is optimally matched with perception, and constantly updated. This is done using interactive communication technology of the kind that has only recently been available, which work online and real-time, and without which it would be impossible to depict complex systems.

Figure 6: An Operations Room at Malik Management

In the Operations Room it is possible at any time – just as it is with GPS navigation – to ask "What if" questions; the respective consequences will immediately be simulated and indicated by the system. It is a *desicion environment* designed according to neuro-cybernetic laws of function, a man-machine interface which synergetically combines the abilities of man, the potential of the situation, and the possibilities of modern technology. It does not really matter so much whether the *Operations / Control / Cyber-Room* exists as a physical or a virtual center. What matters is that people refuse to let themselves be deceived by mere projection and presentation techniques. The essential content does not lie here, on the surface, but in the deeper structures of the algorithms organizing the data, and of the hypertools configuring the information.

The *Operations Room* is the functionally optimal environment for what top managers' brains are supposed to do – that is, for *thinking* rather than enduring unbearable presentations.[48] The presentation technique currently in use will soon be a thing of the past. It has always been a mystery to me how top managers could ever accept the following: invariably darkened rooms where it is impossible for presenters to see the faces of other participants and thus to capture their responses, which leaves them without any feedback except for the occasional verbal comment; 50-feet rectangular conference tables; presentations of 30-plus crowded slides showing very complex structures and diagrams. In times of sophisticated communication technology, this can hardly be the solution.

Three Purpose-Oriented Models

After these explanations about models and their functionality in the context of the overall management process, let us go back to navigation itself; that is, to the formation of opinion and will, to decision and control, and to the organization of the required feedback loop.

Just like nautical or topographical maps, cybernetic management models are always created for a specific purpose. They model what is important for that purpose, and are of no use for other purposes. A map of Eu-

---

48 An exhaustive description can be found in Volume 4 of this book series.

ropean expressways will provide information that is different from what maps of local roads or hiking trails entail.

The navigation of an institution is based on three of the known elements of the basic model: the models for the environment, the corporation, and its management.

When models are understood and used correctly, even a *hypercomplex* system can be captured by a model that is surprisingly simple – provided the management model is designed in such a way that its effective complexity will not be permanently destroyed by that simplification, but can be retrieved as required.

The models of the Malik Management System presented here meet that requirement, and as far as I can tell, they are the only ones that do that in their entirety. In other words, these models serve the purpose of *science of simplification*. They are models suitable for generating yet other models which, depending on their respective uses, may contain more details.[49]

Basic Model for Corporate Policy

As you may remember, corporate policy governs three things: what the institution should be doing (the business), where the institution has to function (the environment), and how the institution is to function (corporate management.)

The *first* dimension, the "what", comprises the company's business operations, purpose, and mission. To the extent that the purpose and mission are affected by corporate governance, they belong to this dimension.

The *second* dimension, the "where", refers to the environment in which the institution operates, its understanding of that environment, and the role and attitude required. The shareholder and stakeholder issues of corporate governance are also part of this dimension.

The *third* dimension, the "how", comprises the institution's *management system*. This dimension also includes those aspects of corporate gov-

---

49 At this point, allow me a quick reminder of the terminology hints given at the beginning of the book: The models used must always be understood in three dimensions: systemic, content and form.

ernance that refer to the actions and behavior of the top-level corporate bodies.

For practical purposes, the starting point for all models of my management system is the model shown in figure 7. It was already part of the original St. Gallen Management Model. It is the cybernetic basic model, from which the so-called *Viable System Model* (VSM)[50] will later originate – the model that every organization must conform to in order to function. The VSM will prove to be the first model ever that is of any use for the structuring and organizing of complex systems.[51] It is one of the most fruitful and far-reaching discoveries in cybernetics.[52.]

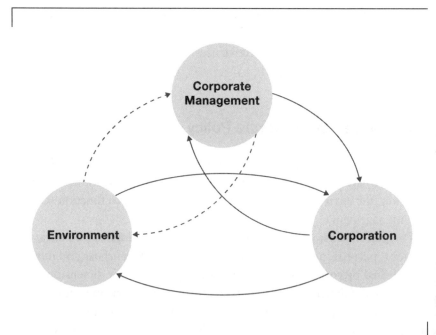

Figure 7: The basic system of corporate policy

50 Beer, Stafford, *The Heart of Enterprise*, London, 1979.
51 The VSM will be explained in detail in Vol. 4 of this series *(Structure)*.
52 I therefore ask my readers to bear with me until Volume 4 is available. For those who are impatient, I refer to the writings of Stafford Beer, as listed in the References section.

The basic model is the inner core of the model for overall corporate policy. The arrows in the graph symbolize the complex interrelations between the subsystems *environment, corporation,* and *corporate management.* Dotted arrows mean that management as a *function* influences the environment not directly but indirectly, through the organization. This thought may not be immediately intuitive, but it is important. As persons, executives obviously have direct access to the environment. As managers, however, they always also act as corporate organs, representatives, and agents--and that is what the dotted lines symbolize.

To function as a Master Control, corporate policy must comprise all three subsystems. Understood in this way, corporate policy does not only refer to the corporation as such, as the term would suggest, but to the *entire system,* that is, the institution in conjunction with its environment and management.[53]

Farewell to Hierarchy: Embedding Replaces Ranking

Before I go on to explain the model further, I want to take the reader one logical level higher up, to the *master model* of complex functioning systems, because here we will accomplish a *paradigm shift* in the understanding of future organization or system structures. This shift is about *abandoning the hierarchical organization model.* About one-third of executives find this hard to do. For the rest – as I have increasingly experienced over the past 10 years, on a daily basis – it is the transition to a better understanding of what they have been feeling intuitively, without being able to put it in words. The reason is that the hierarchical model – the organization chart – still prevails in the perception and depiction of organizations, although it provides very little information about the way a system truly functions.

It is one of the greatest hindrances in advancing towards new approaches to organization in the society of knowledge and complexity.

---

53 At this point I should add a quick note to system specialists: from a logical point of view, corporate policy thus invents itself, as it were, in a recursive act of creation It is the act of systemic closure, corresponding to the logic of systemic self-reference.

Even young people, after having graduated from university and gathered some practical experience, tend to project the hierarchical model onto reality, even where there is really no hierarchy at all – despite their constant talk about networks and such. It is yet another example of what I mean when I speak of the *Copernican effect*: precisely the same data, observations, etc., can be understood in both a hierarchical and an embedding-related sense. The former prevents complexity-compatible thinking – the latter facilitates it.

Figure 8 shows interrelations as they *really* are. They are the systemic master-relations of *embedding*, familiar to anyone from personal experience. The corporation is embedded in its environment, the management in the corporation, just like man is embedded in a family and his regulating brain/nervous system in his organism. As we will see later, *embedding* is a constitutive, or system-defining and system-creating relationship for my management models.

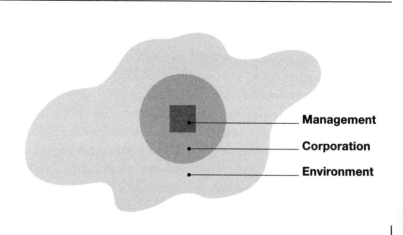

Management
Corporation
Environment

Figure 8: Embedded systems

In figure 8 the environment is modeled in an *amoeboid* form because we *cannot* be entirely sure of the boundaries of the environment, and thus of the system. This uncertainty, which is a consequence of complexity, must be expressed in the model itself; that is to say, it must not be modeled or defined away. System boundaries conform to a very specific logic which we are not familiar with by education, but according to which we lead a major part of our lives. It is the type of logic that is referred to as *fuzzy logic*. This logic is preeminent for developing the environment concept.[54]

Embedded in the environment is the *corporation*, which is depicted as a circle because we have, or can have, much more knowledge about it than about the environment. The circle stands for what the institution does in its environment, and by which it fulfills its purpose. The square embedded in the circle represents the *corporate management* in all three dimensions: functional, institutional, and personal.

The different sizes of the three subsystems signify their *differing degree of complexity*. The environment is always more complex than the institution, which, in turn, is more complex than its management. This is a natural fact, and the basis for the *Law of Requisite Variety* (or complexity) discovered and formulated by W. Ross Ashby, which I had briefly mentioned in Volume I.[55] According to that law, it is absolutely necessary to make use of one's so-called *self*-capabilities (as mentioned in chapter 1), that is, *self*-organization and *self*-regulation, in order to master complexity. Managers or management teams who believe they have the organization or – even worse – its environment directly under control are given to self-deception.

In functioning systems, *embedding* takes the place of *hierarchy*. Contrary to what some may think, this does not reduce one's influence in and on the system – quite the opposite: embedding helps to expand one's influence, only it will be indirect rather than direct.

Functioning societal systems are structured in a *federalist* manner, as this is the only way they can organize themselves. This does not mean that we have established the *right* kind of federalism, but it is a start. As anyone knows, a functioning nation consists of embedded sub-states or regions, in which cities and rural communities are embedded, in which families are embedded, in which persons are embedded,... – down to the smallest elements of microcosm, the atoms, quarks, etc. The same is true for the macro-direction: every system is embedded in one or several comprehensive macrosystems.

As I said before, this does not reduce one's possibilities to exert influence but rather enhances them, as it changes their character from unidirectional to bidirectional, from non-communicative to communicative, from

---

54 The next part of the book will show how this is done.
55 See Vol. 1 of this book series.

uncontrolled to feedback-controlled. Exerting influence in complex systems is something interactive; it requires inputs and outputs rather than issuing commands. The molecule is not the "boss" of the atoms of which it consists and which constitute it. Even in the very system one might surmise to be the origin of hierarchy – the military – the system architecture is based on embedding rather than hierarchy, as a regiment consists of battalions, which consist of companies, which consist of platoons, and so on. This is the case *a fortiori* in modern armies, but even the classical ones had this exact system structure. They could not have functioned any other way. The ancient Romans were the first to clearly realize that, and the first to use it systematically. This system structure helped them build their world empire.

The smaller units *form* the bigger ones, which means a regiment cannot even exist without battalions. And while everyone is at liberty to map this embedded structure by means of hierarchy, as is commonly known from the usual organization charts, this will not help to understand how these systems function. Therefore, no one in their right mind will try to depict a family as an organization chart.

Under particular circumstances – for instance, in cases of emergency – in the mesocosmic realm these systems can change their *mode of operation*, switching into hierarchical mode and back. That, however, does not change their structure. It only changes the mode of use of the communication systems within these systems, in order to be able to cope with certain problem situations.

In order to facilitate working with the models, the subsystems are separated from each other as shown in figure 9 – disembedded, so to speak – while strictly maintaining their systemic interrelations, which are then depicted by using arrows.

The letter V stands for variety; its differing size represents the fact that the variety of management – that is, its controlling and regulating capacity – is always less than the variety of the corporation, which, in turn, is less than that of the environment.

The term *embedding* as such is well established. However, I do not know of any technical term for the opposite operation – drawing the elements of a system out of their embedding in such a way that the system is not destroyed. For the time being, I will call this procedure disembedding. The important thing is that any associations with *separating* and the like are prevented, as that would put the wholeness of interrelations at risk.

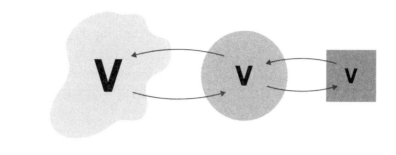

Figure 9: The disembedding of systems

Recursive Logic for Cybernetic Systems

Now let us come back to the three part basic model, which has another graphic depiction but is based on the same logic.

This three part model, which is shown in figure 7, provides the structure for corporate policy. Being a part of the overall management system itself, corporate policy covers all three interacting basic systems: the *environment,* the *corporation,* and the *corporate management.* In figure 10 we see that the subsystem *corporate management* in turn comprises the *whole* system.

It is really quite simple: *the part is* in *the whole and the whole is* in *the part. The part* is *the whole and the whole* is *the part.* It does not require any particular knowledge of philosophy to recognize the basic thought, which keeps recurring since the beginning of time – to capture the systemic nature of the world.

General managers are well familiar with this phenomenon, even if not all of them are aware of it or use it as systematically as they could. The decentralized units of a corporation are parts of the whole but, if done the right way, they are also laid out as viable systems or subsystems. They are entireties for their own part, with their own management, infrastructure, decision-making powers, and responsibility. They are parts and wholes at the same time.

This thought appears in religions, in philosophy and cosmology; it is forgotten and it reappears – because we need it to comprehend a systemic world and to get our bearings in it. What is still a hindrance to understanding is the somber, metaphysical language in which the thought is expressed.

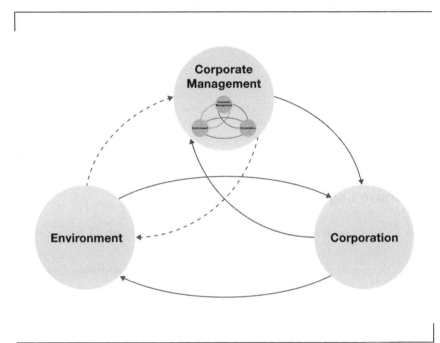

Figure 10: Embedding of the subsystem in the supersystem

The first time that the idea of systemic wholeness was truly understood dates back to around 100 years after René Descartes, when the Scottish moral philosophers of the 18th century such as Adam Ferguson, Adam Smith and David Hume created the first valid theories about society, business, law, language, morals, and custom. These theories were valid because they were based on self-organization and evolution. Descartes's conceptual world – the reductionist and mechanist thinking – was so firmly established back then (because it is quite effective for non-complex phenomena) that the concept of wholeness has largely remained misunderstood to this date. With the model concept described here, we are regaining an understanding of wholes and of complex systems. The definite step from Cartesian-style reductionism to a wholistic system concept of cybernetics and systemic will be characteristic of the 21st century. What people in those times tried to capture with philosophical metaphysics or theological theories – not very successfully, simply because language is not powerful enough – is now elegantly solved by modern mathematics: the mathematics of so-called *recursive functions* can solve the interrelations of embedding in a satisfactory and even descriptive way. It is a point that I feel merits mentioning here, without going into further detail.

Managers have to be familiar not only with mathematics; for their practical work they also need to know the *recursion principle*. It is the most important architectural principle of interconnected systems. To establish *Master Control*, systems must not be interconnected *in just any kind of way*; rather, they have to be *recursively embedded.*

Specialists, Generalists, Specialists for General Subjects

The three part recursive model of the corporate total system, the essential elements of which have now been introduced here, provides the basis for the understanding of management that has been valid from the very start in system-oriented management theory. It is the basis for understanding the arbitrary manner in which complex systems actually function. Experienced executives are constantly and naturally aware of these three fields of reference and act accordingly. In their decisions, they always consider the effect(s) in all subsystems. This is what makes them generalists in the true sense of the word.

The three subsystems are inseparably intertwined. Interventions in each of the systems can always have effects on the other systems linked to it. Due to their complexity, these effects are almost never only intentional ones; in addition, there are many other unexpected and, above all, unintended side effects and repercussions.

A typical characteristic of a truly good manager is that he constantly operates on the premise that there will be unintended side effects – including some he can vaguely anticipate and some he cannot even begin to imagine. He aligns his actions accordingly. A motto I used in the first volume of this series is perfectly fitting here: *the system always kicks back...*[56] Field marshal von Moltke was even more to the point when he said: *"Strategy is about constantly keeping a fallback position open."*

In my 30-plus years of working with executives I encountered two types of managers, generalists and specialists, and I mean both terms in a positive sense because we need both.

A skilled generalist – as opposed to a "high-flyer" – is naturally and intuitively capable of seeing wholes, thinking and acting wholistically. He does see the parts but he is not that interested in them because they do not give him orientation. The specialist, also understood in a positive sense and to be distinguished from the "nitpicker", focuses on the part. Seeing the whole is difficult to him. He sees the parts but they do not join together to form a whole.

We need both categories of executives, as they fulfill two very different kinds of tasks and both are important. In the society of complexity of the 21st century, we will need a third category of managers, which already exists: they are the *specialists for general matters*, namely for *wholes*. They are the true system architects and system designers.

Three Subconcepts for Master Control

As pointed out in the roadmap chapter, corporate policy will ultimately comprise three subconcepts: the concept of corporation, the concept of environment, and the management concept (see figure 11).

The overall system is that section of reality which is important for the given purpose, in this particular case the management of the company or another societal institution. We use the models to capture our knowledge and our nescience. And we use the concepts to define what we want to do.

---

56 The pertinent philosophy and methodology can best be found in Karl R. Popper's and Hans Albert's writings.

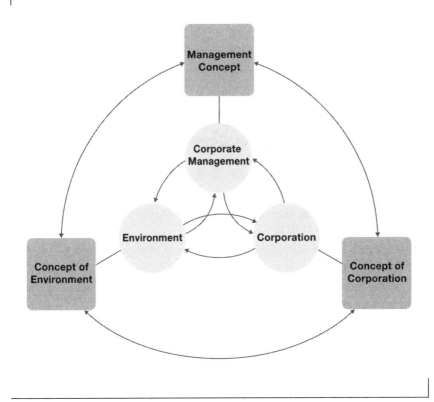

Figure 11: The system of the three concepts of corporate policy

In line with the definition of the terms world ➜ system ➜ model ➜ concept, these three subconcepts comprise what Part III of this book is all about:

- what we already know and what, based on our knowledge, we want to *consider*,
- what, based on our not-knowing, we need to *explore*, and
- what, based on the two, we want to *do* and how our actions have to be organized and regulated, so that as much as possible will organize and regulate itself.

What all these models introduced here, individually and jointly lead us to is not immediate answers but, first of all, questions to be answered by corporate policy. Answers to these questions can only be found in and for the *individual* application: a medium-sized manufacturer of men's shoes will obviously need another corporate policy, in many different ways, than does an international technology group. The intriguing question is what, despite all differences, will be the common and constant elements of a right and good corporate policy – the constants or fixed points of change…

The Best Media for Master Control

At the very beginning of this book, in the introductory part on "concept and logic of the book series", I pointed out that an appropriate understanding of complex systems and their control will require, even mandate, the use of new media.

Although a corporate policy decision should and can ultimately be simple and brief, as was mentioned before, the suitable medium for developing and documenting a corporate policy is no longer the written document. Even with relatively little complexity, we reach the limits of linguistic *descripteveness,* but we are far from reaching the limits of *demonstrability.* If a corporate policy for Master Control is to be clear to everyone concerned across all system structures, this requires quick and safe orientation.

Showing someone a navigation system in a car is easy. *Describing* it to them, if they have not seen one before, is almost impossible. A case in point is instruction manuals for cars, computers, and other devices, which are often hopelessly overloaded – in every meaning of the word.

The best means for designing and documenting a system-oriented corporate policy are provided by the browser technology including all its features, in particular hypertext. Anyone who has ever worked with hypertext and hyperlinks will know how it can facilitate navigation even in highly complex structures. What is more, he will know it is the *only* possible way. It is the ideal and the only means of making visible – in an easy and controlled way – the oscillation between the general and the detail of thinking and understanding.

The importance and usefulness of hypertext and all other visual and auditory possibilities provided by the web, with their three-dimensional, animated, and dynamic presentation techniques, as well as the random links for getting from one point in my model system to any other point in random order, without ever losing orientation, will be explained in a later

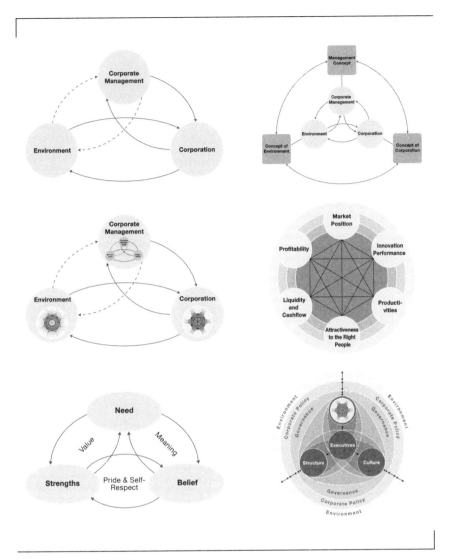

Figure 12: Task-specific navigation models derived from the basic model

chapter and demonstrated on the website mentioned.[57] Figure 12 provides a first impression. It explains how to work with the natural structure of embedded systems.

---

57 www.malik.ch

Part III
Instructions for Self-Organization

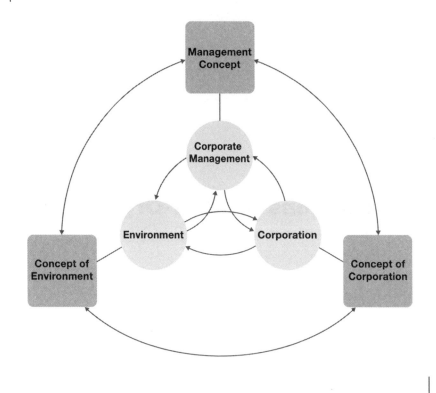

Two CEOs at a business dinner
(A's mobile is ringing non-stop, B's mobile is dead)

A: Say, is your mobile off?
B: No, it's on. I can be reached 24/7.
A: Then why does it never ring?
B: 'Cause we've got our company organized so that my people don't need
to keep checking back with me.

Chapter 1

What the Organization Should Do: The Business Concept

> The business of business is business.
>
> *Milton Friedman, liberal economist and Nobel laureate*

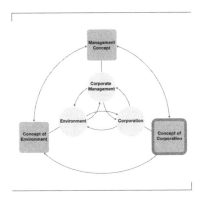

With the first chapter of Part III, we will now start to look at how an environmental or systems policy using *Master Control* is developed and formulated in practice. This chapter focuses on the concept of corporation, and therefore on that part of overall policy that concerns the institution directly. The issues relating to the company will, however, continue to be reflected in the context of the total system, as the illustration shows. The total system is always the same. However, in this step, attention will be focused like a searchlight entirely on the institution.

From the corporate policy point of view, there are three key questions that are equally important to *every* institution and – in my opinion – can be answered in a universally valid way. The specifics of the individual case have to be considered by further questions.

The key questions common to every institution are:

1. What should the purpose of the institution be?
2. What should the mission of the institution be?
3. Where should the institution carry out its mission?

The answers to these three questions have the *greatest* directing influence on an institution's activities. They are the most powerful and complexity-rich *Master Controls* when they are "set" rightly. Conversely, when the "switches" are in the wrong position, they have the most negative impact. This is the core of the big, comprehensive, all-determining feedback regulators – the laws of nature acting within the system, so to speak.

The widely discussed ethical problems of the last few years originate in these three questions, as mentioned in chapter 2, and they can only be solved there. This is also where the errors of corporate governance have arisen, the cases of mismanagement through shareholder value, the excesses of executive pay, the false compromises of the stakeholder approach with the resurrection of management's potential escape routes from responsibility, the re-opening of social gaps. Also, should any turbulence occur in the financial system and a crisis arise in the economic system – a possible and highly probable development due to years of mismanagement – this is where the causes lie.

The Purpose of the Organization

The purpose of the institution determines every aspect of how the organization as a system should be designed and operated. We are thinking entirely on the system level here, in terms of management and content. The central cybernetic importance of the corporate purpose can most clearly be illustrated on the basis of errors that are made in defining purpose.

What people now call corporate governance took the wrong turning at the crossroads of "purpose" when it went in the direction of the shareholder instead of the *customer.*[58] As a result, both sails and rudder were set wrongly. The wind of the *zeitgeist* created the illusion of being on the right course. Once the error was noticed, another false signpost was followed: the stakeholder approach.

It was obvious to eight out of ten top managers from the start. Instead of spending their time concentrating on the business, they would now have to get ready for a balancing act. As one of the most outstanding CEOs told me in a discussion: *"In the morning I have to tell the financial community and the media what they want to hear – and inside the company, in the*

---

58 I gave an extensive description and reasons for the thinking and points of view presented below in my book *Wirksame Unternehmensaufsicht*, Frankfurt am Main 1997, a 3rd edition of which was published with a number of additions in 2002 under the title "Die Neue Corporate Governance". I will confine myself here to core issues.

afternoon, I have to make sure that the opposite is done, without the financial world noticing ..."

The Best Ones Remain Concealed

The shareholder eyeglasses blinded people to the overwhelming number of companies that had always worked well and did not abandon their principles even in the era of the Wall Street scandals. The corporate governance debate only saw and considered the large, listed corporate groups – a relatively small number of companies. However, more than 90 percent of all firms worldwide are not listed on stock exchanges. Today's corporate governance and the governance codes that have now grown up are simply irrelevant to them.

Essentially, people have allowed themselves to be led astray for a whole decade by a few Wall Street scandals and a tiny minority of greedy egocentrics and white-collar criminals. In addition, a problem that is solved with total ease in every country every day is grossly overestimated by one particular economic theory: the *principal agent problem* – that is, the question of how owners can control and monitor persons acting on their behalf in such a way that they will not be able to systematically cheat them. That may be a problem in the ivory tower of economic theory-spinning. We can draw on several thousands of years of experience for the practice of right corporate management.[59] Assuming professional management and subject knowledge, corporate governance functions in a way that does not require any sophisticated financial constructs, which invariably prove to be fair-weather models.

The true gems of the corporate landscape remain virtually undiscovered and disregarded[60] – which is fine by them, since they want no truck with financial publicity. They want their products to be well known, but in their view, the internal details of their companies, ownership structures, finance

---

59 See the historical overview by Paul C. Martin in: Krieg, Walter/Galler, Klaus/ Stadelmann, Peter (Ed.), *Richtiges und gutes Management: vom System zur Praxis, Festschrift für Fredmund Malik*, Berne/Stuttgart/Vienna 2004.
60 Hermann Simon shows good examples in his book *Hidden Champions*, Frankfurt/New York 2007.

etc. are no one else's concern. Presenting their strategy to competitors in road shows is the last thing on their minds.

The one-eyed shareholder viewpoint failed to notice real performers that were not in the stock exchange spotlight, and in the media noise of the corporate governance discussion the gentle tones of the true goldmines went unheard. The truly functioning economy finds no place in MBA programs.

I am not talking about small to mid-sized companies, which are often cited reflexive – and frequently with mocking condescension – as the supposed opposite pole to the listed corporations. I am talking about a quite different category of extremely successful businesses, including many global market leaders. To make my meaning clear, I have coined a new term for these companies: entrepreneurially managed enterprises – which can be abbreviated as EMEs, to separate them from the category of SME, the small and medium-sized enterprises. With this type of company, the key feature is not the size but the type of management.

Examples speak louder than words. In the German-speaking region, which is the second- or third-largest economic region in the world, depending on the method of calculation – and in fact the strongest – examples include Boehringer Ingelheim, Würth, Dr. Oetker, Stihl, the Claas Group, Otto Hamburg, Bertelsmann, Braun Melsungen, Ina Kugelfischer, ZF, Aldi, Lidl, REWE, Bosch, Porsche, BMW, Springer, Hilti, Patek Philippe, Migros, Coop, Logitech, Liebherr, Maxon, EmsChemie, Kaba, Swarovski, Red Bull, Plansee, Spar, Doppelmayr, Miba, Blum, Raiffeisen, Zumtobel and many others, which I unfortunately cannot mention here for lack of space.

It is evident that entrepreneurial management is possible and successful regardless of industry, size, form of finance or ownership structure, and also regardless of whether a company is listed on a stock exchange or not. With regard to the last point in particular, it is frequently said that listed companies have no option but to operate in accordance with shareholder-oriented principles. That is not true, as can be seen.

This type of companies exists in other countries and economic areas as well, and almost everywhere they are the most successful in their fields. They contribute the major part of the gross national product and provide the biggest share of jobs. Corporate governance should learn from them, not the other way round.

Only One Right Purpose: Customer Value

The purpose of the institution must be clear, and it must be right. Conventional corporate governance sometimes set an unclear purpose, but mainly the wrong one. The purpose defines the relevance of events inside and outside the enterprise. Only a clear corporate purpose enables a correct environmental analysis, otherwise you do not know what you are supposed to be looking for and what you should take into account. The purpose determines what will be managed and how. If you have the wrong purpose, you have loaded the wrong program and will inevitably arrive at the wrong results. In contrast, the right, clear purpose makes everything easy, even with a high level of complexity. The corporate purpose defines the relevant feedbacks for the Master Controls at all levels. This is essential for decisions on what should be considered information or misinformation, data and data clutter, and what parts of the institution can and should organize themselves in which direction. The corporate purpose defines what comprises right results and what does not.

Creating clarity about the purpose of the institution, communicating, giving reasons and explaining it internally and externally, is a top priority task for top managers, perhaps the most important one of all. One of their most difficult tasks in this context will be to convince shareholders that they are harming themselves if they hold management to the purpose of shareholder value. What is supposed to be good for the shareholders according to their own intentions will actually lead to the opposite, their disadvantage. The really competent top managers know that. However, they also know how difficult it is in the present climate to communicate that fact. Managers have a hugely important task of enlightenment here[61], which I will expand on further in Part IV.

The better the company's profitability is to be, the less emphasis there should be on financial ratios such as shareholder value. Particularly when a company wants to maximize its financial performance, it has to target a fundamentally different purpose and objective. Companies obviously need profits, and liquidity even more. However, it does not follow that the purpose of the company is to make a profit.

---

61 One contribution is the previously mentioned book *Anders ist besser* by Wendelin Wiedeking, the former CEO of Porsche, Munich 2006.

The right purpose – the purpose that is relevant to decisions for steering the institution – is diametrically opposed to this and places corporate governance on a different basis. The shareholder value approach has shown more dramatically and convincingly than ever that businesses are not just economic, but also human, political and moral institutions. However, regardless of whether social and other reasons also argue against shareholder value, it is possible to stay entirely within the logic of business management and economic thinking and still set the right objective. This is important to the weight of the arguments in my view, because too many people are too quick to argue on non-economic grounds, which, of course, cannot make any impression on economic and financial convictions.

My solution is not aimed at either the supporters or the opponents of neoliberalism. It falls into a different category. There is a *third* way which has been overlooked in the corporate governance debate.

And yet this is the clearest and most obvious purpose if you detach yourself from interest groups – of any kind whatsoever – and think the problem through from the point of view of the *management function*, in other words: including the perspective of navigation and control, from the point of view of the institution ,and how to steer it. To the best of my knowledge, neither the champions nor the opponents of neoliberal thinking have so far found *arguments* to successfully refute my proposal.

The purpose can be formulated simply and clearly:

The purpose of the business is to transform resources into value.

Whose value? As a first possibility, the value of individual or all *interest groups* may be postulated. Any of the solutions conceivable on this basis will damage the institution in the longer term in some way or another and undermine its ability to function, systematically and inevitably. In addition, such purposes will ultimately not be achievable at all, with intrinsic inevitability. A purpose oriented towards interest groups, whether shareholders or stakeholders, will render itself obsolete; it will make its own fulfillment impossible because the decision-making and actions of management will be programmed and incentivized in the wrong direction.

Particularly when the interests of these groups are to be borne in mind, the purpose has to be viewed from a completely different angle: that of *value to the customer*.

The corporate purpose can thus be formulated clearly and simply in practice, and is:

The purpose of a business is to create satisfied customers.

Figure 13 shows the clear and simple relationship. No one is forced to accept this proposal, since we are right at the heart of normative management here, in the realm of true value decisions. However, as explained in Part I, values of this nature should not preempt the decision, but should result from the consequences of the decision. The decision in favor of value to the customer is the only one to deliver the consequence of *right* corporate management, because only the customer pays bills. This, in turn, has the consequence that all interests are served as well as possible. No other purpose can achieve that. It is logically impossible to find a right strategy if it is not explicitly focused on solving customer problems and generating value to the customer. There is not a single strategically relevant question that can be answered rationally without an orientation towards customer value.

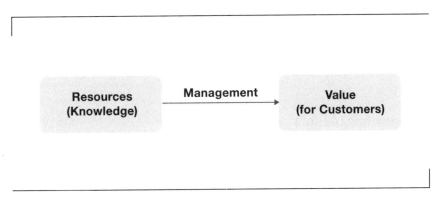

Figure 13: The corporate purpose as the transformation of resources into customer value

If this purpose is accepted, it has to be adapted to the *individual case* in developing the corporate policy. From this point of view, the question has to be asked:

• What is *our* purpose?
• What resources do *we* transform into what value?
• Who are *our* customers? Who should they be, who can they be?

Resources are all types of goods and services that are needed to create value for customers. The key resource in the 21st century will be knowledge, as is already the case today in many areas. Added to this is the (meta-)knowledge that is needed in order to transform knowledge into value, in other words, knowledge about management of and in complex systems.

Value, in turn, is all kinds of goods, services, information and knowledge that *solve a problem* for the customer for which he is prepared to pay a *bill*. I therefore propose *customer value* as the corporate purpose.

If we extend corporate policy into a policy for all types of social institutions, or in other words, into a *general systems policy* as discussed in the introduction, the purpose for non-profit organizations would in principle be:

> The purpose of social institutions is to bring about desired change in people and society.

Thus, the contribution of both business enterprises and non-profit organizations is defined in *social* terms. This is where their ethic lies. It lies in their impact *for* society, in line with CybernEthics by the great cybernetician Heinz von Foerster[62] and his associated observation: *It's not "what should other people do?" but "what should I do"?* The ethics and decency of the person and the institution are founded in this, and not in regulations and codes.

The Function of Profit

The form of organization that has proven most effective to date for the transformation of resources into value is the free-market enterprise. However, the output of the transformation process is not profit, which is the way it is normally seen and which the economic disciplines postulate in particular - over-hastily, as a premise that has not been thought through or tested. The output is the economic *object*.

Naturally, this does not mean that a business can or even should survive without profit. The economic function of profit as a return on capital and risk premium is still valid. However, as mentioned before, the undisputed fact that companies need profits and, still more importantly, liquidity by

---

62 Foerster, Heinz von, *KybernEthik*, Berlin 1993.

no means implies that profit is the *purpose* of the company. Likewise, the fact that people have to eat does not imply that the purpose of humanity or indeed the meaning of life is food. However, every individual is free to make his or her own decisions in this regard. Therefore, the question is not so much what the purpose *is*, but which purpose involves the greatest probability of right decisions.

From the point of view of the company's navigation and control, profit has a different function: that of *control information*. My proposal is to understand profit as a test of the *rightness* of the corporate mission, which I will discuss below, and as a gauge of the *quality of fulfillment* of that corporate mission.

Profit thus provides two key pieces of information for managerial navigation, that is, whether the business is doing the right thing – which encompasses the *effectiveness* of its actions – and whether it is doing the right things well (and right) – which encompasses the *efficiency* of its actions.

As an indicative guide, the more right the business mission is and the better it is fulfilled, the higher will be the profit – not as the objective but as the *consequence* of effective and efficient management. Profit is a variable that should typically be aimed at *indirectly*. Long before you can even think of making profits, other variables which I will deal with later in this chapter have to be brought under control.

A free economy, by the way, is not *defined* by profit, contrary to the majority opinion and superficial economic doctrine. The capitalist system is defined by *liquidity*, that is, the ability to pay creditors. So long as a person can meet his payment obligations he remains in the capitalist game. If he cannot, he drops out of the game. It does not matter to the creditor where the money to meet the payment obligations comes from.

One last point should be mentioned with regard to profit: the opinion – which is also an unproven postulate – that profit is the dominant motive of entrepreneurial activity. No one knows the motives of people who are active in business. Some are in fact motivated by profit, and many of these go bankrupt within a short space of time. Others maintain that they are profit-driven when you ask them, but their actions speak a different language, which shows the wide-spread belief that people are clear about their motives to be a fallacy.

The debate does not include two motives that are easy to spot when talking to real people in real situations, rather than applying the results of questionnaires. The first motive is the desire for independence: in order to avoid ever having a boss, people in small and medium-sized enterprises in particular will make almost any sacrifice, and it is completely immaterial to them whether it pays off in economic terms or not.

The second motive is the deep conviction of being able to do something better than others – and having the will to prove it. This can be seen, among others, in entrepreneurs who appear to be arch-capitalistic and entirely profit-oriented, until you scrutinize them closely enough – such as John D. Rockefeller. Rockefeller was deeply, almost pathologically, convinced that he understood more about the oil business than anyone else. He provided excellent evidence of that in his day.

After almost 40 years of experience, when working with such people I invariably hypothesize that there is not one successful entrepreneur, nor one successful corporate manager, who is profit-driven. Without exception, they act in the service of a thing, an idea and a conviction – and for their freedom and independence.

Understanding Customer Value Correctly: Two Fixed Points for Navigation

The two "fixed stars" by which the enterprise is guided are *customer value* and *competitiveness*.

The economic as well as the social contribution of the institution lie in the transformation of resources into value. This implies the creation of assets that go far beyond *value added*, which is almost exclusively understood in financial terms nowadays. However, it is also evident that the social contribution of the enterprise cannot lie in some kind of social welfare objectives with this solution.

The creation of assets can and should include financial assets, if that is what customers want. That will be the case in the financial sector. Outside the financial sector, however, it is not purely monetary assets that create value in the form of problem solutions, but assets in the form of all the products and services that are purchased every day. Prosperity for society and the individual does not lie in the possession of money, but in what can be bought and done with money. People find this concept hard to grasp from today's one-dimensional financial perspective. Even if, however – as a conceptual experiment – banks and stock exchanges were to be closed, people would still have to live, eat, drink and dress, their children would have to go to school, sick people would have to be nursed and babies born. Life is not defined by money, and neither, by any means, is a functioning society.

Using *value creation* in the financial sense, whether in terms of stock market prices or of potential selling prices, as a criterion for the performance of the company or its management is a grotesque distortion of economic logic. There are only two cases in which a company should be *valuable* in the financial sense: when it is to be sold, and when a hostile takeover is to be fended off through the stock exchange.

In the first case, the entrepreneur ceases to manage as an entrepreneur. It is legitimate for him to want to get the highest possible price for his firm. The true business problem is then simply transferred to the buyer, who has to make a company for which he has overpaid so competitive that it will, in turn, find enough customers for whom it creates value.

Defending against hostile takeovers, by contrast, can be done more cheaply and effectively: by restricting the transferability of the shares. This course is usually condemned vigorously by neoliberal circles, citing the argument of deregulation. However, anyone wishing to be truly liberal – and not just *neoliberal* – will have to accept that every institution has to have the freedom to do what it considers right with its shares. If the necessary decisions are made by the high managerial agents of a company, on the other hand, there is no rational objection to them from a liberal standpoint. One decision-making parameter may be the way in which the stock exchange takes such actions. However, it is impossible to order anyone to make him- or herself the prey to takeover moves, either voluntarily or on the grounds of ideological dogma.

A frequent objection to my proposal of making customer value the supreme purpose is that people do not know what customer value is. That is a remarkable testimony to unfamiliarity with the state of the art. What customer value is can nowadays be determined with great precision, particularly thanks to the biggest empirical strategy research program in the world, the legendary PIMS® research.[63] One of the biggest breakthroughs

---

63 Buzzell, Robert D./Gale, Bradley T., *The PIMS Principles. Linking Strategy to Performance*, New York 1987 and various PIMS letters of the Malik Management (www.mzsg.ch). Also Gale, Bradley T., *Managing Customer-Value*, New York 1994.

in management and business administration overall was achieved with PIMS, particularly in strategy research, in as far as we now know how to distinguish a right strategy from a wrong one very accurately, and what matters when an optimally effective strategy is to be developed. Customer value is the central anchor-point for this.

In the sector of customer value, which has to be a key factor in any right strategy, PIMS created the *"theory of relativity"*, as it were. Customer value is the ratio of *relative price to relative market-perceived quality*, with "relative" being a two-fold relativity: *relative* from the point of view of the customer and *relative* to competitors.[64]

Customer value is the clear, simple and logically compelling purpose on which to base the *control* of the institution, of top management's duty to steer it through the complexity of industry and society. From the point of view of the institution's functioning, that is the only robust management perspective vis-à-vis every conceivable interest group, or in other words: all stakeholders.

Customer value means *value to the customer* – to be absolutely precise, because the neoliberal financial orientation could understand even that wrongly: as the value *of* the customer. The customer and the value to him, captured in the word *satisfied*, is the original fixed point for the safe navigation of the enterprise.

The orientation towards customer value maximizes the probability of making fewer wrong decisions than right ones. Every other orientation maximizes the probability of wrong decisions.

A company that has satisfied customers, or in other words, that is successful, will always have enough investors because they will be happy to make capital available. However, in an apparent paradox, such companies do not need investors because their success allows them to self-finance. They do have *owners*, often through generations of the same family, but these do not have to provide capital. To the contrary, they often obtain the best returns precisely because their companies are rigorously and uncompromisingly oriented towards the customer – and they therefore have no reason to sell their shares.

The best capital does not come from the stock exchange, as present-day miseducation would have it, but from *customers* who are so satisfied that they

---

64 Volume 3 on Corporate Strategy discusses this further.

will pay such good prices that the enterprise can basically do without outside capital. Good firms finance themselves. There are more such firms than is perceived by the public, and in particular by the media. They do not need or make any headlines, which is why they are of no interest to the media.

Customer value is the *first* and primal fixed point by which to orient the steering of organizations. The *second* fixed point results directly from, or is incorporated in the *satisfied* customer himself. Does "*satisfied customer*" mean that one has to give one's market performance away for free? This question, too, is frequently advanced as an objection to customer value as the corporate purpose, which shows how far some people have strayed from a sensible understanding of business.

Naturally, nobody needs to give anything away; rather, the company has to better deliver its market performance, its products and services to the customer than any competitor can. Creating satisfied customers means proving your competitiveness every day and maximizing it constantly.

This brings us to the two most powerful *Master Controls* for corporate guidance, which have to be fixed points of navigation, and therefore fixed points of any corporate policy.

The Most Powerful Master Controls

The logic is clear:

Customer value instead of shareholder value.
Competitiveness instead of value creation.

Only this orientation maximizes the probability of right decisions. Every other orientation maximizes the probability of wrong decisions.

This is where the concept of corporation and the concept of environment meet. Both *Master Controls* are *absolutely objective benchmarks that cannot be manipulated*, that are tested afresh every day "*out there*" in the market and against which companies have to measure and prove themselves. They contain neither subjective nor financial judgments. This logic has to be clearly stipulated by corporate policy. All top management tasks follow from this position. If top management fails on these points it has failed on its most important entrepreneurial task. If investors prevent top management from carrying it out they are damaging the company and therefore themselves.

Setting the purpose also defines the *social* responsibility of the enterprise. As outlined before, this is not a diffuse social obligation that can be defined at random, but it consists in strengthening the institution's performance capability for satisfied customers by constantly improving competitiveness.

The two control variables keep top management from being led astray by the *zeitgeist*. They are the most powerful regulators of complexity, and an example of how simple *Master Controls* can be and how much regulating power they can develop. They eliminate all inadmissible circumstances, concentrate all efforts on the right purpose, and thus focus the regulating power on satisfying more and more customers. This regulating power is needed because customers develop considerable complexity in the form of a variety of needs and behaviors. Customers do not see it as their task to behave *rationally* in the sense of some economic theory or other, or of a promotional strategy.

The only objectivity in business is the subjectivity of the customer.

And as every experienced corporate leader knows, competitors can also develop enormous complexity in the war for customers, in the form of creativity, innovativeness, price maneuvers and marketing, to name only a few areas.

Corporate Capitalism instead of Shareholder Value

Customer value as the corporate purpose places the *business* itself in pole position, and not – as is erroneously common and only seemingly rational – some sort of *interest* or *stakeholder groups*.

The logic is plain to see: what is good for the organization cannot be worse for the sum of its interest groups than any other orientation. With customer value instead of shareholder and stakeholder capitalism, we arrive at what can be termed *corporate capitalism*, if we want to retain the obsolete concept of "capitalism". My thesis is that this – putting the organization first – is the *only* way to find satisfactory solutions to the unresolved questions that have been addressed to the economic system to date, as well as to the doubts about it and the apparent contradictions of the system.

Customer value as the corporate purpose also applies – perhaps most of all – to the strongest advocates of shareholder value: financial institutions.

De facto, these companies do nothing other than maximize customer value, although they claim the opposite. With their demands for shareholder value they naturally fulfill the wishes of *their own* customers, the investors. They create satisfied customers *for themselves*, and thus are rigorously and strictly oriented towards customer value. The finance industry, too, has to prove with every day that passes that it can satisfy its customers, and every individual company in the financial sector has to try and do so better than its competitors. The logic I propose above therefore applies consistently to all types of institutions.

In the finance industry, the shareholder value of equity investments is identical with customer value for investors. In the real economy this is not the case. In zeitgeist-driven mass psychology, however, real-economy enterprises are led astray or actually forced to follow suit by the pressure of analysts and media. As a result, they direct their gaze away from their customers and towards the opposing direction of the shareholders, which – as we will see in a moment – are a strange species nowadays, with a few exceptions.

The rhetoric of the finance industry changes the *appearance* of the market, but not its *logic*. In line with the logic of the market, a company must focus on the group that pays actual bills. That would be the customers and no one else. To say that ultimately the shareholders "foot the bill" is a misleading slogan. It may be that the shareholders will post a loss if the enterprise can no longer find customers who pay real bills. The shareholder bears the owner's risk, but he does not pay any bills. He does not pay for the economic output of the enterprise, but he does bear the loss if the company fails to perform its most important task, that is, to deliver an economic object to the group that will pay for it.

Particularly when owners are interested in the value and value growth of their shares, they have to do everything in their power to enable the institution to create customer value, and they have to empower the management not to have to think about anything else.

In actual fact, shareholders should turn their logic and rhetoric by 180 degrees. Rather than asking what the enterprise can and should do for them, they should ask what they have to do for the enterprise so that its business goes well. In other words: shareholder *interest* is not identical to shareholder *value*. Particularly *when* the shareholder is to be well served, the central focus must be on customer value as the purpose. The tycoons of every epoch have always understood that, as have the entrepreneurial dynasties that survived through the epochs and fads. It determined their actions in the past, and still does so today.

This logic applies *a fortiori* to the pension fund investors, the future pensioners. They rely on receiving their retirement income in 20 or 30 years' time. As a result, their most vital interest has to be aimed at the *long-term* performance of the company, and not the short-term share price. The trick is to first *generate* the economic object – only then can it be distributed. Figure 14 demonstrates this. The shareholders can certainly be first in line when it comes to distribution. However, unless something has previously been generated, there will be nothing to distribute. Precisely these long-term interests, however, are undermined by the shareholder value doctrine, because the fund managers are forced to orient themselves towards short-term performance.

Business performance	
Distribution	**Production**
World of money and fictitious value	World of customers and competition
World of stock exchanges and of securities and book values	World of real assets and performance power
World of investors and gamblers	World of entrepreneurs
Reported earnings	Real earnings
Pro-forma earnings	EAIT, EAE
eBIT (DA), EBA	
Analysts, investment bankers lacking experience financial side of mergers and acquisitions	Engineers, salespeople, researchers and developers, marketing, personnel, logistics, procurement

Figure 14: The two worlds of creating and distributing economic objects

What Is an Investor Really?

The term "investor" has become more or less meaningless due to the development of the financial markets and the funds industry. Its meaning has to be meticulously analyzed in each individual case. Investors and shareholders are identical in purely formal terms as owners, if they hold shares. However, that is far from meaning that they have the same interests.

Those shareholders are a *homogeneous* interest group is one of the dogmas postulated by neoliberalism, but rarely examined. For that reason alone, the demand for shareholder value makes no sense anywhere. In addition, shareholder structures have changed fundamentally over time. Here are some facts.

In 1950, around 90 percent of all US shares were held by private households. Today, the figure is just over 30 percent. By contrast, institutional investors hold almost 70 percent of shares now, while they only possessed 9 percent in 1950. The 100 biggest money managers in America manage almost 60 percent of US shares. That the interests of these two investor groups are radically different needs no explanation.

This is demonstrated, for example, by the so-called churn rate, or the percentage of shares that change hands every year. It was just under 20 percent per annum for the funds in the 1950s and 1960s and has risen to more than 90 percent since the start of the 1990s.

In truth, therefore, the shareholders, although they are the formal owners, are no longer shareholders in the sense of entrepreneurial owners. They do not invest in shares in order to hold them because of the company and its performance capabilities. This type of shareholders is not really interested in the institution, but in fast performance for funds managers and unit holders. This is perfectly legitimate and fulfills an economic function. I am not criticizing it per se. Crucial questions arise, however, when it comes to corporate governance, or to the rights granted to such investors to influence the management and decision-making bodies of the company.

A shareholder has every right to do what he wants with his shares. If, however, he only has short-term financial interests he should not be allowed to take part in determining the company's *Master Control* decisions. He can then quite happily buy shares where he will get the best immediate return. However, since the churn rates prove him to be not interested in the business abilities of the enterprise – otherwise he would hold his securities for a longer period of time – he should not be allowed to interfere in its business interests. This can easily be arranged: anyone who has a hand in appointing the supervisory board, and thus in corporate governance, should have to observe a holding period. Anyone refusing to do so should have no voting rights at the general meetings of shareholders.

If the purpose of the institution is determined from the point of view of the management's control function, all conflicts arising from the one-sidedness of a corporate governance that focuses only on financial concerns can be neatly resolved.

Prey to Stakeholder Groups

What remains to be discussed is the variant of the stakeholder approach, which was revived when it gradually became clear that the shareholder approach led to problems. As I already mentioned in the introduction, the reformers of the shareholder approach do not appear to be aware that the *breakdown* of the stakeholder approach led to the rise of the shareholder approach in the first place.

The stakeholder approach, however, makes the enterprise the object and ultimately the prey or hostage of changes in the balance of power among interest groups, whether the interests are those of capital, organized labor, governments or political parties. That is the reason why the stakeholder approach, although it has been tried out in every form, has never worked anywhere. Every variety of the stakeholder approach has ultimately led to economic ruin instead of healthy companies. The stakeholder approach provides management with innumerable ways of escaping from responsibility for the company's economic performance capabilities.

Even if one was to champion the stakeholder approach, this would make customer value all the more essential as the supreme corporate purpose. If the company passes the tests of customer value and competitiveness, it has a good chance of fulfilling the legitimate demands of stakeholders. If it fails them, on the other hand, it will not be able to fulfill any of these claims, because the company will not function. This also solves the problem of the demand for job protection, for example. Only a company that is healthy in the sense of competitiveness and customer value can create and maintain jobs. If, however, the job is positioned ahead of customer value as a purpose, the company will sooner or later be unable to achieve either.

Another fallacy arises here: the opinion that the customer is also a stakeholder – one of several flaws in the reasoning behind stakeholder theory. The customer is *never* a stakeholder. In the usual definition, stakeholders are groups that can make legitimate claims on the company.[65] However, customers *do not make claims* in this sense. *They buy or they do not buy.* They make claims in the sense of fulfilling their purchase agreements. That has absolutely nothing to do with stakeholder claims.

Customers are basically not interested in the institution as such, their interest is in its *output*. They are interested in what they can buy. That is also why you should never depend on customer loyalty. It may exist, but you can never rely on it. Customers want better goods and services (economic objects) than they can get elsewhere. Customers are people who can say no – because in a competition-based economy there is not just this one supplier but others as well. Every entrepreneur with any sense keeps more than one supplier so that he does not become overly dependent – even if he has to pay higher prices for doing so, as is usually the case. This furnishes further proof to refute the economic profit maximization thesis: entrepreneurial independence and freedom of choice are more important than the last percent of profit.

Whether and in what way claims of third parties – or in other words, stakeholders – can be fulfilled and how these gain legitimacy is another question. It is clear, however, that no claims can be met if an enterprise does not fulfill its original purpose: delivering things to customers and doing so better than competitors.

As far as legitimate claims on the company are concerned, we do not need to use the fuzzy concept of the stakeholder to begin with. First of all, the company has to meet claims that have their legitimacy in *contracts* and *legislation*. No one in his or her right mind would talk about stakeholders in this context. The fact that the enterprise is integrated into a multi-faceted, complex network of contractual relationships which it must comply with goes without saying, as does the fact that it has to observe the dictates of the law. The employees' claims, for example, are manifested in employment contracts and labor law. These are not claims, but *rights*. The same applies to the state, which asserts its statutory rights to taxes, contributions, environmental compatibility etc. The same considerations apply first and foremost to all groups or institutions that can make legitimate

---

65 Ulrich, Peter, *Ethik in Wirtschaft und Gesellschaft*, Berne/Stuttgart 1996, p. 13.

claims on an enterprise in this sense. Further questions of claims and their legitimacy only arise after and beyond that point.

The justified concerns that have come to the fore because of the social incompatibility of neoliberalism, for instance the demands for social responsibility and corporate citizenship, cannot be satisfied unless customer value is the purpose, whichever way the status of legitimacy of such claims is derived or postulated.

Everyone Is Free to Make Wrong Decisions

No one can be forced to make the decision on purpose exactly as I propose here. Those who wish to regard a company as a profit maximization system are free to do so. This decision can only be judged by the likely consequences. I think it can be proved that a company cannot function in the long run if it aims at profit maximization.

In a free society, however, people are free even to make wrong decisions. After listening to all the arguments for and against, a supervisory board or owner can decide freely *not* to have the enterprise managed by customer value. Long debates can be held on whether or not to make the connection with ethics here.

If we accept the Hippocratic principle of *"never knowingly doing any harm – primum non nocere"* as an ethical principle, it is unethical to decide against customer value. However, taking customer value as the supreme purpose does not follow just from this ethical principle, but much more directly from the fact that every purpose orientation that is not focused on the customer hampers the proper functioning of the institution.

As mentioned at the beginning of this book, Milton Friedman, the most extreme of the liberal economists, once gave the best answer – possibly unintentionally, though I cannot verify that: *"The business of business is business"*[66]. If he had meant to say *"profit"*, he probably would have done so. After all, he was a Nobel laureate. But on this occasion he said *"business"*. You can only do business with customers ...

---

66 *Neue Zürcher Zeitung,* online edition of November 18, 2006.

The Business Mission

I dealt in detail with the question of corporate purpose because the biggest and most critical risk of mismanagement and wrong developments lies in decisions about that purpose. As mentioned, corporate governance went off the track of right and good corporate management at precisely this point – despite good intentions. It can only be corrected at this point, too. The purpose determines the whole system and its way of functioning.

The second basic decision about the concept of corporation which has the effect of *Master Control* consists in defining the corporate or business *mission*. It determines what the institution has to accomplish on the subject level. In other words, the mission determines at the system level what the institution should do – or its business activities. Its contents ensure functionality on the subject level.

As a word, *mission* is not necessarily better than *vision*, a buzzword that I have always regarded critically. The fuss about it has died down, which I regard as progress. You can undoubtedly start with a vision, but it is not enough on its own. The problem is that to this day no one has been able to demonstrate how you can distinguish a *right* vision from a *wrong* one, or a useful vision from a useless one. As a result, any act of charlatanism could be justified for a while using the term "vision". On the other hand, we know exactly what is needed for a right and good business mission.

The business mission is not identical with the purpose, as is often assumed. Rather, it tells us the means by which the purpose of the enterprise will be fulfilled. For example, I never thought it was a good decision for DaimlerChrysler to build the Smart – not for reasons of taste, but on the basis of the requirements that a good mission has to fulfill. As you will see in a moment, the Smart decision failed to meet two key criteria of a good mission, which was why its prospects of success were, though not quite zero, fairly small indeed.

I can keep this section on business mission short, because it is absolutely clear what has to be considered and what has to be decided. Here, we have one of those cases where the simplicity of good Master Control decisions even for the most complex systems is clearly evident. Viewed in this light, the business mission is as simple and effective a tool for the management of an institution as a traffic circle, which I described at the start of the book as a prototype of self-organization. The questions, answers and decisions associated with the business mission, in contrast, are anything but simple.

Three Elements of the Business Mission

A useful business mission must comprise three elements – that is, it has to rest on three pillars. From these three pillars, three fields of interaction arise, each being the source of capabilities that are decisive for success: requirements, competencies and conviction.

A business mission can never start with the *formulation* of a mission statement, and certainly not with finding the most memorable slogan. These things come at the end of its design. They are tasks for the corporate communication, marketing and advertising departments. The beginning has to be a close conceptual examination of the decision on the company's business activity, based on the three key questions below. After that come the related detailed questions, which I will present in later sections. The search for memorable wording does not come until after these stages. The key questions are:

- What is the need? Or: what does the customer really pay us for?
- What are our strengths? Or: what can we do better than others?
- Where does our belief come from? Or: where does our inner force come from?

Need

The first question thus directs the gaze outside, towards the customer as dictated by the corporate purpose, or in other words towards the center and source of proliferating complexity. I am talking about a *need* here, not of a want or even of a demand. A need is more, it is more comprehensive and it is objective. Sometimes a need and a want are congruent; sometimes a perceived want has to grow out of the objective need. Of course, not all needs are covered and not all of them lead to demand. As you can see, we are at the heart of the most difficult questions of strategy, marketing, and the communication that is central for the age of complexity. The starting point is disposable income and its use by the customer.

The key questions are:

- What is the customer paying us for?
- What is he really paying for?
- Where and for what are *non*-customers paying?

Trivial as these questions may seem, it is difficult to find really substantial answers to them as a guide to action. Every manager who is not content with superficial slogans is familiar with this experience. Barely a third of the companies I am familiar with have really thought the answers through as adequately as the Master Control impact of the mission decision requires.

The third question in particular is a puzzle to corporate managers. Of course they think about customers every day, but do they also think about non-customers? If someone holds a 30 percent market share, he can be justifiably proud of a major business achievement. But then there is 70 percent of the market which he has not been able to reach. Why not?

Strenghts

The second element of the business mission arises from the following questions:

- What are our strengths?
- What can we do better than others?
- As a consequence, where does our superiority come from?

These questions direct the attention from the environment to the institution itself, on the institution's strengths, that is, inward but always in *comparison with others*, or in other words, using a reference point that lies in the environment. It is not just a matter of looking inward – things are not that simple. It is a matter of looking *from inside out and back inside*, which will be discussed further in relation to the environment concept.[67]

There is no great art in identifying the institution's weaknesses. That can be left to consultants – and they should not be paid too much for it. By contrast, finding out what you can do, and what you can or must be able to do better than others in order for the customer to notice, motivating him to buy from you and not from others – that is a high art, and the responsibility of the corporate top management. The thinking of the best top managers revolves around this point day and night.

---

67 For systems experts: this is an example of the communicative closure of the system through self-referential relationship.

The third pillar of a business mission concerns the question of what really moves people deep inside, what mobilizes their performance capabilities and above all their performance reserves. It stems from the following questions:

- What are we really convinced of?
- What do we believe in?
- Where does our commitment come from?
- Where do we get the energy to deliver performance?
- Where does our energy come from, particularly when all our motivation is exhausted?

In other words, it is not just about motivation, incentives and so on, but about something much more fundamental: the energy with which people can still master even apparently hopeless situations. So long as you can *motivate* people to do something, no real problems exist. If, however, their motivation is exhausted before the objective is reached, that element of the business mission comes into play which mobilizes the last reserves of performance beyond the lowest ebb. Every endurance athlete is familiar with this situation, doctors and nurses possibly even more so. It happens in the life of every human being. Whether you face up to it is a question of conscience.

No institution can be successful in the long run unless it at least gives its employees good reasons to mobilize their last performance reserves voluntarily, beyond normal motivation or any thought of money. The example set by superiors who can motivate themselves beyond their superficial limits is one such reason. The most important ones, however, lie in what the institution is really capable of and in what the customer really needs.

The Interaction of the Three Elements

The result of the interaction, or, to put it another way, the cybernetics of these three elements, is a whole – a system. It comes about because three further systemic skills or characteristics result from it: value, self-respect and pride, and meaning. They are what the system sciences describe as *emerging properties*. These are typical results of indirect control, which only appear in complex, self-organizing systems. They are perfect examples of systemic self-organization in the sense of *results of human action, but not of human intention*. The reader will remember this notion or system type from Part II. Naturally, our intentions are focused on the stated objectives of the corporate purpose and business mission, and are therefore an element in the game. However, the actual results of our actions still depend on many other influencing factors over which we have no direct control. We can create conditions in complex systems that increase the probability of occurrence of desired results, but we cannot influence the results themselves directly.

Source of Value

Customer value arises from the interaction of the need and the company's strengths. Where there is a need but the company has no strengths, no value can emerge. On the other hand, no value exists if a company can do something for which no need exists. The creation of value – value to the customer or customer value – requires both. Value is an emerging property arising from the interaction of created conditions, in other words, an indirect result of directly created conditions.

Source of Pride, Self-Respect, and Self-Confidence

From the interaction of what the institution can do and what its people are convinced of – because the institution has its strengths – the crucial *collective* and *personal* values of the corporate culture arise: pride in the firm and its performance and *self-respect* and *self-confidence*. You cannot be proud of something the enterprise *cannot* do, and under such circumstances conviction and commitment cannot exist either. It hardly needs stressing that we are touching on the very innermost heart of corporate culture here.

Source of Meaning

Finally, what I call *meaning* arises from the interaction of belief and the need. Meaning does not have a metaphysical or philosophical significance here; I am using the term as defined in practice by *Viktor Frankl*, the Austrian creator of the theory of existential meaning.[68] It is the meaning – in-

---

68 Frankl, Viktor, *Man's Search for Meaning*, New York, 1957.

dividual and collective – that lies in serving a cause or a task. Meaning is far more than motivation as it is commonly understood, and is therefore a first class asset of a good corporate culture. Motivation is not sufficient to mobilize the final reserves of strength – that can only be done through meaning that every individual can perceive in his task and in his service to the institution's cause. Meaning is the *basis* of all motivation. Frankl quotes *Friedrich Nietzsche* in this context: "He who has a why to live can bear almost any how ..." Where there is no meaning, motivation is powerless.

Business Mission in a Systemic View

In figure 15, the elements of a business mission and their relationships are shown as a whole. They form an interactive system. By interpreting the terms appropriately, we can generalize from the *business mission* to the *corporate mission*, and beyond that more broadly to what can be termed the *organizational* or *institutional mission*. In a sense, all social organizations – schools, hospitals, administrative authorities, cultural organizations, universities, etc. – need a mission and they have to ask the same questions when it comes to determining that mission.

By now it should be clear where my above-mentioned skepticism about Daimler-Benz's Smart decision came from. Of course there is a clear need for small city vehicles. However, other companies, such as VW, Fiat or the Japanese players can build them better than Daimler; they have gathered experience in that field and a proven track record to show. They have the credibility, brand impact, and the necessary infrastructure on their side. Small cars were never one of Daimler-Benz's *strengths*; on the contrary, the firm had deliberately avoided this field. Also, building small cars is not what Daimler's engineers and Swabian automotive workers are proud of, the source of their self-respect, commitment and meaning. They have proved dozens of times that they will do everything in their power for the Mercedes car and its success, and that this is where their success and skills lie. But for the Smart ...?

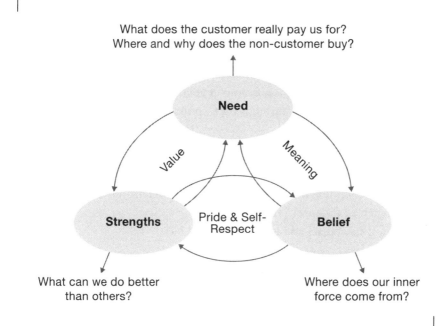

What does the customer really pay us for?
Where and why does the non-customer buy?

Need

Value

Meaning

Strengths

Pride & Self-Respect

Belief

What can we do better than others?

Where does our inner force come from?

Figure 15: Business mission

Concentration as a Master Control Effect

The business mission is all the more realizable, the more it forces the enterprise to *concentrate* its energies and attention. This produces a further Master Control effect. Exercising the discipline to concentrate[69] on the minimum, on a small number of focal areas, is one of the most important rules for the effectiveness of people and likewise of organizations.

The opposite of concentration is diversification. I am not saying that diversification cannot work. There are successful examples. However, one thing is frequently overlooked: these examples are *few*. General Electric is regularly cited as an example of good, successful diversification. Rightly so, but how many General Electrics are there? How many companies have

---

69 Malik, Fredmund, *Managing Performing Living. Effective Management for a New Era*, Frankfurt/New York 2006, p. 95.

been able to successfully resolve the enormous management problems that are typically associated with diversification?

The control problem is that diversified companies belong to the most complex systems in existence. In order to function they need *perfect* management; just good is not enough. Even rough calculations of the varieties of such systems show their enormous regulation requirements. Such companies can only function through correspondingly highly developed self-organization skills.

The need for *Master Control* through a business mission is all the greater,

- the more complex, turbulent and opaque the environment is,
- the bigger an organization is,
- the more specialists and brain-workers it has,
- the more risks it entails.

Also, it is all the more important to communicate the business mission effectively and interpret it rightly. In today's organizations, decisions are taken at many levels by many people, and potentially each of these people has a different business mission in his or her mind; each one has a different mental model. Alignment and cohesion are impossible without the *Master Control* impact of the business mission.

Opinion and will-forming for a business mission are among the most difficult and time-consuming communication and decision-making processes, because they are the most complex. Here, the previously mentioned *Syntegration method* brings about a revolution in effectiveness and efficiency. It is by far the most powerful and reliable approach for such purposes. If you want to make fast and reliable progress, it is essential to apply it in such cases. Once you have experienced the impact of this optimized cybernetic communication process, you will never want to be without it again in resolving your most difficult problems. The impact of Syntegration does not just lie in the quality of the resulting decisions, in the speed and efficiency of the process. It much rather lies in the level of commitment by the people involved, which cannot be achieved in any other way. That is also the reason for the unrivalled level of efficiency with which the measures decided on are implemented – typically 90 percent within twelve months.

In addition, corporate policy must insist on the application of solid *decision-making* principles in formulating and applying the business mission. They are a component part of the *Malik Management System* and are described in detail in *Managing Performing Living*.

Performance of the Institution: The Cockpit

We seek the *constants in change* for reliable orientation and navigation. These include, in addition to the *corporate purpose* and the *business mission*, a *central guidance complex* of *six key variables*. These are the so-called *essential variables* of the system, whose interaction determines the institution's success.

Together, these six key variables form the "central performance scorecard", so to speak, and in conjunction with the operations room the "cockpit" of top management:

- Market Position,
- Innovation Performance,
- Productivities,
- Attractiveness to the Right People,
- Liquidity and Cash Flow, and
- Profitability.

According to the present status of research, precisely these six ratios – highly complex in themselves, yet very simple as Master Controls – comprehensively determine the action and guidance of every business organization. Peter F. Drucker has been working on such key variables since the 1970s, and they were always a subject of our discussions. In the context of the PIMS research and its practical application, I experimented with them myself from the early 1980s onwards, together with friends from top management. My first published work on the six variables presented here was in 1995, in an issue of my monthly Management Letter, as the *Cockpit of Management*. I have modeled them since as an active complex in the appropriate cybernetic order.[70]

---

70 These six essential variables are discussed in detail in: Malik, Fredmund, *Effective Top Management. Beyond the Failure of Corporate Governance and Shareholder Value*. Wiley-VCH, 2006. A revised and amended version entitled *The Right Corporate Governance* is expected for late 2012 (published by Campus).

Whatever a company or any other kind of institution does, it is reflected in these six essential variables. In a business, market position is strengthened by ever improved customer value, while in non-profit organizations the recipient of the output is central. But "market position" will be under discussion in the latter area, too, in the future, because not even government organizations will have a monopoly. They will be in a competitive situation and thus will be operating in a market.

Central Performance Control (CPC)

For the above-mentioned complex of six essential variables a special term is required. I call it *Central Performance Control*. Any institution that has the active structure of the six variables of this control complex permanently under control is on the safe side, so to speak. It is no guarantee for success, but the probability will help managers because the drift of events sort of finds its anchor in these variables. Conversely, if they are not under control the company is as good as programmed for failure. This also pinpoints the principal locus of corporate risks.

The *Central Performance Control* complex made up of these six relevant control variables is situated *together with* the *purpose* and the *mission* at the *highest level of order of the Master Controls*. It creates cohesion and ensures *central control* throughout the system. Figuratively speaking, it is the neural power center – the "six-pack of control" with a highly sensitive "solar plexus". Should further variables be needed for central control one day – of which there are no signs at the present time – they can easily be added to the system on a modular basis, in accordance with the evolutionary, development-friendly logic of all my models.

The purpose and mission dictate the direction. The way the two elements are understood here, it is evident that these *Master Controls* take effect down to the capillaries of an organization, and are essential to make the distinction between performance and non-performance. They therefore install more of the large feedback loops that are needed as controls in order to master complexity.

In this next step towards *Central Performance Control*, the business mission is made concrete by projecting it into Master Controls that determine concrete action and control. The business mission is thus operationalized and made actionable at the object level of the organization. For the control of the institution, these Central Performance Controls are the bridge between policy and strategy.

The Cybernetics of Success: Essential Variables

One of the greatest achievements of cybernetics is the discovery of the so-called *essential variables* by W. Ross Ashby.[71] He coined this term for those variables that are *critical*, or *essential*, for the survival and viability of the organism, and whose range of fluctuation must always remain within certain so-called *physiological limits* to ensure that viability. Examples of essential variables in the organism are body temperature, blood pressure, pulse rate, body fat levels, uric acid, blood sugar count and many others. The values of essential variables must be neither too low nor too high; they have to keep within the specific limits of the "organism-environment" system. They define normality, health and functionality.

The *essential variables* define the organism's survival. The concept as such is universally valid, while the actual variables and their physiological limits are species-dependent. We find a special optimization strategy in nature to ensure survival. It is much more sophisticated than those we apply in social systems, particularly companies, because of the complexity of natural systems. The organism neither maximizes nor optimizes its essential variables; instead, its control system keeps them in precisely the flowing equilibrium that maximizes a quite different, *superordinate systemic variable* – the functionality and viability of the organism.[72]

Exactly the same applies to complex social and industrial systems. Profit maximization corresponds to the maximization of *one* of the essential variables of an organism, for example, the blood sugar count. The result would be first the collapse and then the death of the organism. The same would happen to a company if the doctrine of profit maximization were actually applied. Clever managers never do it for this very reason.

Keeping your eye on one variable only, even if it is as important as profit, is *never* sufficient for the control of a complex system. In order to

---

71 Ashby, W. Ross, *An Introduction to Cybernetics*, London 1956, 5th edition 1970, Pg. 197 f / *Design for a Brain. The Origin of Adaptive Behaviour*, 3rd edition, London 1970, Pg. 41 f.
72 For specialists: this is a typical example of an emergent meta-variable.

function and survive, the institution needs to keep a whole series of variables within its institution-specific, "physiological" limit values so as to fulfill the superordinate purpose of customer value.

The CPC Complex and Its Threefold Function

The interaction of the above-mentioned six variables has a *threefold impact*: they are simultaneously fields of performance and assessment parameters for corporate performance. That means the institution has to deliver its performance in these six areas. All entrepreneurial actions have to focus on them. At the same time, the results serve for continuous assessment of corporate performance – they are performance measures. That makes them *risk sensors* and *risk controls* at one and the same time.

The concept of the essential variables goes far beyond that of the *balanced scorecard*. Measured against the one-sidedness of shareholder value,

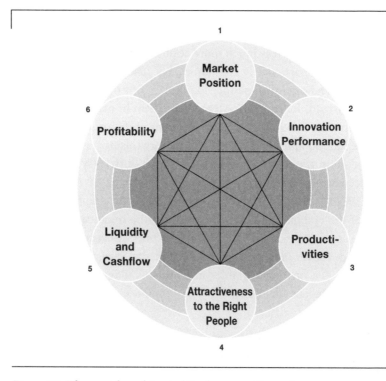

Figure 16: The complex of Central Performance Control

the balanced scorecard was clearly a step forward, but it still does not go far enough. The variables typically contained in the balanced scorecard are largely arbitrary and normally much too biased towards finance.

The guidance-relevant variables for overall systems control, like the essential variables, have to be empirically verifiable as *right*, have a sufficient *guiding effect*, enable control of *complexity* and ensure the *viability* of the institution in its environment. Precisely that is achieved with the six essential variables of *Central Performance Control*.

The six essential variables and their interactions are shown in Figure 16. They form an integrated *system* because they are interconnected and interdependent. Any kind of isolated study or analysis, or isolated interventions, would typically be unsystemic and reductionist. It would make it impossible to understand and steer the system.

Each of the six essential variables is, in itself, a complex field of influencing factors and sub-variables which, however, is comprehensible and easy to handle due to the arrangement in six groups.

The content of the individual performance fields is not fully defined in advance, because they partly depend on the specifics of a company's business activity, or in other words, they can be used adaptively and situation-specifically. In addition, the internal composition of the six variables may alter, depending on the evolution of the market and the economy and in particular on the success of the institution itself. That means that the system has to be capable of evolving.[73] However, the basic factors are given by the PIMS research and will be discussed in detail in volume 3 of the series, in the context of corporate strategy.

It is obvious that market position, for example, has to be defined differently for a retailer than for an automotive company or an airline, apart from certain invariant parameters such as market share. Although every company has a market position, different aspects and factors may be important to it.

One of the core tasks of *corporate strategy* lies in precisely determining those contents of the six CPC variables and their limit values which determine the individual situation, and in constantly re-adjusting them to

---

73 In order to have sufficient complexity for the steering of the total institution-environment system, the aim of the research was to project what happens in an organization onto the smallest possible number of variables. Nevertheless, however, the system is open to extension.

changing circumstances. As a result, we arrive at a new concept of strategy, as a continuous process of anticipative and adaptive evolution.

The CPC Variables in Detail and Their Potential

In the following, I will give a sketch of the CPC variables that is brief, but adequate for the *Master Control* level of corporate policy.[74] Although all the variables are equally necessary, the sequence is important. First of all, the CPC variables generate questions, because questions lead to information. Asking the right questions is always the starting point of *Master Control*. This skill is particularly highly developed in experienced top managers. Some of them can literally be said to guide their firms through and with questions.

Market Position

The first complex variable is the company's *market position*, relating to each of its fields of business. The question has to be: What determines market position *for us?* – not: what determines market position *generally?*

There is no *single* ratio that enables an adequate description of market position on its own. Naturally, customer value in the sense of the relative price/performance ratio must be included. Market shares and their structures should be determined according to customer groups, sales channels, purposes of use, direct customers, and end consumers, as well as by substitutes in the market. Awareness and image can be important, share of voice, market rankings, turnover rates and many other factors, depending, as I mentioned before, on the company's business activities.

Continuous improvement of the market position as a whole has to be the core of any corporate strategy. This is where growth takes place. Errors can rarely be made in expanding and strengthening an institution's market position, and if they are, they are noticed relatively quickly. It is difficult to imagine a market position that is too good.

---

74 Further details form part of volume 3 on corporate strategy.

Innovation Performance

The second key performance variable is *innovation performance*. Companies that stop innovating are on the slide. Innovation concerns the exterior and the interior of the institution. Above all, it relates to the rest of the six CPC variables because it forges the link between today and tomorrow. Constant renewal has to be a standard chapter in the corporate strategy.

Typical ratios are time to market, the hit versus flop rate and shares of sales with new products. There is a proprietary startup database in the PIMS Program which documents the innovation parameters in full. Internally, these are continued renewal of systems and processes, methods and practices, structures and technologies.

Similarly to market position, every institution has to think through the fields of innovation that are relevant to its individual situation and define and track suitable ratios. Flagging innovation performance is a warning sign of a declining business. It can be recognized long before its consequences become visible in accounting tools.

Productivity/Productivities

The third CPC variable is *productivity*, or more accurately: productivities. Productivity is also a factor that influences all the other CPC variables. Continuing productivity improvement in all areas forms part of the foundation of all corporate success.

For many years, it was sufficient in most cases to measure one kind of productivity: that of labor. Today, at least three ratios are required: the productivities of labor, capital and time. And managers are well advised to consider a fourth one at this early stage, the productivity of knowledge, even if no one so far can tell what that really is.

Productivities are only meaningful when they are expressed in the dimension of value added, for example value added per employee (labor productivity), value added per invested cash unit (capital productivity) and value added per time unit. Not every institution can grow continuously, but they can all improve continuously in the sense of becoming more productive. So far, there is no indication of limits to productivity improvement.

Knowledge productivity, which is still not understood to a large extent, will become the key to affluence just as labor productivity was some 120 years ago. Knowledge and knowledge workers incur enormous investments before they can ever be used. We must have every interest in making these resources productive and applying them to solving the right problems.

Attractiveness to the Right People

The fourth measure of success is the field of building and assessing the institution's skill potential. This is also where the center of the corporate culture is located. In contrast to earlier publications, I nowadays prefer to talk about the *right* people instead of *good* people. This is because the idea of *good* people is largely dominated by clichés. You only need to read the job advertisements to see that. The question cannot be aimed at specific standard training programs, so-called interpersonal skills and so on, but at the specifics of the institution on the one hand, and people's individual strengths on the other. *Good* in the abstract sense does not exist; it has to be *good – for what?* I have always seen it that way, but the original formulation was misunderstood too often.

Liquidity and Cash Flow

The fifth of the essential CPC variables is the institution's ability to pay, or liquidity. As you can see, it comes before profit. It is an old truth that an institution can get by without profit for a relatively long time, but never without liquidity. It is dangerous to increase profit at the expense of liquidity, for example, by buying higher margins with longer payment terms. In a profit squeeze, a company normally does the right thing – it parts with the bad businesses. In a liquidity squeeze, however, people almost invariably have to do the wrong thing, because they have to part with the best businesses. These are the only ones that can be sold quickly enough and at a high enough price to bridge the liquidity gap promptly enough.

Profitability

At the end of the list, with the sixth variable, I arrive at the first topic in mainstream thinking, and at one of the many differences between economics and cybernetics. It is an apparent paradox: if you want to earn a high profit, you cannot start from that point. And you absolutely cannot take the profit maximum as your goal, as demanded and practiced by management theory and economics. No one has so far been able to say what a profit maximum is. It is practically impossible to define, let alone to determine in concrete terms.

Profitability that is relevant to the management of a company must be viewed from the opposite of the profit maximum, that is, from the *profit minimum*. The question relevant to the guidance of the company has to be: what is the minimum profit we need *to remain in business tomorrow*? The profit minimum as understood in this way is normally much higher than most of us can imagine as a maximum.

The profit maximum is oriented towards the past and towards what the accounting department can show. The profit minimum used here is oriented towards the future, that is, towards what the company has to earn as a minimum in order to have a future. Doing business is one thing – staying in business is another, and it requires a 180 degree turn in perspective.

This completes the brief descriptions of the six variables in the *Central Performance Control* complex. Further discussion of this subject can be found in volume 3 on corporate strategy.

Radical Restructuring of State of Information

Everything in the institution should be mapped in or projected onto the *Central Performance Control* variables. Marketing campaigns, branding technology, price changes, et cetera only make logical sense by virtue of their impact on these six *Master Controls*. As a rule, one and the same action can and will affect several of the controls. A price increase, for example, contains risks for market position, but is firstly and directly a positive factor for liquidity and profitability. Investments in production equipment have an effect on the productivities, innovation performance and market position, and at the same time on cash flow and profitability. Changes in recruiting or training policy will affect attractiveness to the right people, time and knowledge productivity, innovation performance and market position; in the medium term and indirectly they will also have an impact on profitability.

So much for actions taken inside the institution. The same thing applies to the external world. You can picture for yourself the scenarios under which CPC variables are affected by changes in the economic situation, by competitive reactions, technological innovations in the outside world, strikes, the opening of national borders, deregulation, and so on. Everything is projected onto the CPC screen through the *master model of the environment* and thought through in real time, with or without the support of simulation. This leads to actions that correct, strengthen, accelerate, damp down, and/or change the total system, depending on what is required.

PIMS® as an Empirical Basis for Safe Navigation

Here, the PIMS program in the *Malik Management System* proves to be of inestimable value, because it enables the greatest possible certainty in assessing the situation and analyzing the impact of competitive actions. As you will recall, the minimum and maximum values of the six essential variables define *survival*. Their *permissible* configurations within the limit values define *success*. Having them on the corporate policy radar is an essential prerequisite for business *success* and the *viability* of the institution in its environment.

To my knowledge, the PIMS research results are by far the best toolset in the world for defining, measuring and assessing the six essential variables of *Central Performance Control*. The relevant variables are *empirically quantified* and their statistical influence on profitability is known. The empirical limit values are known for each of these parameters and their sub-variables, as are their interrelationships and therefore the optimum system configurations.

Anyone who fails to keep one or more of these essential variables permanently under observation risks losing his *viability*, because he runs the risk of these variables getting out of control unnoticed. This will sooner or later be reflected in others of the six variables, possibly irreversibly.

In order to be able to capture the complexity of the interaction of the essential variables in a way that is suitable for corporate guidance, they are mapped using *Vester's sensitivity model*, which I mentioned above in the chapter on navigation.

The systemic configuration of all six variables – in other words, the relationship of all six values to one another, which varies constantly – is crucial at all times, just as the interaction of the essential variables in an organism is constantly changing. It is well known that there are 30 possible different relationships between six elements. If the *physiological limits*, in other words the permissible fluctuations, are taken into account as well, the whole adds up to enormous complexity, which is captured in the apparently simple model of *Central Performance Control* and which can be generated from there.

These six essential variables define the institution's fields of performance. Performance has to be achieved in these areas, and must be assessed by these variables. In the *Malik Management System,* the empirical basis is supplied by the above-mentioned PIMS program.

ᴿEvolutionizing Corporate Control through CPC towards Brain-Like Processes

The importance of brain-like processes to management in complex systems has already been mentioned. The way in which data are organized by the CPC concept into control-relevant information is one step in this direction. There is practically no aspect of corporate management that is not affected by the essential variables in *Central Performance Control.* The design and steering of the organization are ᴿEvolutionized by control and assessment using these performance controls. Through the six performance variables, the Master Controls of the organization can be restructured in a way that allows them to evolve for long-term success, because the fields of performance and assessment as such do not change. They are among the *constants in change.* The signals they emit, on the other hand, change constantly, because they map the current situation at any given time which will demand specific actions in response to different signals.

CPC – Relevance to General Management

All management actions have to focus on keeping the six essential variables of CPC under control and constantly improving the organization performance in these areas. Corporate strategy, structure and culture are at the service of these six performance controls. The same applies, for example, to investments, information technology, process management and use of the internet. They are all determined by the requirements of the six performance fields and can only be justified by their contribution to improving these controls. Anything that cannot be represented within the categories of these *Central Performance Controls* cannot be justified.

CPC and the State of Information

The six performance fields of CPC will revolutionize the corporate information function. We need the same kind of reliable information about each of the fields that we obtain at present from the accounting department for variables 5 and 6, liquidity and profitability. When the system is fully developed, the necessary information should be kept available at all times in the *operations room*, and be prepared there accordingly as a guiding tool.

As you can see, this entails a quite different and radically new view of the state of information which has little in common with accounting or balanced scorecards. Accounting covers only two sixths of the total information repertoire required and not even these adequately. The central control variables cover all four of the institution's *existential coordinates* at a stroke: *internal and external, present and future*. Only this leads to an integrative information platform that is properly balanced and control-oriented.

Experienced management accountants with whom I have discussed this type of *Central Performance Control system* over the years have immediately seen its enormous navigation and control potential. Above all, they noticed without prompting the integrative, cohesive function that it gives to corporate guidance. Control is therefore no longer incremental, as it inevitably must be when the information is disorganized. Control evolves from *aggregated* to *syntegrated*, a characteristic of the Syntegration method I have mentioned several times and of cybernetics *per se*.

CPC is comparable to a fitness assessment for a human being. Regardless of what sports he or she does and irrespective of which organs account for what share of overall fitness, fitness itself as a systemic property can be judged, roughly speaking, by stamina, mobility, speed, strength and balance. There is no need to go to the level of the individual organ counts for that. To apply this to a company, the way in which, for example, production plants, technology, in-house training, process management or value chains contribute to total productivity is not initially relevant for an assessment at the total system level. In contrast, it is naturally important at the object level for targeted improvement of the productivities.

In most companies, the information for the CPC system is not immediately accessible. The data are available, but scattered over many different departments and offices in a disorganized form. Well organized accounting figures are only available for variables 5 and 6. However, these are only relevant for the assessment of the present operational efficiency of the institution, but are not meaningful for the *future* performance capability and the performance potentials of the institution. They only tell us how well the *existing* potentials built up in the past are currently being used – and profit data do not contain the minimum level described above. Furthermore, the accounting system gives practically no meaningful information about the external dimension of the organization.

Effective control, however, needs the information from the CPC areas, organized in that way and no other. The *Central Performance Control complex* delivers this.

Inside – Outside – Present – Future

The monitoring of each of the six key variables is projected onto a coordinate system as shown in figure 17 which, as mentioned, consists of the dimensions "outside – inside" and "present – future". Each of the six variables has effects both on the world outside the institution and on its internal workings, and the effects develop both in the present and in the future.

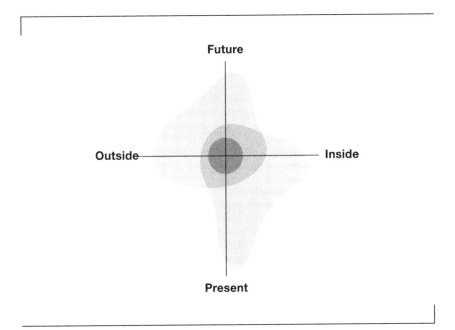

Figure 17: Coordinate system for CPC monitoring

Sub-Policies

Consequently, the essential variables determine which specific sub-policies the institution needs. In relation to market position, for example, it is easy to deduce that these will include the customer value policy as well as quality, price and brand policies. For innovation, the policies will relate to innovation and technology, design, research and development and so on. The human resources policy belongs to variable four, financing and profitability policies will also find their control-relevant locus.

Direttissima to Strategy

The use of the six variables leads to radical improvements in the effectiveness and efficiency of strategy development. I call the specific approach that I have developed and tested over a period of years in close collaboration with managers the *strategy direttissima*. It shortens the time required to less than one third of the normal strategy process and makes it possible to design strategy as a genuinely continuous process. This had always been desirable from the logical point of view, but could not be realized in practice with the traditional methods. In conjunction with the operations room, it leads to a radically new type of adaptive strategy work.

Planning and Objective-Setting Systems

All planning and objective-setting systems have to be oriented towards these six performance fields. An investment plan is only useful and justified in so far as the individual investments serve the improvement of the individual performance fields. These define where investments are needed and what they will be. The same applies to sub-strategies and objectives of functions, departments etc. From the guidance point of view, the widespread practice of preparing an investment plan as a mechanical financial projection, and deciding on it in the responsible management committees, is basically useless. Any type of planning can only be usefully assessed in relation to the effects it has on the *Central Performance Controls*. This does not necessarily require different data, but it does require different organization of the data so that it becomes control-relevant information.

Early Warning

Despite the fact that they are of relatively equal importance, working with the six variables means in principle using a specific sequence, starting with market position and moving clockwise. This relates to the early warning effect of the information about the individual performance fields. All information about a potential or actual erosion of market position must trigger immediate action, because corrections in this area take a relatively long time. Reliance on the Accounting department's information about the financial ratios would leave any useful anticipatory action and up front control too late. Among other things, it is this informational time delay that makes a strategy necessary in the first place.[75]

Risk Monitoring

The *Central Performance Controls* are the crystallization points for recognizing, assessing and monitoring risks. Irrespective of where the individual sources and causes of risks may lie, they will be revealed in the CPCs. As a reminder: as I mentioned in chapter 2, Part II, risk is a typical systemic phenomenon, an emergent property of situations and systems. Risks can rarely be located monocausally, or if they can, they are no longer risky because it will be clear what needs to be done.

Four types of risk can be distinguished, each requiring different decision-making and action:

1. First, there is the risk that is inevitably associated with any type of business management, normal business risk. It is great enough – in principle, there is always the danger of bankruptcy, and no one in business can ever really escape it.
2. The second risk is the risk over and above the first one which is affordable – because it will not threaten the institution's survival if it occurs.
3. Risk of the third type is risk that is not affordable – because it will drive the institution into insolvency if it materializes.
4. Finally, the fourth risk is the risk that managers cannot afford *not* to take – a risk, in other words, that they *have to* take because they will otherwise arrive at the point of no return.

---

75 Readers of volume 1 will remember the sketch of the background given there.

Peter F. Drucker distinguished these four types of risk early on. They are indispensable for any sensible risk management because they are complexity-oriented. By contrast, many of the risk management systems in vogue today are only complicated without capturing the true essentials. This will quite certainly be demonstrated in the event of the expected turbulence on the international financial markets, where a false belief prevails that executives have the risks under control because they are using these complicated systems. It seems probable that the opposite will be demonstrated in dramatic fashion.

Sketch of a Brain: System Monitoring Based on In-Out-In Logic

As previously mentioned, we are literally heading towards the *Brain of the Firm*[76]. The performance controls also define to a large degree the environmental information needed to control the environment-enterprise system. Figure 16 shows how the six essential variables are embedded in the dimensions of the corporate environment, which are represented by the concentric circles. I will explain their significance in the next chapter, which is about the concept of the environment.

The six essential variables thus become like six windows on the outside world, as shown in figure 18. They form the basis of one of the most important cybernetic solutions for mastering complexity, the *in-out-in logic* for scanning and monitoring the environment, which is also dealt with in the next chapter. The six essential variables *define* what parts of the environment are really relevant to the institution – that is, everything that relates to these six variables. Figure 18 illustrates this.

The Right Compensation for Corporate Managers

Not least – and this is a particularly important topic these days – the concept of *Central Performance Control*, or of the essential variables presented here, will revolutionize the *determination of manager's compensation*. It will be based on a comprehensive performance assessment that encompasses *all* necessary dimensions of a company's activities, the prerequisites for their success and the actual success. The application of these six variables prevents any sub-optimization that is programmed in by per-

---

76 Beer, Stafford, *Brain of the Firm*, London 1972, 1994.

formance assessment systems with a purely or mainly financial orientation, which can only capture current operational achievements.

Executives should be paid partly, but not solely, on present results. The future has to be taken into account as well. It is easy to present a super result today if you do not have to consider the future. Likewise, it is easy to build an excellent potential for the future if you do not have to consider the present.

Doing both together is the task that makes top management difficult. Performance should be rewarded on the basis of the integrated, wholistic result, which is only possible using a system like the CPC.[77]

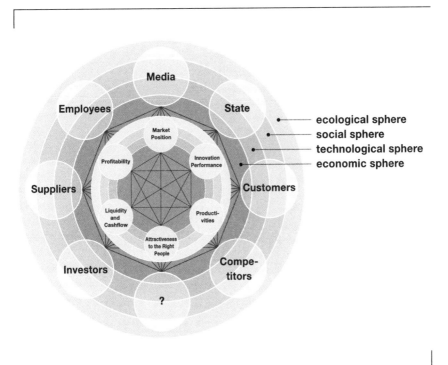

Figure 18: CPC in relation to the outside world

---

77 This topic is discussed further in Part IV of this volume, and in particular in volumes 5 and 6 of this series.

As stated at the beginning, these *essential* or *key variables* are the transitional zone to *corporate strategy*. In corporate groups, the essential variables are used as control ratios for every given business area and generally for all units with profit accountability. We have here another example of a modular and recursive control system that can be multiplied an unlimited number of times, thereby contributing to a common language, common understanding and to system-wide self-organization.

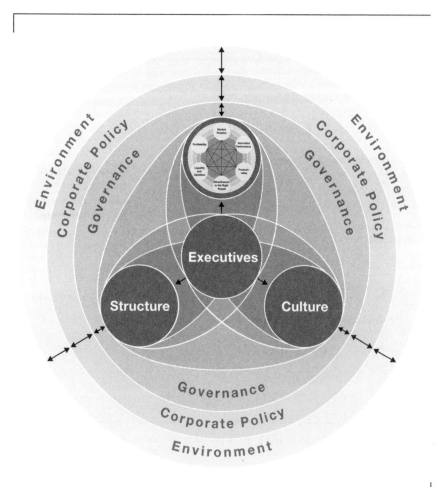

Figure 19: Embedding of CPC in the general management system in the field of strategy

Detailed management accounting systems are not suitable for controlling complex corporate group structures, because people will get bogged down in details. Coarse systems, particularly those which focus on just a few highly aggregated financial ratios, are dangerous, too, because they flag up wrong developments far too late. The CPC system has precisely the right degree of resolution or granularity for the Master Control of corporate groups. The system is particularly valuable for monitoring network structures, in other words alliances and cooperative ventures, in which control is needed but command is impossible.

Figure 19 shows the locus of the *Central Performance Control complex* in my general management system. It is embedded in the strategy subsystem.

The Cybernetic Power of Purpose and Mission

What are the corporate purpose and corporate mission for? Specialists will realize that the issue here is to avoid or resolve cybernetic problems of the so-called *second order*, which is often misunderstood even by systemic experts.

In determining the corporate purpose and corporate mission, the one right purpose for the institution is selected from the number of *basically* possible purposes, and the one *right* route is chosen from the immense number of routes that are possible in principle.[78] That is variety regulation at the highest level, and these are *Master Control* with the greatest range and impact, as Heinz von Foerster understood his first and second order cybernetics. Second-order matters are reduced to first-order matters through appropriate regulation or rules. In this way, open complex systems are closed informatively by natural means, and thereby made as effective as nature allows.

In the following, I summarize the *Master Control* effects of the purpose and mission. The purpose and mission are the only way of achieving the following as a *relative* Archimedean point:

---

78 As I repeatedly emphasize, there are an infinite number of possibilities to do something wrongly and badly in complex systems, but always only one way to do them rightly and well in the sense of effectiveness and efficiency.

1. Integration of fluctuating, short-term, conflicting interests, claims, objectives and wishes and their alignment with the corporate purpose.
2. Assessment of the relevance, clarification and weighting of criticism of and attacks on the organization, for example, by the political sphere and media, the trade unions or consumer associations.
3. Estimation of the importance of environmental changes.
4. Rise and creation of identity, team spirit, commitment, pride and self-respect.
5. Derivation of sensible sub-controls in the form of objectives and performance standards.
6. Ultimately, performance and performance assessment of the organization as a whole and its operating, result-producing units.

The cybernetics of right and good management in the sense of my motto and management system can be clearly seen from the business purpose and business mission. The control effects are obvious: the regulating effect from the head to the center and into the capillaries of the organization, through very simple controls which can normally be described on half a page.

Although opinion- and will-forming takes a great deal of effort, the complexity of the decisions required, their range and the number of influences, variables, etcetera to be taken into account is enormous. However, once the manager knows what matters, a reassuring orienting power sets in. The corporate purpose and mission have an inestimable regulatory power as controls. They form part of the basis of self-organization because they have an impact reaching even the peripheral boundaries of the organization. Comparatively speaking, they act like the Rule of St. Benedict, which I mention because it has stood the test of all changes, confusions and crises. Institutions are not monastic communities, of course, they have different functions, so we should not overdo the comparison. However, the monks do provide an idea of the effect of rightly designed *Master Controls*.

On the basis of the purpose and mission, the six essential performance controls become the pivot of the continuous flowing equilibrium of the *institution* as a system.[79] They are the crucial elements of system coher-

---

79 See also: Probst, Gilbert/Raisch, Sebastian, "Das Unternehmen im Gleichgewicht", in: Krieg, Walter/Galler, Klaus/Stadelmann, Peter (Ed.), *Richtiges und gutes Management: vom System zur Praxis*, Berne/Stuttgart/Vienna 2005.

ence: central control. The "six-pack" is the design, control and development platform. All actions are projected onto it, and the control stimuli emanate from it. In conjunction with the operations room and its simulation and decision support systems, this gives us the real time and online regulatory environment for the top management level.

Chapter 2

Where the Organization Has to Function: The Environment Concept

We spend the first years of our lives
learning that we end at our skin;
and the rest of our lives learning that we don't.

Saul Garn, computer philosopher

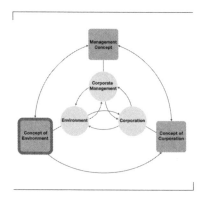

Now that we have clarified what the organization should do and the contents of the concept of the corporation have been defined, this chapter will be about the *Master Control* for the environment. This is formulated as the concept of environment. It will show how managers can go from data overload to relevant information. That is done through a model which creates the context needed to sort out data clutter. It makes it possible to determine what is relevant information and what is just "noise". The model of the environment defines what top management has to know about the external world. It must be designed to incorporate continuous updates.

To capture and assess environmental developments, the ability to think structurally and a wholistic context are particularly important. In this chapter, I will address the methods and tools suited to the development of a cybernetically effective environment concept which will form the basis of top management's continuous assessment of the current situation. The term *environment* means much more here than ecology, as it is normally understood in everyday language. It stands for the entirety of all relevant aspects outside the institution.

What Needs to be Considered?
A Common Topographical Map

The contents of the environment concept are obviously some of the most important information top management can have. Surprises rarely come from the organization itself; they come from its external surroundings. Innovation, substitution, technology, politics, competitive maneuvers, hostile takeover attempts etc. come from outside the firm. Even more importantly, the external environment is the source of opportunity. Managing entrepreneurially means managing *from the outside in*, identifying and tapping opportunities in the process.

Thinking in broad lines of corporate policy demands that a manager repeatedly travel mentally through systems embedded in one another – in an informational fast-forward process, so to speak. The ideas have to start from the company, then go out into the industry, from there into the extended field of the whole economy, into the global dimension and back – metaphorically speaking, a journey through a cosmos of systems. Every *chunk of information* – not just formal analysis results, but also, for example, what comes up in conversation, what you read in the paper and what you find on the web – is filtered out according to relevance, integrated, and will change the picture. Sometimes it will even change the mode of operation of the institution, right through to emergency mode, as I will show later.

Corporate policy principles for the Master Control management system can be generalized almost entirely, because the *control principles* of complex systems, I may remind you, are always the same although they occur in innumerable forms. In contrast, the concept of the environment and the concept of the corporation are heavily dependent on the specifics of the concrete case in which they are applied, the concept of the corporation even more so than the one of environment.

The model of the environment ensures that decision makers have an overview of the entire position and can assess the situation at all times. They have a common *roadmap* – a system topography – and can review the probable impact of decisions on the basis of the model by mental and computer-supported simulation.

The future cannot be forecast, but on the basis of cybernetic laws, properly applied, it is possible to identify necessary measures that help to shape the future and predict the effects. On the basis of simulative anticipation, a desired future state can be enabled by decision-making and action. This is the function of management, in contrast to academia: management cannot let things rest after they have been recognized and understood. It deals with the consequences of academia, which demand decisions and logically consistent action.

Forecasts are thus replaced by flexibility and adaptability, whether proactively or reactively. That is nature's solution, which has proven its value over four billion years because it has been tested over and over again. Evolution is not forecasting, but constant trying, testing, acting, trying, testing, acting and so forth.

Requirements to the Environment Model

Mankind can only survive in one environment, and an institution can only function in one environment. The environment and the enterprise define each other *mutually* and *interactively* more than many executives realize. The environment is an organizer of the institution and the institution is an organizer of the environment. Together – and only together – they form a whole, a functioning system. The "six-pack" of *Central Performance Controls* from the previous chapter is the basis and the guideline for this system.

The *environment* subsystem is the most complex system component. All *conventional* notions of analysis and understanding fail to capture its complexity. Nevertheless, we need to obtain a picture of the environment in which the institution is supposed to function. What kind of picture can and must it be? In accordance with the chapter about navigation, the only possible answer is that it has to be a cybernetic *model* of the environment which serves the purpose of steering the company within the environment. In somewhat abridged form, you may envisage it as follows.

For this purpose, may I remind you of the description of the *mental model* in the chapter about navigation. The model of the environment for steering an institution has to approach as closely as possible to its functionality, that is, to the brain function principles described there.

In many small companies that is no problem, provided that its environmental models are in the heads of the boss and his closest associates, and are properly congruent in those heads. This enables shared perception, thinking, communication and action. In *large* organizations, it is not enough. Here, too, the decision makers have their individual mental models. But the more people are involved and the more diverse their tasks are, the less their models have in common. As their perceptions of the system drift apart, so does the system itself. Each individual gives of his best, but this is defined by a personal model, not a *common* one.

As I have explained, self-coordination, self-regulation and self-organization need a common basis, otherwise the system falls apart. The more complex the system becomes, the more regulatory effort is needed to ensure the coherence of perception, recognition and communication. Ultimately, this effort would reach insurmountable limits. The system would fall apart due to lack of communicability and the resulting unmanageability. Additional tools are therefore needed to capture the complexity at source, in order to achieve and maintain a common base. I will present the required tools below.

Cybernetic Modeling Toolset: From Data to Information

At Malik Management, we have developed a set of environmental modeling methods which integrate the relevant methodological and content-related research results. We call these methods the cybernetic modeling toolset. One of its core elements is the *Sensitivity Model Prof. Vester (Sensitivitätsmodell Prof. Vester®),* which I mentioned in the chapter on navigation.[80]

A crucial factor is the so-called *meta-organization of information,* as it is called by Japanese cyberneticist Masao Maruyama. Meta-organization means three things: classification – relations – relevance.

Classification – Relations – Relevance

These are the three crucial steps to enable *guidance-relevant* information to be generated from data: the *Sensitivity Model* makes it possible to simulate environmental information; see figure 20 for a first impression. Other

---

80 I enjoyed long-standing bonds of friendship and collaboration with Frederic Vester. After his death, his intellectual estate with all rights became the property of Malik Management.

methods, such as *logistical systems analysis,* extend the possibilities of what is erroneously called *forecasting* far beyond normal trend research.

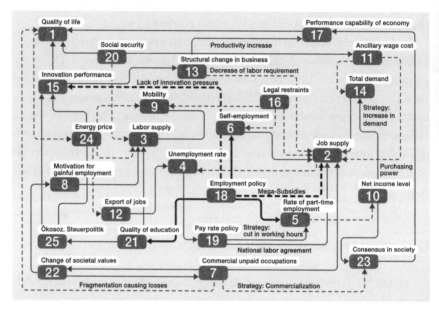

Figure 20: Exemplary Sensitivity model – partial view

Corporate policy itself cannot and should not contain any *content-related* statements about the environment on the *object level.* That is the responsibility of downstream management systems. In the *integrated management system* these things are the task of corporate strategy on the level of the profit-accountable operating units.[81] Corporate policy's only task for *Master Control* is to determine the broad outlines of the following by basic decisions:

• what the nature of the environmental picture has to be,
• by what means it should be created,
• what particular ways of thinking and methods are to be applied in doing so.

The purpose of these decisions is to ensure that nothing is overlooked that is relevant to the institution as an opportunity or a risk. In principle, the question is simply: *"What needs to be considered?"*

81 On this subject, see the next chapter and volume 1, chapter 6.

Controlling Attention

The *Master Control* decisions on the corporate environment determine the nature of the radar screen, so to speak, with which the environment will be constantly monitored and scanned.

The most important inputs for the model and concept of the environment include the opinions of directors, general managers and senior executives. Their observations, presumptions and thoughts can continuously be fed into the model via the operations room. The same applies, for example, to the more or less systematic observations of a field sales force whose task is not just to sell, but – at least equally importantly – to explore customer needs and competitors. All this is permanent input into the environmental sensitivity model, just as constant inputs from the external world enter our mental model via the sensory organs.[82]

The constantly updated model of the environment is the basis for top management's assessment of the current situation. This assessment is made at regular intervals depending on the business's cycle, as well as on particular occasions due to external or internal events. Again, the environment for this is the *operations room.*

The previously mentioned method of Syntegration is used wherever necessary in order to tap into the knowledge, information and judgment of all the required employees. I may remind you at this point that Syntegration – the term is an amalgamation of synergy and integration – is a communication process totally controlled by cybernetic means which operates on the principle of the shortest and fastest information path. The model for it is the *geometry of the icosahedron*, the most complex of the Platonic bodies, which is shown in figure 21. The S0yntegration method was developed in order to allow a large number of people to communicate with the efficiency typical of a small team. The mathematical optimum in line with the geometry of the icosahedron is around 42 people and three and a half days. By modifying the protocol, the number of people can be varied from around 20 to around 100.

---

82 For specialists: this is an element of the closure between enterprise and environment which makes the two together into a system. The second element is the company's actions.

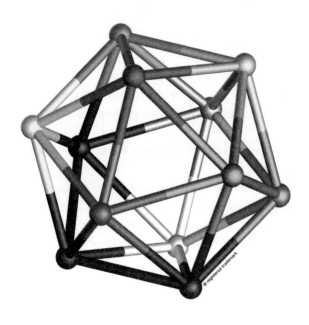

Figure 21: The geometric structure model of Syntegration®

The Master Control Model for the Environment

The *Master Control* decisions for the model of the environment regulate the development of a concrete environment model for an individual institution. This is the basis for the development of the concept of the environment, of scenarios and simulation models and for sub-models of individual corporate areas. The *Master Control Model* for the environment is shown in figure 22.[83] On the basis of this illustration, I will explain some of the most important cybernetic aspects of the model and its use.

---

83 Readers of volume 1 will already be familiar with the model.

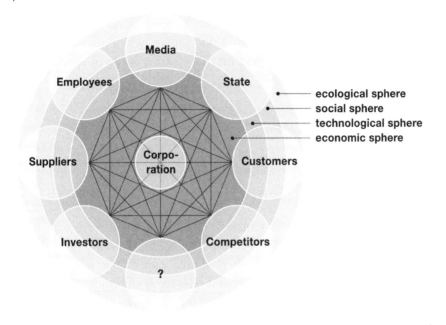

Figure 22: Master Control Model of environment

Work-Sharing Thought Processes

The *master model of environment* regulates the work-sharing thought processes for the observation of the environment in such a way that the focus is always on the whole of the relevant environment. There are two main logical-organic ways of sharing work, by domains and by *institutions*, each of which will be defined shortly. This way, customers, suppliers, and investors can be looked after by one person or work group, and the individual sphere components by another. As may be supposed, the individual sub-models are further resolved based on recursive aspects of embedding, as described in the chapter on navigation, so that the organic system wholes are never broken up or lost.

A model of this type is needed so that such tasks can be performed on a shared basis, but in a coordinated way. The people who work on a model of the environment thus never lose sight of the common context. Nothing is overlooked. Even those areas of the external world which the organization knows nothing about and which have to remain uncompleted permanently or temporarily, are present on the map as "white spots". This prevents the company from slipping into the narrow focus of special areas while losing sight of the whole.

In-Out-In Logic

The *master model of environment* is based on what I call in-out-in logic. I have already mentioned this term in connection with the six performance controls (CPC).

Methods of environmental analysis which only have the usual out-in logic become lost in the infinity of the data ocean. A brain works differently. It takes *itself* as the reference point and asks: "*What is important – to me?*" This perspective defines what is relevant as environment and what is not[84], going from the organism out into the environment and back again.

The model of corporation as a whole, which in figure 22 is contained in small format in the middle of the model, is replaced in the following figure 23 by the model of the familiar six performance controls which I addressed in the previous chapter about the business mission and the six essential variables of the cybernetic scorecard. As mentioned before, they are the *sensory organs* of the institution, so to speak. They define what type of signals and data can actually be turned into information. In the specialist jargon: which signals are *differences that make differences* – in other words, which ones mean information for the company.

The in-out-in logic itself means a revolutionary 180-degree change compared with traditional views of environmental analysis and, by extension, of strategy development, as I described in connection with the direttissima method.

---

84 For specialists: this is the self-referentiality of systemic cognition, one of the findings for which we have the circular recursive logic of Heinz von Foerster and Franzisco Varela to thank.

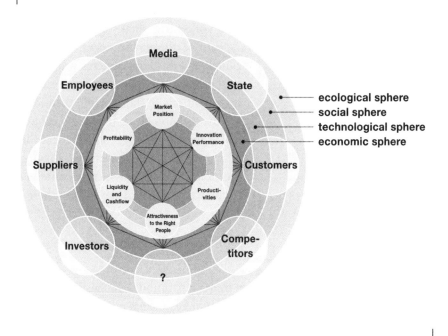

Figure 23: The master model of environment with six performance controls

Spheres-Institutions Aspect: A Dual Perspective

The master model of *environment* combines two points of view: it contains *spheres* on the one hand and *institutions* on the other. Both can be expanded *modularly*. They are mutually complementary because deliberate redundancy is built into them and, in addition, this both facilitates and forces a change of system perspectives. As a result, anything that may be overlooked in one dimension can be picked up in the other. Something that may be insignificant from the spheric point of view could be important from the institutional one. Spheres and institutions can be further sub-divided, depending on the purpose. This shows what is meant by the *control of mental processes*. No one can rely on people to think of all the necessary points. Models prescribed by corporate policy are the way to resolve this problem. Once again, we see the Master Control effect of such prescriptions.

Spheric Dimension

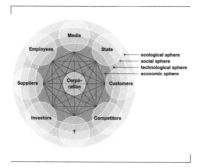

The concentric rings represent typical *aspects* of the environment which are called *spheres*. Four spheres are shown in the chart: the economic sphere is the dominant one in the center[85], then there are the technological, social and ecological spheres. Further spheres can be added in individual cases, for example the political sphere, which is contained in the basic model of the social sphere.

Institutional Dimension

Typical influence groups are shown in the institutional dimension. The element marked with an interrogation point represents a space for further elements which can be added as required by the individual case. Groupings of this kind are generally considered to be stakeholders. In my model, this term is assigned much later, because whether and to what extent such groups have a *stake* in the institution is only revealed by the analysis. To start with, they are groupings with a potential influence which is taken into account in decisions taken by the institution. I consider the stakeholder approach to the discussion on corporate governance to be wrong, and have given my reasons in the first volume and in the previous chapter.

Dynamic Networking

As you will know, complexity results from dynamic networking. This is represented in the model. There are 56 relationships between eight elements, of which every one may be important or unimportant and need more or less regulation, i.e. more or less management. As a minimum, we

---

85 This is imperative for business organizations. If applied, for example, to a social organization, the social sphere would have to be in the center. The model offers every flexibility in this regard.

therefore have 2 to the power of 56 relational contacts or conditions – an enormous variety which is latent in this environment model. When we combine this variety with the six performance controls, we have astronomical orders of magnitude of complexity which are nevertheless conveniently organized in the model's categories.

Geography as Required

As you may notice, the master model does not have a geographic dimension. This is not needed because the model is used separately for every relevant geographic region, in the same way as there are separate roadmaps for every area. That means there is a *master model* for the USA, the EU, China, India, Brazil, etc., or maybe the whole world, or maybe individual cities, depending on the institution's need for geographical differentiation.

From Academia to Practice

A useful environment model does not result from what is generally understood by scientific analyses. These are generated from the point of view of academically defined disciplines. A model of the environment in the sense of my management system, on the other hand, has to serve the practical requirements of corporate management. This means that practical problems, not academic disciplines, form the guideline. Naturally, this does not mean that science is entirely excluded. On the contrary, it is given a much higher but quite different importance and function. First of all, many disciplines have to interact, as shown in figure 24. Secondly, the practical problems form the focus for a synthesis of the disciplinary findings.

Once again, the brain-like functioning of organization in contrast to analysis should be mentioned. The environment model has to process information or knowledge in a way that is relevant for action. Knowledge itself is not enough for management, let alone lexicographic knowledge. Beyond knowledge, an additional step is needed – of a special kind: knowing how to use knowledge. For want of a better alternative, I use the term *insight* for this.

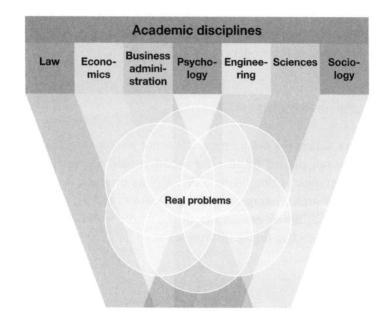

Figure 24: Selective academic disciplines versus real problems

Double Syntegration®

The next step is obvious. The logic and system of figure 23 are amalgamated – or rather syntegrated – with those of figure 24. The six essential variables of the CPC complex determine what parts of the environment are relevant to the institution in accordance with the in-out-in logic. Information and knowledge about it are in turn incorporated into the essential variables using the relevant scientific disciplines. What scientific areas and methods are particularly important here is the subject of the next section. A double process of Syntegration is the appropriate term here. The feedback loops contained in it are among the strongest regulators of information and knowledge processes and therefore of the functioning of systems.

Master Controls for the Environment Model

As mentioned before, the master model of the *environment* regulates the development of a concrete environment model for an individual institution. The discussions above show that every individual area, such as customers, investors, etc., can be easily extracted using this model and entrusted to specialists for handling without losing the overall context, because the controlling and integrating context is always given. Remember the thinking on *shared knowledge and understanding* in the navigation chapter.

A useful environment model demands the application of some important principles and theories. In the following, I will discuss a selection of the most important areas of knowledge and methods that must be used in order to arrive at a *state-of-the-art* environmental model. For example, it is hard to imagine that you can obtain an adequate understanding of global behavioral phenomena, which you need to be familiar with for communication and marketing purposes, for example, without any knowledge of mass psychology.

It would be risky to depend on an assessment of the environment that was not undertaken on the basis of these principles. It is noteworthy how few companies, not to mention other institutions, meet these conditions. Measured by the importance of environmental knowledge, the available resources and current knowledge, consideration of the external world is underdeveloped in the majority of companies, often dangerously restricted to narrow segments of the environment, and totally non-existent in many organizations.

Some of the following recommendations are always important. Others will change in the future, but are *particularly critical* at present, according to my observation, and will remain so for the time being. With the progressive spread of systemic thinking, these rules will one day be taken for granted. Until that time comes, responsible management bodies have to specify them in basic decisions, and demand compliance with them.

The best *Master Controls* for the concept of the environment are the following:

Real-Time Principle: Environmental Modeling and Scanning Must be Done Continuously in Real Time.

This principle corresponds to the perception and thought processes described earlier. The widespread practice of conducting a major scenario exercise every few years and leaving things to rest in between is totally unsuitable for system control, and counterproductive from a cybernetics point of view. This practice almost certainly leads to irreversible mistakes; at the very least it makes the whole tool of environmental modeling lose credibility. Relevant events that require action can happen at any time. The world does not revolve around the dates for scenario reviews. The methods of information gathering and processing must be usable in real time.

Fuzzy System Limits: The Boundaries of Complex Systems Are Always Fluid, and Important Points are Inherently Unknown.

That cannot be changed, and managers should not even try. It only leads to pseudo-accuracy and false demarcations. In contrast, working with fuzzy limits should be explicitly allowed or even prescribed. No one can say precisely where the enterprise ends and the environment begins and vice versa. Managers should have to explore deliberately and extensively. The motto at the beginning of this chapter does mean something. Models of the type required here are deliberately designed as interface models.[86]

Statistics Are Mandatory: Without Correct Statistical Thinking There is No Information.

I would never have thought of proposing a corporate policy rule for information processing if I had not regularly seen how underdeveloped it sometimes is in practice. Two thirds of the presentations that I have experienced over more than thirty years have contained fundamental statistical errors

---

86 The volume on strategy makes clear that a strategy that is useful for guidance purposes always has an interfacing function between the environment and the enterprise.

that led to wrong conclusions and decisions. This happened regularly even in the highest decision-making bodies, such as managing board and supervisory board meetings of prestigious companies. And by the way, this phenomenon has not been declining recently, as you would expect: it is increasing. One could actually say we have a situation of statistical illiteracy. Sometimes the simplest things are lacking. Therefore there has to be a Master Control rule that prescribes the use of professional-standard statistics.[87] Without statistics, mastering complexity is inconceivable.

Demographics Is a Compulsory Subject.

It is essential to process demographic developments. Demographics is one of the few areas from which reliable conclusions about long-term developments can be drawn in a complex society. Peter F. Drucker has constantly pointed this out since his first book, and consistently also derived his own thinking from demographic facts. In the environmental model, demographics belongs in the social sphere. At present, demographics is in vogue, which, however, does not say anything about the quality of the opinions disseminated. The interest in demographics has come too late for a lot of actions, because it only led a shadow existence for decades. It therefore received too little or no attention in many companies. Too little consideration is given, for instance, to Gunnar Heinsohn's youth bulge theory, which deserves more notice not just because of its demographic, but also its general political urgency.[88]

The basic demographic facts are available. However, many managers find it astonishingly difficult to accept the conclusions from them.

---

87 Gerd Gigerenzer presented this idea very nicely in his book *Calculated Risks: How To Know When Numbers Deceive You*, New York 2002. I agree with his demand that we have to reform mathematics education and should teach statistics instead of analysis. For the professional use of statistics, Walter Krämer's books are mandatory reading.

88 Heinsohn, Gunnar, *Söhne und Weltmacht*, Zurich, 2006.

The Financial System is Crucial. It Needs to Be Given a Dominant Position in Any Environment Model.

One of the most complex and unstable systems is the international financial system with its infinite ramifications and internal crosslinkages. It forms part of the economic sphere in the master model of environmental policy, but it can also be included as an independent element. In any case, the financial markets have to be tracked permanently and with the greatest attention – outside of mainstream thinking. Their development may become highly critical and may threaten our survival. Particular points to note include these:

- the overall mechanism of an economy based on unlimited credit,
- the difference between earned and borrowed liquidity,
- the risks of the leverage effect,
- Iiternational debt recycling,
- the dollar in relation to the US trade deficit,
- the financial analyst system,
- the financial media,
- investment banking,
- the pension fund and hedge fund scene and
- generally, neoliberal financial capital-based thinking.

At the time of the mass mania about the new economy and the apparently unending bull market on the financial markets, I modeled the corporate governance system and its shareholder value doctrine cybernetically using the *sensitivity model*. The most important relationships and internal linkages are shown in figure 25.

The system had 79 feedback control loops that were all *positive*, in other words, they had a magnifying and destabilizing effect, while only two *negative* feedback control loops were to be found to stabilize the system. Among the destabilizing booster feedback control loops, the link between shareholder value and CEO income played a dominant role.

This enabled the reliable prognosis that the system would go *out of control*, which was confirmed in the years 2000 to 2002. The developments back then drove previously prestigious companies into bankruptcy. In the meantime, some strong stabilizing influences have been added, including the loud and bold voices of top managers with the personal per-

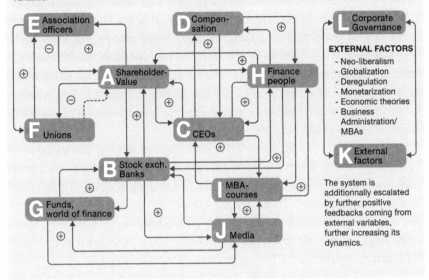

Figure 25: System analysis for corporate governance

formance history to have sufficient authority.[89] Nevertheless, the financial markets are the area which will produce the biggest surprises and the greatest turbulence.[90]

Current Management Theory is Questionable in Significant Areas and Wrong in Many

The understanding of business today will have to change fundamentally before any sensible pronouncements can be made about the management of the complexity society. One of the new paradigms in management theory that is of importance to corporate policy is the property economics of

---

89 I remind readers of the previous quotations about Wiedeking and Buffett.
90 Some readers will remember my scenario in chapter 8 of volume 1, first published in spring 2004 in my monthly newsletter Malik on Management (m.o.m.) It is still valid. I see no occasion so far to change any of its material points.

Bremen-based academics Gunnar Heinsohn and Otto Steiger.[91] My premise is that this theory will bring about a fundamental revolution in the understanding and explanation of business in the 21st century. It should therefore be processed in good time and built into situation assessments.

The current economics, especially as followed in the USA and passed on to the rest of the world as dogma, is likely to be recognized soon as the false doctrine it has been from the start.[92] The American wealth theory is untenable because values and prices are confused. Indeed, all value-based theories are wrong or irrelevant from the economic point of view, whether for the valuation of companies and shares, the determination of executive incomes or any other purpose.

Such "values" may be suitable for defining negotiating tactics between business partners. From the economic point of view, the value of a good does not result from valuation methods, but is the price paid for the good by the next purchaser. There are no values in business, only prices. Furthermore, there is still no useful theory of the knowledge economy, about knowledge work and knowledge workers, which and who are already management realities.

The problem is not so much the lack of relevant theories, but the fact that decision-making and action are led astray by wrong ones, as well as the illusion and presumptuousness that accompany them.

Comparisons between the USA and EU Are Misleading. The Strongest Economy Is the Euro Zone.

The economic data of the USA cannot be compared with the data of the EU or of other countries. The US economy is shown much too positively in significant areas due to the statistical methods applied in the USA. Growth and productivity are overstated by an order of magnitude of 1.5 to 2 percentage points, which means that the USA's alleged lead over Europe proves to be statistical hot air. America does have a very *large* economy,

---

91 Heinsohn, Gunnar/Steiger, Otto, *Eigentumsökonomik*, Marburg 2006 and in impressively succinct form Heinsohn, Gunnar, „Warum gibt es Märkte?" as well a Steiger, Otto, „Eigentum und Recht und Freiheit"; both in: Krieg, Walter/Galler, Klaus/Stadelmann, Peter (Ed.), *Richtiges und gutes Management: vom System zur Praxis, Festschrift für Fredmund Malik*, Berne/Stuttgart/Vienna 2004
92 I addressed some of the key weaknesses in volume 1.

but that it is a *strong* economy is a myth. The structural weaknesses are conspicuously obvious. The fact that the opposite is constantly repeated in the media is one of the remarkable phenomena of "copy-paste journalism" – that is, copying data without checking them – which I will discuss soon below.

The *largest* economy will soon be China, though it is even further than the USA from being the strongest. The largest *and* strongest economy in the world today is the euro zone, a fact which is constantly overlooked for one simple reason: the EU does not represent itself in the media as a single economic unit. It does not exist in economic terms, so to speak, because it only presents itself in the form of its individual states and their economic performance. It is as though the US states were to act individually instead of as a single economic area. Apart from demonstrations of state sovereignty, the reason for this individualism lies in the flaws in the *political* unity of the EU. However, this is virtually irrelevant to the unity of the *economic area*, or rather, it is no more than a source of friction. The unity of the EU as an economic area has long been just as much reality as that of the USA.

The world's dominant economic power is not the USA with its population of 300 million, but the 500 million or so Europeans in the euro zone, most of them with highly developed economies and above all with a common currency. This tends to be overlooked due to their lack of a single face to the world. For example, the USA is omnipresent in the perception of the Chinese public, while the strongest economy in the world is literally unknown.

Within the euro zone, Germany – or rather, the German-speaking area with around 100 million inhabitants – is undoubtedly the strongest economy. It is therefore pure nonsense to believe that this area should be Anglicized, as some media appear to be trying and a few "gurus" would have the Germans believe.

What Everyone Thinks Is Correct Is More Wrong than Right.

There is an almost irresistible tendency for most people to side with the majority. That is dangerous for managers, particularly those in the top ranks. It is proven fact that the truth almost never lies with the majority. Historically, it has been individual minds that discovered the errors in majority opinions, such as Copernicus, Galileo, Einstein, Karl R. Popper, Rupert Riedl, Peter F. Drucker, Robert Prechter, Gunnar Heinsohn and Otto Steiger. They were, or are, what are called *contrarian thinkers*, and were only able to create the new paradigms for progress by this approach. The successful entrepreneur is also a contrarian thinker. Going with the flow of the majority rarely brings business success, and leadership is definitely not based on majority opinion. Top managers have to be strong enough to split off from the mainstream, review it critically from a superior position, and in some cases run counter to it. That is one of the foundations of true leadership that rarely gets a mention. Leaders distinguish very precisely between facts and opinions, particularly when they use mass opinions to their own ends.

Without Mass Psychology, Complex Systems Cannot Be Understood.

Majorities are formed by the mass-psychological *lemming effect*. That *is* the reason for the above-mentioned postulate that the truth never lies with the majority. Knowledge of mass psychology which, after all, is a theory about a complex system, is of central importance to the top level. How can you understand markets without the psychology of the mass?

Mass psychology was neglected for decades. It is now receiving attention again, but only a few researchers have a profound knowledge of the subject. One of the great experts is the Austrian Professor Linda Pelzmann[93], who made decisive contributions to the understanding of the masses, of so-called *mass-manufactured wills*, during her time at Harvard. It was knowledge of mass psychology, in addition to other system properties, that enabled me to correctly assess the nonsensical nature of the new economy and the true character of the financial markets in the 1990s, and to predict its impending collapse at the right time.

---

93 Pelzmann, Linda, Malik on Management Letters 11/02, 02/03, 12/04, 11/05, see also the paper by Constantin Malik cited above.

What the Media Have to Say About the Future Is Already in the Past.

Trend research based on media clippings is largely without value. The media can only report on trends when they are drawing to a close, not when they are just beginning. This lies in the nature of the media, because at its very beginning a trend is not a trend, and therefore cannot make headlines. This is easy to prove: one simply needs to examine, firstly, what *discontinuities* of trends have ever been reported in the media in advance, and secondly, which of the media forecasts about stock market developments have proved true. It can easily be argued that you have to do exactly the opposite of what the media recommend if you want to succeed in the financial markets. There are successful traders who build their decisions on that.

Media Construct Realities.

It has to be mandatory practice to constantly integrate the media (including the internet) as well as journalism and the functioning of the media as a whole into one's decision-making. Media construct realities in accordance with laws of which they themselves have only a limited knowledge. They themselves are constantly struggling with the complexity of the world, and at the same time against it, because they believe they have to keep simplifying as the facts grow ever more complex. They put across images of the world which do not have to be accurate, and generally are not, but have an effect on people.

Familiarity with the media and how they function is all the more important as for the majority of people they increasingly become the source of misinformation, or of the knowledge they only think they have. For example, the things that are reported about the sciences and meet with widespread public interest are of dubious value. This is true, for example, of large areas of medicine, psychology, environmental and biosciences, and in particular of gene and brain research.

The bulk of the images of management created by the media have almost nothing to do with the reality of most companies, and nothing at all to do with soundly-based research results about management. News about management in the media is nevertheless the only source of management "knowledge" for most people in organizations, while most of what is offered on the subject in the media is utter rubbish. Most journalists lack the yardsticks to evaluate management issues – on the one hand, because they do not have the training or practical experience, and they have not read serious literature on the discipline; on the other hand because their profession does not leave them the time to do that reading, or even for the most essential research in many cases. The ignorance of journalists thus multiplies the ignorance of society.

Consequently, the mavens on management issues produced by the media are academics from a very wide range of disciplines with no practical experience themselves, who are selected on the basis of equal ignorance and who ensure the illusion of seriousness. By this means, a worrying degree of misinformation and, literally, intellectual malformation has arisen in this area.

Quite possibly, no other field displays a wider gap between the information content of serious literature and the media message. That is an enormous obstacle to professional management and education about it, because it prevents the accumulation of knowledge and makes it essential to explain every aspect from scratch every time. It is wrong to believe that reading articles and journals about the field is enough. Because the media often fail in this area and the insightful messages of individuals drop out of sight immediately because the vehicles are short-lived, no one is spared the pain of working systematically through the serious specialist literature – bearing in mind that even here, authors ultimately cannot start every piece of information about management at the 101 level.

It has always been an illusion – one which has become even greater and more serious in the age of complexity – to expect magic solutions for management that can be communicated in simple and even pleasant patent recipes.

It is impossible to overestimate the importance of the media to the world of the age of complexity. This applies in particular to the internet. Top managers have to know the laws of the cybernetic functioning of the media system intimately and independently of PR questions, and study them constantly.[94]

---

94 There are plenty of studies about journalism and PR. On the other hand, there is practically nothing about the cybernetic regulatory effects of the media system. An illuminating study of the cybernetics of the interaction of media and management has been made by Maria Pruckner, and can be found at www.mariapruckner.com.

Discontinuities Are More Important than Trends.

It is not trends that are the most important thing, especially not those that feature in the media. It is the discontinuities in trends – those that are the most dangerous on the one hand, and offer the greatest opportunities on the other. To the alert spirit, discontinuities are often indicated early enough to be prepared when a trend actually does reach the tipping point. That applies in the financial markets, for example, and in technology as well. Real surprises are extremely rare; yet, those who have not previously tuned in their antennae do feel surprised. Trends as such are soporific, and the more pleasant they are, the sleepier they make people. This provokes a false sense of security. Managers fail to take note of the early warning signals of radical change and are surprised – often by apparently new phenomena which took several decades to develop, such as computer technology or the internet. Despite frequent insistence to the contrary, basic innovations are not speeding up, but tending more in the opposite direction.

Linear Thinking Must Be Prohibited; S-Curve Analyses are Needed Instead.

Complex systems do not operate in a linear fashion and have a non-linear structure. There is no getting around this. It is a well known fact, yet nevertheless people mostly think in linear mode. Therefore, linear thinking and linear analysis have to be absolutely prohibited. The dominant pattern in the world of complex systems is the S-curve, not the straight line. Once this insight has become widely enough disseminated, the postulate can be deleted from corporate policy. For the time being, however, it must be given central importance.

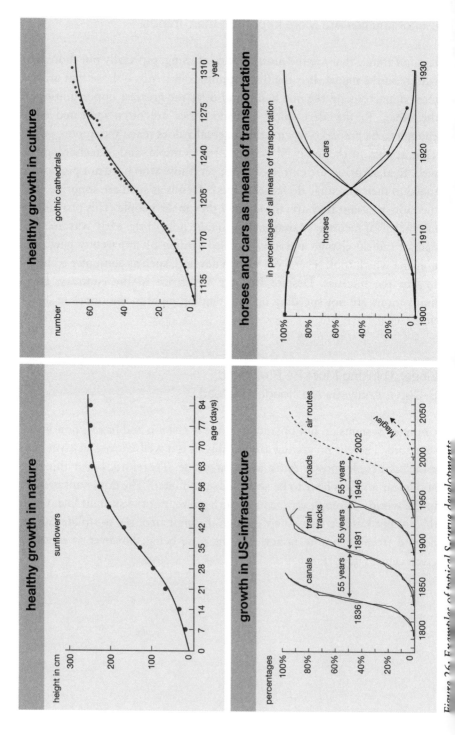

healthy growth in nature

sunflowers

height in cm

healthy growth in culture

gothic cathedrals

number

year

growth in US-infrastructure

percentages

canals   train tracks   roads   air routes

1836   55 years   1891   55 years   1946   55 years   2002

Maglev

horses and cars as means of transportation

in percentages of all means of transportation

cars

horses

Figure 26: Examples of typical S-curve developments

Figure 26 shows only four examples out of some thousands of cases.[95] A glance is sufficient to see the typical *S-pattern*. Complex systems generate a stable behavior pattern on the output side which corresponds to an S-curve because of their inner regulatory systems – their Master Controls. This is one of the few methods for reliable forecasts about complex systems. These are not forecasts of the normal type, which are practically always extrapolations, but extractions of the natural dynamic of systems, in other words, the basic pattern of their functioning. Cesare Marchetti's method is closely related to bionics.

These methods are indispensable for market analyses to determine saturation levels, market volumes, growth rates, turning points of growth, substitution, and innovation. These are key issues in every strategy decision.

The examples: first a glance at nature, which teaches us about these things. The issue here is not the details, but an intuitive understanding of the so-called *logistical* phenomenon, that is, of the s-shaped process of system developments. It is particularly important for top executives to know that this phenomenon exists and that there are methods for analyzing it.

The curve of the normal growth of a sunflower over time is shown at the upper left of figure 26. Anything that shows healthy growth in nature grows in an s-shape. Growth that does not lie on an S-curve is diseased. The upper right shows the rise of Gothic cathedrals in Europe as the cumulative number of foundation stones laid in those cathedrals that were essentially completed. The process stretched over about 200 years. On the basis of the data, its curve can be estimated early and accurately enough for practical purposes.

The figure at the bottom left shows the almost aesthetically arranged sequence of transport infrastructures in the USA since 1800 – canals, railways, roads and airlines – classed according to their percentage saturation curves, that is, the relative exploitation of their ecological niches.

The bottom right shows how the car replaced the horse as a means of transport. The process went amazingly quickly. At late as 1900, the horse

---

95 The pioneers in this field are Cesare Marchetti and Gerhard Mensch. Theodore Modis, Nebojsa Nakicenovich and Arnold Grübler have also made important contributions. In the context of my own research, two dissertations have been written in this subject area, by Andreas Eggler and Herman Pengg.

had practically a 100 percent market share as a traction engine, 15 years later it was half that, and by 1930 it had been displaced by the automobile.

As I said, the details are not important to the main message. The toolset for S-curve analysis lifts the exploration of technology development, technological substitution, competitive analysis and generally of market and societal analysis to a new and higher level which allows enormous insight into the way complex systems function. This methodological tool is part of the state of the art.

Benchmarking and Competitive Analysis with PIMS®: Evidence-Based Decisions

PIMS, which has been mentioned several times, is the acronym for the largest empirical strategy research program in the world, which bears the name *Profit Impact of Market Strategy*. This was its title at the launch of the program in 1965. Today, we go far beyond profit and market strategy with PIMS. PIMS has the only reliable knowledge base about the actually relevant, empirically proven factors of influence for the performance of businesses. To this extent, PIMS represents a paradigmatic breakthrough in business studies and strategic planning. The results of this research are indispensable for all strategic planning if you consider evidence-based decisions to be important.

Using the PIMS results and methods for competitive analysis and benchmarking is recommended for the concept of the environment in particular.

Bionics is Mandatory.

The superficially surprising but systemically expected similarity in the behavior patterns of complex systems as shown above and the similarity of the cybernetic laws in social and biological systems lead straight to *bionics*, the combination of biology and technology.[96] My use of the word goes far beyond the rather restricted meaning it has in some circles, to do with

---

96 See on this subject the wealth of references in the bibliography: of particular importance for management are the 1ˢᵗ and 2ⁿᵈ Congresses for Bionics and Manage-

artificial limbs and the like. Bionics means learning from nature and applying the lessons to technology. The fundamental concept of bionics is as simple as it is convincing: *if you have a problem to solve, look at nature to see whether solutions already exist there.* You will not always find something, but frequently enough for the results to be a bonanza. After all, nature is a research and development laboratory that has been testing solutions for four billion years. You do not just find solutions in nature, but ones that have been optimized in every respect.

Bionics transfers findings from biology to technical applications in the broadest sense of the term; it actually transfers them into applications for society. This young discipline, unknown to many, has a revolutionary innovation potential for materials and production methods in terms of design, structural and functional principles. In particular the structural and functional principles that nature can teach are of central importance to management of and in complex systems.

The basic concept of bionics goes beyond technical applications to meet cybernetics, where this concept was actually developed much earlier. The previously mentioned founder of cybernetics, mathematician Norbert Wiener, had realized that *control and communication* are subject to the same laws in the animate and the inanimate worlds – or *the animal and the machine,* as he called it.[97] Bionic thinking is when we mimic the regulatory systems of nature, and in particular the neurophysiology of human beings.[98]

Socionomics for the Analysis of Social Systems

My final proposal for a corporate policy rulebook for the analysis of the environment is that *socionomics* should be used to analyze social systems. Socionomics enables analyses of systems and forecasts about their future behavior which – metaphorically speaking – are comparable with computer tomography in medicine. This is possible through the combination

---

ment, which were held in the years 2006 and 2007 by Malik Management See the bibliography for the proceedings.

97 Wiener, Norbert, *Cybernetics or control and communication in the animal and the machine,* Cambridge, MA, 1948.

98 The work with the Viable System Model in volume 4 will demonstrate how.

of mathematical chaos theory and the theory of so-called *Elliott waves.* The details are irrelevant here, and it should be pointed out that this is the absolute cutting edge of basic research. Curiosity, openness and the courage to experiment are therefore needed. Socionomics is totally compatible with the other approaches recommended here and complementary to S-curve system analysis. I presume and expect that socionomics will turn out to be one of the most revolutionary theories of the 21st century and have a radical impact as soon as it begins to spread.[99]

Cybernetic Sensitivity Analysis is Imperative with Complex Systems.

Finally, I will once more mention system modeling of the environmental relationship using the sensitivity model's toolset. On the one hand, it is used to model the object level of a system and make it capable of simulation. Other modeling methods could do the same thing, however. The actual progress lies in the fact that the cybernetic properties of a system can be analyzed, explored and tested with the sensitivity tool. That is the brilliant feature of Vester's development. The fact that the software and programming technique of the sensitivity model enables extremely intuitive and simple modeling and is therefore far superior to many common simulation tools is an added advantage. The crucial factor is, however, that we can test how good the *self*-regulation of a system is, where it is susceptible to going *out of control*, and how it can be got *back in control.*

As mentioned above, Vester's sensitivity model is the critical tool in my method set for the environmental concept, allowing the environment to be recorded in concrete terms and simulated. It is only with this and related tools that a picture of an integrated system can be made out of informational jigsaw pieces, as shown in figure 27. The use of systemic networking models for the exploration of environmental systems must be prescribed by a corporate policy directive. Methods of this kind will be more important than accounting for controlling and using the complexity of the age of complexity. They are of even greater importance to the management of a

---

99 Pioneer work in this area is Prechter, Robert R. Jr., *The Wave Principle of Human Social Behavior and the New Science of Socionomics,* 1999, and *Pioneering Studies in Socionomics,* 2003.

complex enterprise today than the invention of accounting around 100 years ago, which at the time sparked off revolutionary progress in business management.

Categorical Change

Categorical change, which I mentioned at the beginning, also requires categorically different methods. Metaphorically speaking, flat roadmaps are not only useless in a round world, but wrong and misleading.

An environmental analysis according to the principles discussed here, and bearing in mind the research results and new sciences mentioned, lifts the consciousness of top management and indirectly of the institution to a much higher level than is possible with conventional methods.

A useful record of the environment for the overall guidance of a system must, however, always be wholistic. It must start with general changes relating to society as a whole, because it the importance of individual circumstances can only be judged in that context.

The following hypotheses at least should be on the observation screen of every institution's environment as premises:

• Growing and accelerating complexification in every area of society, with ever increasing integration of more and more areas, the reduction of certainties, non-linearity of almost all developments with unexpectedly steep exponential rises and equivalent drops.
• Global competition in all areas and for all companies, regardless of industry, size and radius of action; even if a company is not itself active in China, for example, new, threatening competitors could arise there over night. That means that while there is absolutely no need for every institution to operate globally – it would not be possible in any case – companies do have to observe global developments.
• Low labor costs will no longer provide anyone with competitive advantages. Labor in the conventional sense is becoming increasingly unimportant, so it is becoming increasingly meaningless to risk strikes because of wages. The share of labor costs in total costs is no longer a decisive factor in most industries these days.
• Protectionist tendencies will increase worldwide, although they will in

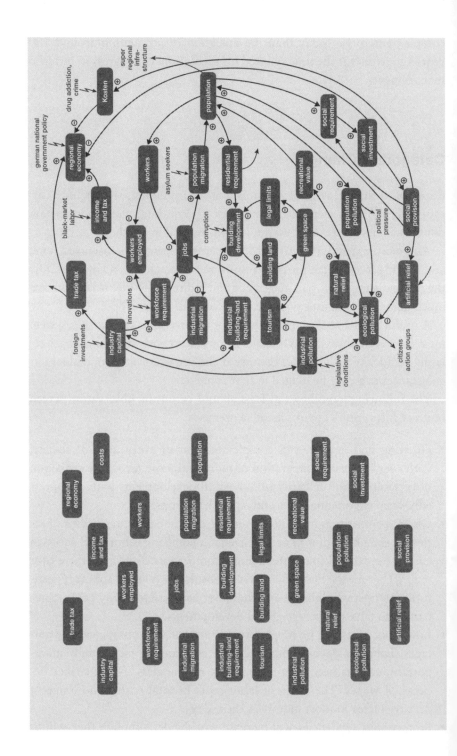

fact have very little effect. A great deal of rhetoric will be involved here, which will be aimed at domestic voters but will nevertheless put a strain on the climate of global business.

- National politics will remain important. It will not help anyone any more, but it will be the most important source of friction. People will have to live with that.
- Knowledge in the singular and even more in the plural – knowledges[100] – that means that more and more differentiated types of special knowledge, and consequently knowledge-based work and knowledge or mind workers, will be the economically and socially dominant dimensions – basically, they already are in that position today. The quality and productivity of knowledge, the costs of knowledge and its value, but above all the interdependencies of knowledge and its owners, will introduce previously unknown difficulties, risks, but also opportunities for management. Knowledge as a resource will lead to new forms of mobility, but above all to new forms of influence and the exercise of power. The owners of knowledge, specialists of all kinds, will be more important than today's shareholders, regardless of how knowledge is owned in the future. Ownership of money will have less and less economic influence relative to knowledge; indeed, the classic rights of ownership will be transformed generally. Whether or not knowledge workers will have formal rights of influence at annual general meetings remains to be seen, but it must be assumed that they will. Their de facto influence will become greater than that of the financial investors regardless of formal power, but faster than the provisions of law can keep up with. That is already the case today in the finance industry, in marketing, advertising, design, consultancy and similar knowledge-based areas, because whole teams can and do "change fronts" overnight.
- The internet should be mentioned only for the sake of completeness, since it is well known in any case. Its potential for change is probably still being drastically underestimated.
- Not each of the postulates is equally important to every institution. Corporate policy on *where the institution has to function* will be based on the specifics of each case. It is evident that the contents of the environment model or environment concept will be different in an insurance

---

100 With this term, which strictly speaking does not exist in the plural in English, I am following a suggestion from Peter F. Drucker.

company than in a food production company, tourism business or private equity firm.

With regard to the management system that follows in the next chapter – how should the institution function? – generalizations can be applied more or less across the board, because the functional principles of right system guidance are the same everywhere. Individual cases are only crucial in relation to environment and enterprise, as I pointed out at the beginning of this chapter.

Chapter 3

How and With What the Organization Should Function: The Management Concept

> Management is the moving force …
> Hans Ulrich,
> founder of systems-oriented management theory

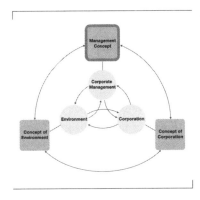

Following *Master Control* through the concept of corporation and *Master Control* through the concept of environment, the question of practical implementation remains unresolved. In other words, a concrete management concept is missing, and it is not just advisable but absolutely mandatory to set down this concept in the corporate policy as well. *Master Control* through the management concept is the crucial prerequisite for actually being able to fulfill the requirements of the two previous chapters. Corporate policy decisions should be used to determine how and with what the institution should be guided within its environment – the management system has to be established.

Management is regulation and regulation is management, I gave reasons for that in the introduction. You may recall that in accordance with the terminology laid down in volume 1, I use the term *management* a lot more frequently than *leadership*. The frequent attempt to make a contrast between management and leadership creates confusion. Leadership is a dimension of management, not something fundamentally different, a subject which will be addressed among others in Part IV.

In this chapter, I will now describe the controls for the design, steering, and development of the company in its environment, the cybernetic regulatory systems that have to act as Master Controls to manage – that is, regulate and steer – what happens on the object level. I will keep this chapter short because all the parts of my entire management system are available fully elaborated and have been published in a range of literature. In addition, the individual subsystems are discussed in detail in the four subsequent volumes.[101]

The Same Management Everywhere and for All

For the institution, the management system is functionally similar to the operating system of a computer or the genome of a cell in an organism. It is therefore logically compelling that throughout the *whole* institution

- one and the same management system is used,
- *the same* ideas about management prevail,
- all actions are guided by the same concepts and contents, and
- the same methods and tools are used.

Clear as this principle may be from the point of view of logic, it is little observed in many companies. This is one of the other main reasons for the poor functioning of companies, particularly for the omnipresent difficulties in communication, the previously mentioned sloppy use of language, the omnipresent misunderstandings and the apparently increasingly necessary programs to improve corporate culture, interpersonal skills, emotional intelligence and so on.

1. The demand for management to be the same everywhere normally raises two questions. What is actually understood by *management* in a company? In a discussion with the CEO of a company employing nearly 50,000 people, I recommended him to focus on management training because the company was underdeveloped in that area. Agreeing enthusiastically, he said *he would put it on the agenda immediately,* and that *seminars on conflict management and personality development were urgently needed.* This notion of management is out of date. In the age of complexity, it has about as much to do with management as a Roman chariot race with Formula 1.
2. Can and should multicultural companies really be managed by *the same* principles everywhere, or do individual cultural differences have to be taken into account? On the basis of my management system, there is a *clear* answer to this question: *right and good management is the same*

---

101 Volume 1 gives an overview.

everywhere because the cybernetic laws are universally valid. The cultures and their requirements may be different. However, fulfilling these requirements calls for the same things everywhere. This question once more demonstrates the enormous advantage of cybernetics for a functioning management system.

Because of the general validity of the laws of cybernetic control, I have been able to design my management system by the criteria of *"right"* and *"good"*. I explained this in detail in *Managing Performing Living.*[102] Tests in a very wide variety of cultures, particularly in China, where the greatest cultural differences would perhaps be expected in this regard, confirm: *right and good management* is *the same everywhere and is culturally invariant.* By contrast, wrong and bad management is to be found in innumerable variations all over the world. Tolstoy had the same insight in his own way, when he says in Anna Karenina: *all happy families are similar; every family is unhappy in its own way.*

Tapping the Performance Potential

An enormous potential to improve, professionalize and perfect the management function lies dormant in society as a whole and in most of its organizations. Many problems would be solved faster and more permanently by better management than by legislation – including the following:

- the functionality and reliable working of organizations,
- improvement of prosperity, education and health,
- protection of natural resources, and
- improvement of the quality of life.

What Peter F. Drucker says about underdeveloped *countries* also applies to underdeveloped *social institutions*: *there are no underdeveloped countries, there are only undermanaged countries.* A large share of organizations in the non-profit sector is "underdeveloped", although this sector also features the best examples of excellent institutions. The majority, however, are still deeply rooted in the mindsets of the 20th century. They

---

102 Malik, Fredmund, *Managing Performing Living. Effective Management for a New Era*, Frankfurt/New York 2006.

are *underdeveloped* because they are "undermanaged" – not in the sense of management by command, but in the sense of the *self*-organization and *self*-regulation that are the subject of this book and of the whole series.

Strangely, however, the term "management" is nowhere to be found in the debate in the public media and political spheres when it comes to improvement, change and reform programs. Management as a social function of design, control and development is simply not present in the public awareness. It can be safely forecast that no reform will be successful if it does not include the laws of functionality. It is hopeless to want to achieve something by going against the nature of complex systems, however much money is spent.

Inducing Self-Organization

The above-mentioned basic corporate policy decisions about the management system to be established thus determine how the institution is to be managed and how its operational level is to be controlled.

The design of the *Master Control* system determines innumerable controls and regulating systems that are responsible for guiding the object level. If the *Master Control* system is correctly designed, you can "lean back", so to speak, because from that point onwards the downstream systems take over its work: the subsystems and elements of the *Malik Management System*, that is, the subsystems of corporate strategy, corporate structure and corporate culture which are shown in the following models. These subsystems serve the *implementation* of the corporate policy; as such, they are implementation systems for the purposes, intentions and principles of corporate policy.

Master Controls which create systems of controls which in turn create controls and so on are therefore the way *to organize systems in such a way that they can organize themselves*. This is not a metaphysical construct. It means empowering people on all levels and in all functions to manage themselves and their immediate work, their teams and areas of responsibility independently and with full responsibility, or in other words, to design, guide and further develop them. Management for *people* and management for *institutions* are the two dimensions in which my management system is applied, and through which self-organization is created. At its core, self-organization in social institutions means enabling every individual to make an independent contribution in the service of the institution at his own initiative, using his skills, intelligence and knowledge. It means empowering people and offering the environmental conditions to transform their strengths into performance and to be successful by this means.

Management Models for Master Control

To make my management system a part of corporate policy, it usually suffices to include a few sentences stating that the institution's managers should perform their management tasks according to the principles and contents of this management system.

This is possible because my system is available to use in all dimensions, in a modular structure that can be composed and configured for every type of application. This is where one of the advantages of this system lies: it leads to a high level of efficiency in its introduction and application, a fast pace and an extremely favorable cost/benefit ratio, because all the possibilities of communication technology available today are used for it.[103]

I have already discussed the basic model in the chapter on navigating by means of models. Building on this basis, there are two *Master Control Models*: first, the *Malik General Management Model* for the overall management level, and second, the *Malik Standard Model of Effectiveness* for the level of individuals and teams. The latter has rapidly become known in practice as the *Malik Management Wheel* because of its graphic depiction. An overview of both is shown in figure 28 below.

The General Management Model is used for the management of an institution as a whole, while the "Management Wheel" is used for the management of people. Each can be integrated within the other because they are *recursively* designed as described in the navigation chapter. As I will go on to discuss, a special form of application is derived from these two basic models, the *Integrated Management System (IMS)*.

---

103 A brief description of my management system, its modular structure and the resulting ease of configuration is to be found in the appendix to this book. The main modules themselves are the subject of the individual volumes of this series.

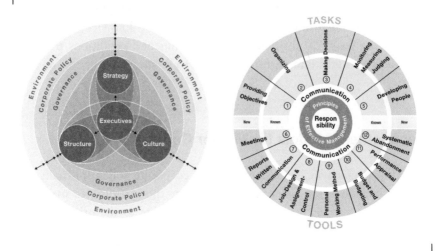

Figure 28: On the left, the General Management Model, on the right, the Standard Model of Effectiveness

As a first step, it is enough to stipulate in a corporate policy decision that these two models are prescriptive for the performance of management tasks throughout the organization. These two models should be specifically mentioned in the written documentation of corporate policy, because this serves for better orientation.

The General Management Model

Figure 29 shows the model of the *general management* functions. As mentioned previously, the book format is an obsolete vehicle for describing and understanding complex systemic structures. I will therefore confine my description to essentials.

The graphic form of the model represents the *embedding* of systems into one integrated system complex which is typical of complex structures, and which I discussed and explained in the navigation chapter. Each individual part is a complex control mechanism in itself, which has to regulate certain parts of the overall complexity of the company. Together with the

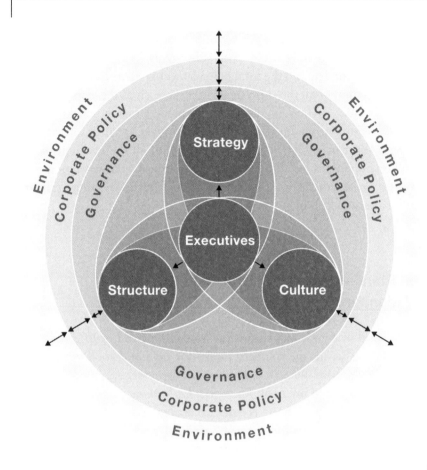

Figure 29: The Malik General Management System

other linked systems, they form the overall structure of the control system at the *general management level*.

The outer ring represents the environment. Corporate policy follows, embedded in the environment. Embedded in this, in turn, is corporate governance. I treat this as part of corporate policy in my management system, for reasons previously discussed. Inside these three "embedding shells", the subsystems for *corporate strategy, corporate structure* and *corporate culture* can be seen, with the *executives* in the center. The links can also be seen in the graphic, but require animations to be properly visible and comprehensible. Each of these subsystems and their interconnections is explained in another volume in this series.

The design of the interaction of all subsystems – and that applies to all the following models and the total management system – is comparable to the coordination of all the subsystems of a car, such as the engine, chassis, electronics etc.. Anyone familiar with Formula 1 racing will know how high the requirements are that professionals make on themselves in this context. Another comparison can be made with all the instruments of a symphony orchestra, or all the participants in the overall work of art that is opera. Professionalism in management does not have lower standards than professionalism in any other area.

The Standard Model of Effectiveness – or "Management Wheel"

On the level of people and teams, the *Standard Model of Effectiveness* is used, in other words the standard model for *right and good management* – the *"Management Wheel"* in figure 30. The model and its contents are described in detail in my book *Managing Performing Living*.

The *"Management Wheel"* is designed around four elements of the professionalism of any job: tasks, tools, principles and responsibility. It contains the norms for professional effectiveness in the sense of the actions needed to ensure this effectiveness. However different managers may be, the actions of effective people show a pattern. It is not *being* that is crucial, but *doing*.[104]

The element of *responsibility* is in the innermost core of my model, as the most important part of a good corporate culture and corporate ethic. I advocate a culture and ethic of performance, effectiveness and responsibility. Ethics in the management of people means enabling people to perform

---

104 The model of the actions of effective management is summarized again concisely by Peter F. Drucker in his contribution to the book *Kardinaltugenden effektiver Führung* which he edited together with Peter Paschek in 2004.

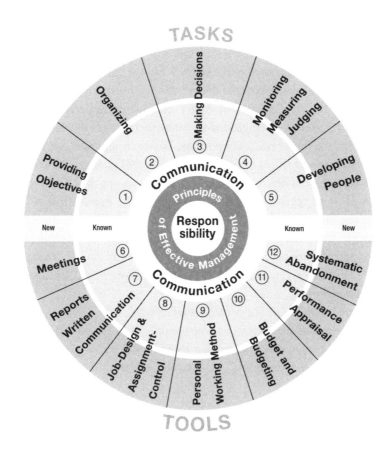

Figure 30: The Standard Model of Effectiveness or "Management Wheel"

in those areas where they have their strengths, and to be successful as a result. That is the responsibility of managers.

The next module is the *principles* of effective management. There are six of these, which I have distilled from the actions of effective people as Master Controls. The *tasks* and *tools* modules are shown in the upper and lower semi-circle respectively. They contain the necessary and sufficient elements of professionalism for every function. The Standard Model of Effectiveness comprises what every person needs at all times and in all places to be an effective manager. It defines the kind of management I describe as *right* and *good*, which promises effectiveness and efficiency and on this basis can be applied uniformly and culture-independently all over the world.

The "Management Wheel" – and this is a key advantage – is equally valid for the management of tasks already *known* (management of operations) and *new* tasks (management of innovations). In my experience, many people find this statement pretty difficult to understand, because they allow themselves to be guided by mainstream ideas of management.

In contrast to the prevailing opinions, however, separate, specific *innovation management* is *not* needed. Innovation and change – things new – are managed in the same way as things known, except that for new things a higher level of control, a greater *mastery* of the application is needed than for the known territory. The situation is comparable to driving a car. It is always the same as such, but will require a higher level of routine, mastery and experience depending on traffic conditions.[105] This second model must also be prescribed as binding by corporate policy, and documented accordingly.

The application of the six *principles of effective management* as Master Controls alone has an enormous impact on self-organization, all system levels and the corporate culture. I list them here without giving details of the content, which is dealt with extensively in *Managing Performing Living*.

1. Principle 1: *Results are the only thing that ultimately counts in management.*
   As mentioned previously, management is the transformation of resources into performance and results. This precept must therefore determine the activities of the people at all levels of an organization.
2. Principle 2: *Making a contribution to the whole is important.*
   It is not just an individual's own position, status and privileges, but the institution as a whole whose purpose, mission and fields of performance have to be the guideline of his actions.
3. Principle 3: *Concentrating on a small number of important things is important.*
   Few professions are as exposed to the danger of unproductive hustle and bustle, and of dissipating one's energies, as management. True pro-

---

105 For further explanations, please see *Managing Performing Living*.

fessionalism is revealed by confining oneself to a few things that are genuinely crucial. That is the first road to results.

4. Principle 4: *Utilizing existing strengths is important.*
Performance can never come from weaknesses, only from strengths. Identifying people's strengths and designing their tasks in a way that enables them to use these strengths is the second road to results.

5. Principle 5: *Mutual trust is important.*
Motivation and performance can only thrive on the basis of trust. Trust makes systems self-organizing, intelligent, and robust.

6. Principle 6: *Thinking positively is important.*
Positive thinking leads away from a fixation on problems and in the direction of an orientation towards opportunities. This is also the road from motivation to the much more important skill of self-motivation, and therefore to personal emancipation and independence of outside motivation.

The impact of these principles alone on Master Control as described in this book requires no explanation.

Application of the Management Wheel in the Standard Situation

The corporate policy decisions for the management concept become even more precise when the standard situation for the application of the "Management Wheel" is also explicitly stated. Figure 31 shows the systemic context in which every manager acts. It is the same all over the world in all well-run institutions.

The standard situation of every manager is a network consisting of five elements: himself, his boss, his colleagues, his subordinates and the outside world, including his customers. This system is invariant, independent of the company, industry, level and culture. Even the CEO has a "boss" – the supervisory board chairman, and ultimately customers and shareholders. In every component of this system, the Management Wheel is applied as the Master Control on the relevant level, meaning that a high degree of systemic self-organization is programmed into the system. A comparison with the genetic code suggests itself: the code ensures that every individual cell functions, and therefore at the same time ensures that the total organism also functions.

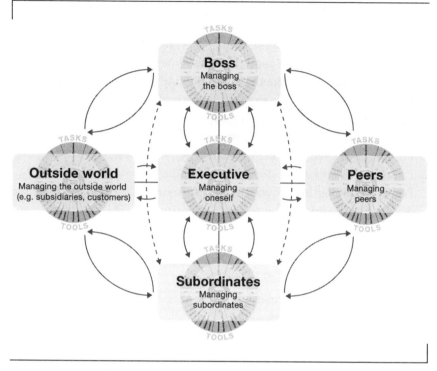

Figure 31: Five different areas of application of the Management Wheel

The Integrated Management System (IMS)

In the next step, the two models discussed above are combined to form the *Integrated Management System (IMS)*. This is the *Master Control* version for the most *frequent* purpose of use: the management of a *result-producing unit* (RPU). The term "result-producing unit" is the generic title for the operating units of an institution, which may have very different names. Typical ones are business units, divisions, subsidiaries, profit, cost, result and performance units.

An overview of the IMS is given in figure 32.

Figure 32: Integrated Management System (IMS) – overview

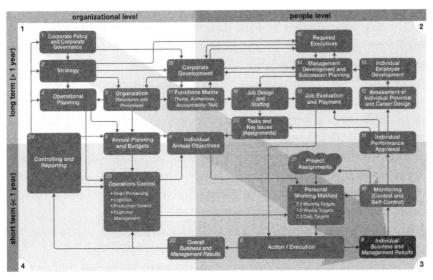

Figure 33: Integrated Management System (IMS) – detailed view

Figure 33 shows the IMS in detail.[106]

---

106 There is a detailed description in volume 1.

All elements and subsystems of the *Integrated Management System (IMS)* are underpinned with the knowledge needed in practice, the necessary tools and the methodological instructions for its application and procedures, including the training of managers and employees in how to handle the management system. The *Malik Management System* is thus fully developed and tooled up in every respect. I refer readers to the description in the appendix.

In a complex corporate group with numerous subsidiaries and affiliates, which, in turn, are typically large companies with a corresponding internal structure, there are therefore dozens to hundreds of applications of the IMS. This has the major advantage that *the same* control systems are used everywhere, and are absolutely compatible in terms of structure and content. That is the only way to launch practical self-organization of any preferred scope, and to start basically unlimited organizational expansion with the simplest possible functional model.

The first introduction of these models is achieved by making the required basic corporate policy decisions, followed by the essential internal training of the managers.

The two basic models and the Integrated Management System configured from them embody all the principles that are needed for right and good management. It does not make much sense to reinvent the wheel from scratch and in the company's own style, as frequently occurs. The risk of errors is great; also, if the in-house development is to be system-compatible, even a proprietary management system will have to correspond to the IMS because cybernetic things are as they are in management.

In the context of corporate policy, decisions can and should be made about the management system as *a whole*. The detailed design of individual subsystems, for example the various levels and types of planning systems, cannot be a matter for corporate policy decisions. The necessary adaptation to an institution's practical specifics will be carried out on other, subordinate levels.

Corporate policy must concentrate on the really important things. That is not easy in *management*, because in my experience there is a great temptation for those involved to go into details that are not or should not be significant to the normative level of management.

Starting with an Inventory

The normal case for introducing and using the management system will usually be an existing organization where some elements of the management system are already in place, even if they are not in the same form as I intend for my system. However, to the extent that usable components are available, they should continue to be used. Cybernetic management means building on what is available, just like natural evolution, if and in so far as it functions.

Therefore, a decision has to be taken about which parts of existing management practice can be built on, which ones should be restructured and which ones need to be introduced as new. The starting point here is an inventory of the status quo, or in other words, a systematic record and assessment of existing elements. The IMS is particularly suitable for this inventory. On its basis, we have developed a computer-aided analysis tool at Malik Management for quick and complete data gathering: the *Management System Audit* for the corporate entity.

With its help, the existing management toolset can be reliably reviewed on the basis of the parameters of the *Integrated Management System*. On the basis of this inventory, the renovation and restructuring program for a company's management system can be determined in a targeted manner, and the necessary project steps can be directed with the *management system audit*.

We have also developed a comparable tool to analyze managers and their management professionalism – the *Management Effectiveness Audit* for the individual level. This is used to determine both the individual and system-wide training needs, and the personal development of professional management competence in every individual executive.

Watch Out for False Hybrid Solutions

I must caution against making *false* compromises. As I have explained several times, my management system is aimed at *right and good management*. It is also systematically geared towards the control requirements of complex systems, and for these reasons, it must be wholistically adapted to their cybernetic laws.

This means that the components of my management systems cannot be exchanged at random, or even mixed with other systems, without putting their functionality at risk. In the same way, components cannot be mixed at random in computers, cars or organisms. That is why the above-mentioned inventory and the compatibility test of existing practice using the *Management System Audit* are needed in order to see what fits together and what does not.

In this sense, the previously mentioned three dimensions of right modeling are crucial for all the models in this book: *systemic, content;* and *form.*[107] Systemic – that is, the logic of the system structure – and content are mandatory, although the graphic design of their form can be varied if there are good reasons for doing so. However, care must be taken not to change the systemic along with the form.

Interpretation Traps

I must warn readers in particular against the careless use of *terms* and *meanings*. False contents are the landmines in the territory of management.

This is one of the most treacherous sides of the current state of the art. One and the same term often has quite different meanings. For example, the term *strategy* in a presentation does not tell you the slightest thing about the author's notions of the content of strategy.

I am not talking about definitions here. It is easy enough to cope with different definitions. The problem lies in completely incompatible contents. *Strategy* can, for example, mean an orientation either towards shareholder value or towards customer value. The differences could not be greater or the consequences more different. Metaphorically speaking, one means a journey to the north, the other to the south. For example, as shown by this book, I think shareholder value is wrong as a corporate purpose while customer value is right. I have been unable to use the common everyday meanings, not even the meanings in the literature, for almost every term that occurs in my management models because even today there is no recognized, consensus-based management theory or vocabulary. My work consists of creating the basis for such a theory and vocabulary by giving practitioners the opportunity to reflect on it critically, and that is also the purpose of my publications.

---

107 Further details can be found in the German version of *Managing Performing Living* on pp. 374 et seq.

Because of my orientation towards right and good management, I arrive at contents that largely differ from those represented in the mainstream. The worst mistake would be to draw naïve conclusions about ordinary contents from ordinary terms.

Navigation instead of Documentation

As mentioned earlier, only the basic models should appear in a concrete corporate policy. The individual model components need not be described. That would overload the documentation of the corporate policy and undermine its main purpose.

Some companies produce hundreds of pages of documents for corporate policy decisions and so-called *corporate guidelines* and *management manuals* that have no impact precisely because of their volume. The controls are too detailed instead of confining themselves to the fundamentals, and documentation is carried out by unsuitable means.

The *purpose* of the corporate policy is not to have documentation; rather, it is to *support* managers at all corporate levels, including all subsidiaries, business units and other operating entities, in their *practical* management work and to give them a direction and orientation. The corporate policy is supposed to enable and facilitate their *navigation* in and through the complex system structures on the basis of the models. The models provide a *common frame of reference* which enables communication and cooperation – in the sense of the common understanding, common language and required coordination of perception, thinking and decision-making processes.

It is the particular advantage of the cybernetic-modular structure of my management models that no details are needed in order to have an overview and be able to navigate. Basically, all the functional elements of right and good management can be mapped with one *single model*: environment, corporate policy, corporate governance, strategy, structure, culture, the principles, tasks and tools of effective management, and plus responsibility as an ethical basis, forming the core of self-organization. You can navigate from every point at every required level of detail and back again using browser technology and hypertext, without losing your sense of direction.

An Overview of the Master Control "Management Concept"

The different sub-models that together make up the overall management system of the institution are summarized in figure 34 below. Their validity as a *Master Control* for the regulatory level should be declared binding by corporate policy decisions. That is the declaration of intent by the top management as to how and with what the institution should function. Corporate policy provisions for employee training on the basis of this management system must be added to this.

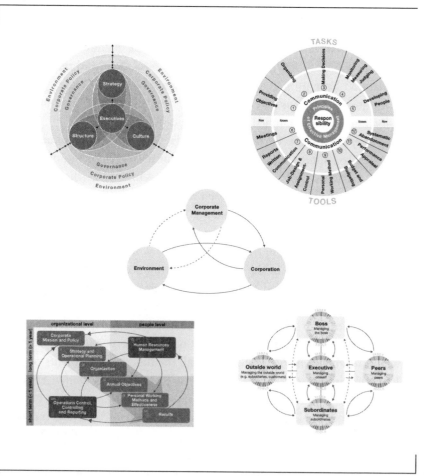

Figure 34: Overview of the sub-models of the overall management system

Implementing Corporate Policy: Order is Law times Application

For the corporate policy Master Controls to be effective, they must be known to every person in the organization in a way appropriate to their level, and every person must be empowered to apply corporate policy decisions and rules. This is only possible through active communication in every conceivable form: continuous education and training are among the most important ones.

> *Self-organization is based on the law:*
> *order is law times application.*

According to my knowledge, we have Rupert Riedl to thank for this insight – in my opinion, one of the most fundamental natural laws of function. He is one of the most productive, thorough and profound researchers in the fields of evolution and complexity.[108]

I see *Riedl's Law*, as I would like to call it, as the twin of *Ashby's Law of Requisite Variety*, which I mentioned in the chapter on navigation. The former provides the latter with the dynamic required for its effect and – what is more important – operational relevance, or in other words, a guideline for action. Riedl's Law – *Order is law times application* – has direct importance for the effectiveness and efficiency of corporate policy. The Master Control effect of all basic decisions and rules depends directly on it.

My management system is structured in such a way that it empowers people to systematically realize this law of Riedl's in practice, syntegrated with Ashby's Law, for corporate self-organization. The *Malik Management System* is the first management system – to the best of my knowledge, also the only one in the world – to offer a solid basis for training all the employees in an organization to a *consistent standard of quality* with the *same knowledge* using the *same terminology* and the *same – right – contents*. The system does this with sufficient training intensity to be able to translate knowledge into skill, such skill as ensures the independent and correct situational application of corporate policy rules – in other words,

---

108 His papers "Die Ordnung des Lebendigen", "Strategie der Genesis", "Strukturen der Komplexität" and "Verlust der Morphologie" are mandatory reading for a serious understanding of systems.

to make *law times application* reality. There are three reasons for this guarantee:

1. The structure and content of my management system.
2. The use of the most effective methods of communication, which are not always identical with what is understood by "modern didactics", which may be "modern", but is not *proven* in every area.
3. The fact that all modules are available in all types of technology and therefore three previous bottlenecks are eliminated:
   - The costs of training, which in its traditional form are simply too high for the lower corporate levels.
   - The shortage of well-educated trainers, as a result of which the volume simply cannot be handled.
   - The quality assurance of knowledge by the freezing of knowledge through technology. My e-management learning programs in particular give companies independence from variable trainer quality and uncontrollable changes in knowledge. In addition, the trainees become independent of place, time, and learning format.

Working with the *Malik Management System* naturally has to be learnt and practiced just like the use of a particular software, a sport, or a foreign language. *Management* as a corporate language has to exist in exactly the same way as *English* as a corporate language, or the standardized specialist language of marketing, control or finance in the relevant functional areas. Corporate policy must therefore also cater for *training* in management, not just for the management system as such, because its control effect only arises from the control-led actions of human beings. That means these human beings have to learn the rules thoroughly. This is the only way to achieve automatic application to every individual situation, which is the only way to stimulate the self-organization that is already built into the rules.

May I remind you here of the distinction between rules that lead to *bureaucratic strangulation* and those that lead to the *liberation of self-organization*. As explained, one and the same rule can require *different* action in different situations. The action demanded by the rule depends on the *information* about the situation. The employees of an institution therefore have to be trained in how to handle the control questions – otherwise they will become rule-executing robots, or bureaucrats, instead of rule-led *self-*controllers. This applies above all to the content issue I mentioned above.

The rules encompass *"frozen knowledge"* about the necessary constants in change. The information for the selection and application of this knowledge comes from the situation. Bringing the two together can be deemed an act of insight. Thus, information, knowledge and insight are the components that are needed by training for self-organization and are made possible by my management system, because its modularity allows for an unlimited number of practical configurations for every type and size of institution.

Management Training and Development: Return on Management Education

The self-organizing, complexity-exploiting and system-intelligence-reinforcing impact of regulations does not result from the rules alone, but – as described – from the combination of *rules* and *information*. This is achieved fastest, most easily and even at the highest financial profit if the group of employees to be trained immediately apply what they have learnt to the solving of company problems. This refutes one of the most important arguments against management training: the opinion that training does not produce results, or at least none that can be quantified.

This is where an innovation comes into play that is the result of my decades of experience with in-house management training. I call the related method and program the *Return on Management Education Program (ROME)*. It is education, development and training in one, simultaneously focused on knowledge and skill.

In an ROME program, participants directly apply their learnings, with guidance, to problems that affect the institution. The return results from direct project results and from cutting out consultants. The costs of such a program generally pay back as early as one third of the way through its execution. The final returns are in the high double-digit percentage range, occasionally in three digits, always depending on the projects the top management select for implementation.

But the financial returns are not the main thing, however pleasing they may be and however little the management would have considered them possible. The crucial elements are the outcome of the reliability and success of application, the visible results, the unity of ways of thinking, approaches and methods. The most striking results relate to the corporate culture and the level of commonality and team spirit that develop as a result of such programs.[109]

It is management education that makes the normal type of consultancy superfluous. The nature of consultancy thus changes fundamentally. It turns into a way to help people to help themselves and to become personally independent. It is basically intuitive, because doctors or orchestra conductors, for instance, do not have to call in the help of consultants after they finish their training.

Management Education is Critical for Success

As mentioned, the management system must be binding on every individual in the organization, and every individual has to have the uniform knowledge and skills to apply it. The managers of a company have to be so well trained in management that no consultants are needed to perform what are the quintessential tasks of management.

To achieve this, management in complex systems demands more than conventional training or development. That is why I call it management *education*, in German *Bildung*, and in French *formation*.

If reliable application of the natural laws of function is to be achieved, which is a mandatory condition for self-organization, both education and training have to be carried out. The education element must be focused on insight into and understanding of the nature of complexity, of systems, their laws, the regulatory processes and controls. The training element consists of continuous training to ensure reliability of application.

It is essential for new hires from outside – regardless of their previous education and experience – to be included in the training as well, because there can be no reliance on their already having a knowledge of right management. Everyone embarking on working life has a certain everyday understanding of management, but few have gotten it right. Experience makes up for it over time, but even experienced people often have completely different ideas of what is important, right and wrong in management. I have already mentioned this several times under the title of the

---

109 This subject is addressed in more detail in volumes 5 and 6.

"Babylon syndrome" which I have been experiencing for more than 30 years in all relevant programs.

Management education and training is a task critical to the success of *all* organizations in society, because it relates not only to the organization's activities, but to the *innermost workings of its functioning*. Metaphorically speaking, it is not just a question of the function of organs and limbs, but of the nervous system and the brain. When these are not working properly, all the organs and limbs are affected as well.

Management education is basically no more difficult than learning a foreign language or a sport. However, it is not easier either. Therefore, the same demands must be made in this training as would be made in learning any other serious discipline.

Wrong management knowledge has the same effect on an organization as computer viruses have on hard disks. Therefore, everything possible has to be done to prevent errors and nonsense – *mind pollution* – from being imported. That it a top priority task for corporate policy. The only remedy for it is consistently identical contents and standards for all those people who perform management tasks and, ideally, for those affected by them as well.

There is basically no serious management education anywhere in the world to this date. This may sound paradoxical bearing in mind the innumerable MBA programs and the tens of thousands of business studies graduates produced every year. Yet, however important these degree programs are, they have little to do with management in the sense of regulation and control, or in other words, with the actual laws of function.

MBA programs and business studies are primarily training for tasks at the subject matter level (HR, Finance, Marketing, etc.), but not really for the management and therefore the system level. To make things worse, people with this kind of degree are wrongly considered as particularly well qualified for management positions, which is why they are soon assigned management tasks for which they are not prepared. That is more or less as if aeronautical engineers were appointed as pilots without any training on the basis of their technical knowledge.

Companies that have realized this systematically invest in their employees' management professionalism, even more than in their vocational training. They do this in a targeted and systematic way, based on the standards of the management system laid down in corporate policy, and not in accordance with the people's individual wishes. They carry out management training on the model of athletic training.

Craftsmanship in management, in the sense of being familiar with the controls discussed here, is absolutely critical for success. There is a reason why I compare right management with a computer's operating system. Underestimating or ignoring these principles is one of the main causes of the management confusions that exist in many companies and almost universally in non-business organizations. Changing this is a matter for basic corporate policy decisions.

As a rule, experienced managers, particularly at the top level, have a high level of intuitive and occasionally explicit understanding of systems. Complexity is their daily challenge. Their closest associates on their staff, often selected for their educational background but with no practical experience, are undoubtedly perfectly trained. However, they are trained in a world view that is not suitable for top management. That is one of the many paradoxes that can only be resolved through Master Controls, as discussed here – above all, with the corporate policy specifications for the corporate management concept. Basically, everything else depends on the management concept. Close scrutiny reveals that the corporate and environmental concepts are part of the management concept.

Charts of the Malik Management System (MMS)

Finally, for a better overview and ease of reading, the main models of the Malik Management System and their interactions are illustrated in large format.

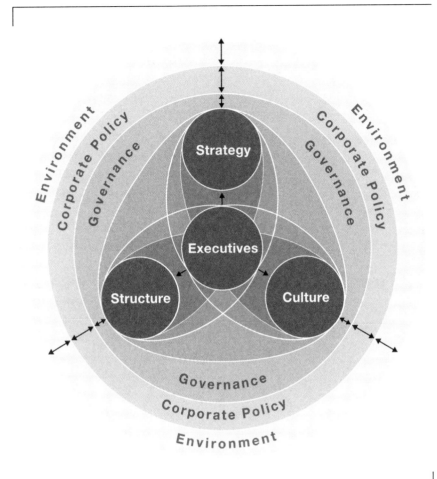

Figure 35: The General Management Model for Corporate Management

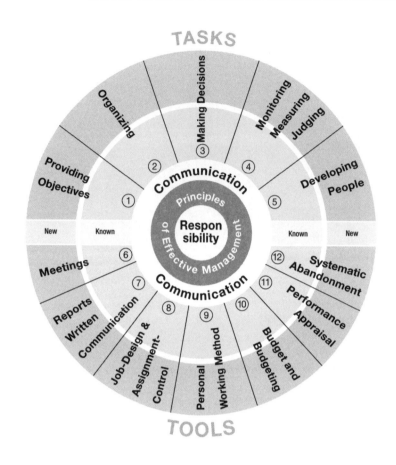

TASKS

Organizing

Making Decisions

Monitoring
Measuring
Judging

Providing
Objectives

Communication

Principles

Respon
sibility

of Effective Management

Developing
People

New   Known

Known   New

Meetings

Communication

Systematic
Abandonment

Reports
Written
Communication

Job-Design &
Assignment-
Control

Personal
Working Method

Budget and
Budgeting

Performance
Appraisal

TOOLS

Figure 36: The Standard Model of Effectiveness ("Management Wheel")

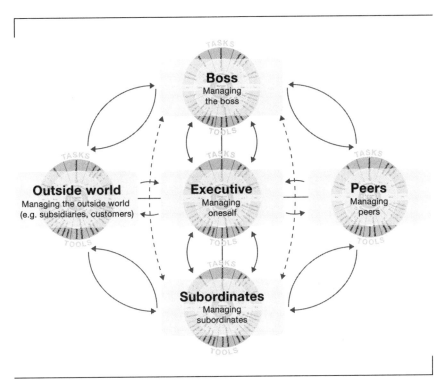

Figure 37: Standard situation for the application of the "Management Wheel"

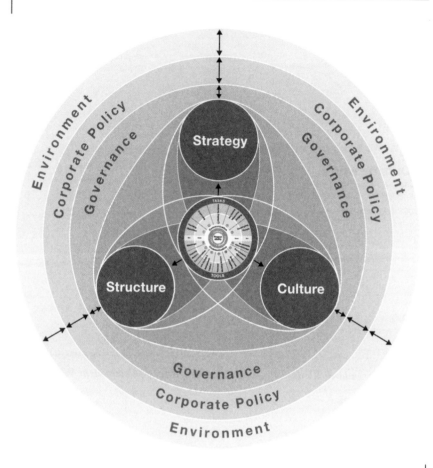

Figure 38: The General Management Model with embedded Management Wheel, with which corporate management and people management are systemically integrated.

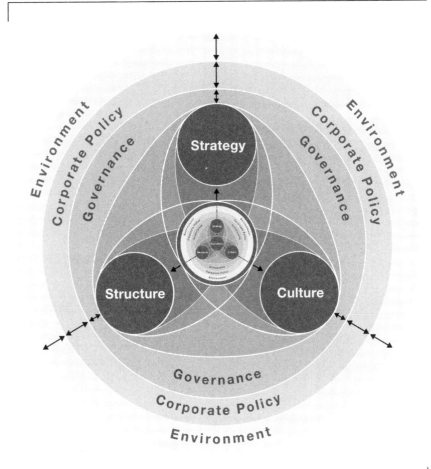

Figure 39: The General Management Model with recursive embedding of the General Management Model, through which recursive system links (that are infinite in principle) can be extended over any number of levels.

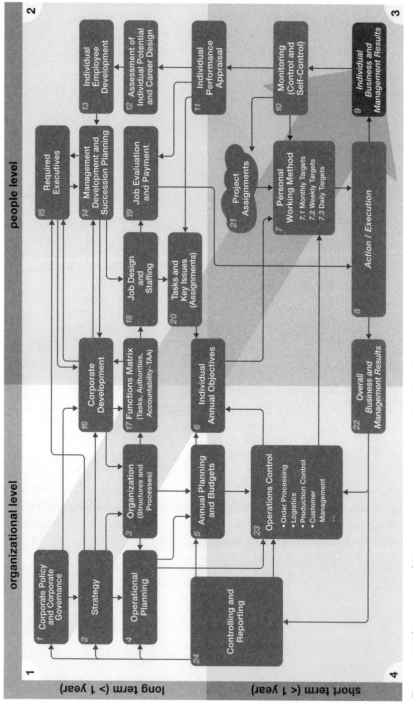

Figure 40: *The Integrated Management System as standard for the management of result-producing units, configurated from the*

Part IV
Sovereignty and Leadership through Master Control

At the end of a very successful shareholders' meeting:

Investor: Congratulations to an outstanding performance!

CEO: Thank you, it's been a good year for us.

Investor: Still, I sold all my shares while you were presenting. Got a good price for them.

CEO: But why? You just told me –

Investor: I'll tell you why. The numbers you presented were great, so that speaks for the past. But there was nothing to convince me that the future of your company will be just as good.

Chapter 1

Order, Time, Peace

<blockquote>
Systems are what they are and they do what they do;
if you don't like it, change the system.

Stafford Beer, Founder of management cybernetics
</blockquote>

There are top management floors which resemble beehives even with business being as usual. And then there are those which, under identical circumstances, exude the silence of a cathedral. In the former, people need to keep *getting* things under control – in the latter things *are* under control. Complexity, tasks, and requirements are the same in both cases; what differs is the way they are handled.

It is entirely up to top management to create either one of both worlds. Only they can change the system – *if they don't like it* – by applying the right system or corporate policy, thus establishing the basic rules that enable the system to function in a complexity-compatible way. Possible approaches and solutions are provided by this book.

Effective managers – or so I quoted Peter F. Drucker at an earlier point – do not make many decisions; rather, they solve problems by establishing policies. Right top management is not operations. Everyone knows that, but not everyone manages to transition to the entirely different solution I am proposing here. The greater the complexity, the more important this will be, however, because operations provide the poorest approach to steering a complex system.

Right top management means establishing Master Control by the means I have been describing. The result is an order which "keeps the system together internally" and which provides cohesion and alignment throughout. To the extent that this is achieved, one is basically free to sit back, as pointed out at the beginning, as the system organizes and regulates itself. There will be peace and quiet on the top floors, and the top managers in such organizations have time – which they use for *reflecting* rather than acting. They monitor the system from a certain distance, and with a constant view to the outside world. They confine themselves to three essential tasks:

1. *adjusting* corporate policy wherever necessary, which usually requires no more than subtle control impulses,
2. tune in their "antennae" to the whole *modus operandi*, the basic pattern of system behavior, and
3. dealing with the so-called *corporate issues*.

These are problems and opportunities arising "out of the blue", and which are to be tackled from the top, because they are important and because they do not fit anywhere else at that point.

Who are the managers responsible for corporate or systems policy? They are the people heading organizations, no matter what kind, whether they be individuals or members of top-level corporate bodies: owners and executive officers, university presidents and ministers of science, board members at corporations, top-level administrative bodies in public service, theater managers, artistic directors and cultural politicians, members of federal and state governments, etcetera. Their top management functions carry a variety of names, their basic functions are the same. By way of generalization, I usually speak of *executives* although I am not too happy with this term, as I will explain later.

Their Working Conditions: Proliferating Complexity

Measured by the requirements of their tasks, corporate top management of institutions still encounter rather unfavorable working conditions. The concepts, knowledge, and technologies for a very different kind of corporate management, however, are in place. It is all but certain that a radical change will ᴿEvolutionize the way top managements function.

If we were to contrast the situation of most executives to the possibilities existing in management cybernetics, it is comparable to aircraft pilots having at their disposal the modest means of aviation of the 1960s, as opposed to full-blown modern-day avionics and satellite navigation.

In other words, most executives are insufficiently equipped, both in terms of system methodology and technology, for regulating complexity in the way required. This is due not so much to their tasks but to the challenges of fulfilling them even in highly complex environments.

The key problem for executives is not so much the size of their organization but the complexity of the systems and the function for which they are responsible. The management of small companies can be much more complex than that of large ones, just as fighter planes put much higher demands on pilots in many respects than big passenger aircraft, to remain within the aviation metaphor.

Their Task: Total System Master Control

Based on what has been pointed out so far, the non-delegable tasks at the top management level are as follows:

1. Making decisions on corporate policy in the sense of the concepts discussed here.
2. Formulating the required principles and rules.
3. Implementing them, according to their degree of validity, through effective communication.
4. Making sure that these principles are adhered to in the organization.
5. Evaluating the results of the institution's operations.
6. Correcting deviations, justifying and modifying the Master Controls as required.

It is hardly surprising that the logical sequence of these tasks is basically that of a classical-cybernetic control loop. In this logical way, the quintessential function of executives can be formulated so clearly and simply that it must appear self-evident to anyone. However, organizing them under the given conditions is anything but simple.

Their Challenge: Change Leaders

As we have seen, the conditions of complexity that exist already, and the naturally ongoing complexification, force Top Management to advance to a higher level of effectiveness. Top Management either manage to install the required Master Controls of self-organization, thus aligning the organization with the nature of complex systems, or do not bring about this kind of system quality, and fail.

The profound changes calling for this evolution have long been in the making:

1. The complexification calling for this evolutionary leap has long been here; and with it the natural forces, driven by intensifying information flows, which control the internal dynamics of complex systems.
2. Information and communication technology has long accomplished the evolutionary leap to real-time monitoring. Correspondingly it accelerates the evolution and effect of system-immanent forces. What was true in one second may no longer apply in the next, as change is a constant state in complex systems.
3. The effects of data and information overload, as well as of overstimulation, multiply accordingly, while under traditional thinking and problem-solving patterns, based on outdated concepts of reality, the brain capacity decreases due to stress.
4. The result is a yet bigger problem, the information *underload*, or put more simply, the lack of relevant information. It maximizes the risk of wrong decisions as well as the probability of a system breakdown, as Maria Pruckner writes in her cybernetic system study *Die Komplexitätsfalle* ["The Complexity Trap"][110]. In a manner of speaking, it is the typical natural phenomenon in the age of complexity wherever systems have not yet adjusted to the 21st Century transformation.
5. Contemporary theories, methods, and technologies for the comprehensive mastering of complex situations and systems, in particular the use of management cybernetics, have long been at everyone's disposal, and the best managers are applying them already. Wherever no higher dimension of controlling and regulating force is used, strong competition will lead to irreversible disadvantages in business.
6. Even top managers cannot permanently work at the limits of their physical and mental performance. Without the necessary controlling and regulating systems, not even the best personal assistants and support staffs can achieve the state of knowledge and information that the Master Control function requires under complex conditions.

---

110 Pruckner, Maria, *Die Komplexitätsfalle. Wie sich Komplexität auf den Menschen auswirkt – vom Informationsmangel bis zum Zusammenbruch*. Norderstedt 2005.

Their Choice: Making Use of Complexity

Top managers in highly complex environments only have a choice between adjusting to global evolution or being overrun by it. What this adjustment requires of them is not so much knowledge or education, for there is not really a major lack of that, but new categories of organization as well as the integration of knowledge and information.

It requires a mental frame of reference which corresponds to their changed reality. It requires them to distinguish right theories from wrong, effective methods from ineffective ones, and suitable tools from unsuitable ones. In other words, the least that is needed is fundamental system-theoretical and cybernetic knowledge, helping them to make the distinctions crucial for success, to tell the relevant from the irrelevant, and to reach and maintain a concentration on the essential.

Their Conflict: Categorical Change

A remarkable proportion of managers has already developed the view required for the age of complexity. Another, by far larger proportion has yet to bid farewell to outdated ideas and concepts, which many of them find difficult to do. According to Paul Watzlawick and co, all pioneers of modern cybernetic communication theory, the reason goes somewhat like this: *man is ready to accept new insights as long as he does not have to give up his accustomed premises in turn*, such as his view of the world or his idea of what management is, how it works, and what makes a manager a manager.[111]

Management in the age of complexity requires letting go of old ideas held dear, because they have become outdated and wrong. With regard to this, the team of authors around Watzlawick points out that it will invariably result in conflict. Nothing is more difficult for people than giving up their accustomed mental models, because they are what give them orientation in the world. But the unfortunate fact is that the world has changed,

---

111 Watzlawick, P., Beavin, J. H., Jackson, D.D., *Pragmatics of Human Communication. A Study of Interactional Patterns, Pathologies, and Paradoxes,* Palo Alto,California/New York 1967.

so we have no choice but to change our mental models. The *Malik Management System* can help do that by offering better models. Whether people can or wish to accept them is up to them.

The following chapter will elaborate on the context in which top managers in the age of complexity operate.

Chapter 2

Top-Management Frame of Reference
for Change Leaders

Top management work requires navigation in the most comprehensive meaning of the word. By analogy to the longitudes and latitudes of the globe, it requires simultaneously monitoring four dimensions of orientation: the *inside* and *outside world* of the organization, as well as its *present* and *future*. It can be depicted using a simple cross-hairs diagram.

In the Cross-Hairs of Total System Control

The axes given in figure 41 define the dimensions of navigation for the dynamic balancing of the continuously moving and changing system *corporation-environment*. It is the field of tension between *conservation* and *continuity* as against *change* and *innovation* – always across the entire *corporation-environment* system, and increasingly also across the entire networked system ecology in which this system is embedded.[112]

The job titles available to us – originating from the Old World – are hardly of any use for semantically capturing the nature of top management tasks in the age of complexity. The top people can be managers, executives, and leaders, but also architects, configurators, composers, and directors of their systems.

For quite some time there will be plenty of experimenting with the understanding of new requirements, tasks, and function of the top level, as well as with new forms of task-sharing and the terms potentially suitable

---

112 What an organization structure should look like, in order to safely maintain and support the required balance through strong yet elastic structures, is described in Volume 4.

for them. Those in use so far are potentially dangerous in that they perpetuate the old ideas, ways of thinking, and understanding.

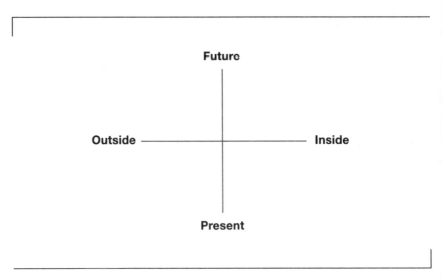

Figure 41: Coordinates for top management

The moving dynamic equilibrium of the total system can be illustrated roughly as shown in figure 42. The tools for mastering complexity in this situation are the Master Controls I am proposing in this book.

The focus of top management is in constant motion, in order to keep the system in a dynamic equilibrium – in a global society – around the clock – across all continents. It is difficult enough to know where the attention, experiences, knowledge, skills, and power of judgment are to be directed; after all, top executives constantly usually have to deal with a number of situations which compete for their attention. Every steering intervention involves decisions which, in turn, entail major consequences and risks. These decisions require a highly complex, time-consuming process of opinion and will formation – with top management colleagues in the narrower and broader sense, with owner representatives, unions, political authorities, and the media.

I am not saying that corporate top managements lack professionalism in the conventional sense. As a general rule, they have experience, business expertise, and power of judgment. What they often lack, though, is the *control toolset* for top management – or in other words. the cybernetics of the overall control situation and the necessary information: the rudders,

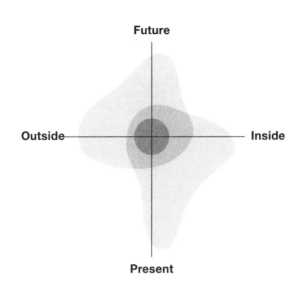

Figure 42: Visualization of the moving dynamic equilibrium of the overall system

levers, and controls for situation-specific measures and the necessary feed-backs for Master Control.

What results from the dynamics indicated in figure 42 is that the concept of *stability* can have temporary significance at best. Complex systems, in the stream of ongoing change, must be multi- and poly-stable. Hence, the foundations of Master Control at the top level are the self-regulation and self-organization of the overall system, based on a corporate policy conforming to the cybernetic principles set forth here. They make self-regulation and self-organization possible across the whole system, from its head to its center and to its periphery.

The Future is Created Now – Or It Has Been Missed

The most important and difficult task at the corporate top is the fundamental reorientation of the institution in times of profound change, which I referred to at the beginning of this book.

Categorical Change: Logic, Chrono-logic, and Psycho-logic

Figure 42 shows, in a coordinate system of possible developments in the course of time, the basic problem faced by every institution in a period of fundamental change: it is the balance of present and future – in all manifestations this change can take – including: current and future business, current and future technology, pre- and post-merger phases. These are typical cases of paradigm change.

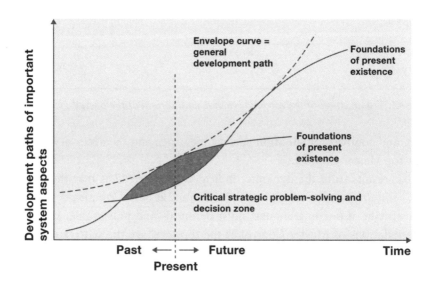

Figure 43: Coordinate system of categorical change

According to the central hypothesis of this book, it is about much more: about categorical change – change from the Old to the New World, comparable to the transition from the geocentric to the heliocentric view of the world, or from "the world is flat" to "the world is round". A change from the money to the complexity society, from a focus on economic profit maximization to the architecture of viable systems.

Change of this kind has its own factual logic: its own logic in the course of time, which I call *chrono-logic*, and its own emotional logic, which I call *psycho-logic*.

The two overlapping S-curves represent the respective foundations of current and future existence. This means that the current operations and innovations for the future, although generated today, are difficult to assess from a current standpoint because the evolution toward the right – hand side of today is uncertain. Above both curves we find the so-called envelope curve – the path of an organization that is successful throughout, even across breakpoints.

Basic questions in this situation are:

1. Where are we now?
2. What will be the probable course of both development curves? How much longer can we keep doing our current business? How well are we prepared for future business?
3. When do we have to start redirecting our key resources from the Today to the Tomorrow?
4. What risks are involved? What risks do we face if we do not make the transition? What risks do we face if we make it?
5. What are the choices that we have?

Only in this logic do we find the true task complexes of top management. There are three of them:

1. The Present curve represents the current place and time. It is the field for *operational corporate management*. Its focus is: what *is* right now and here? Consequently, what needs to be done right *now*, in the *present* context?
2. The Future curve represents the Outside and the Tomorrow. It is the field for *strategic corporate management*. Its focus is: what *could* be – outside and tomorrow? What do we need to do in order to be successful in *new, future* contexts?
3. The critical decision zone represents the *normative corporate management*. Its focus is: what should be – in the light of what *is* and what *could be*? What do we want to do now in order to get from the Today to the Tomorrow? This is where the defining decisions of corporate policy are made.

The steering task of top management is difficult not only in terms of its logic. It is characterized by a lack of information and by risk. In addition, there is what I call *psycho-logic*. People are familiar with the *Present curve*; it is their life and there are many reasons in favor of keeping it that way, while there is no reason to support going towards an uncertain future. The more fundamental the changes are, the greater the future risks appear. In fact, however, the greatest risk is missing out on the change.

Existential Options and Timing

This field of tension between operation and innovation, motion and change, is omnipresent in top management. Complexity increases, decisions must be taken under growing time pressure, timing becomes essential. In addition, what comes into play is what I call *chrono-logic*.

Managers changing S-curves at the lower point of intersection are steering a risky course. If it succeeds it will usually lead to break-through success. That is an innovation strategy under the motto *quick and powerful*. It is the strategy with the greatest payoff – if it is successful. For it is also the strategy involving the greatest risk. If it fails it usually fails completely. There is no second chance.

By contrast, if resources are realigned at a later point – at the second intersection – there will be greater certainty due to better information. On the other hand, the start of the new will clearly be more costly, as the institution will have to match up to established competitors. In most cases, an entry at this later point will only be possible via an acquisition, a merger, or some form of alliance.

The Best Point in Time – Which No One Can Tell

The optimal point in time, which due to complexity nobody knows, will thus lie somewhere in the shaded area of figure 43. In fact, the situation is even more complex, as shown in figure 44. As a general rule, there will be not only *one* possible future but several possible *"futures"*, such as several different technologies competing against each other. Take, for instances, companies developing vehicle engines: should they opt for the gas turbine, the hybrid drive, or the hydrogen-powered engine? No one can tell at this point which of the different potential developments will ultimately prevail.

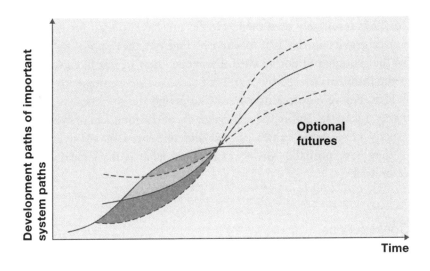

Figure 44: Optional futures

Due to cost considerations, only few organizations are able to experiment with all variants – which they actually ought to do, as the mistakes made in these decision situations can hardly be corrected later. They are not mistakes of the kind that result from the professionalism of top executives, but of the fateful kind, where – despite all professionalism – fate and coincidence also play a role. The question, therefore, is to what extent one has to succumb to fate and to what extent one can influence it, at least in part.

Fate and Destiny

Without venturing too far into metaphysical dimensions, the pragmatic research findings of cybernetics about the innate behavior of complex systems and their self-control, self-regulation, and self-organization does show us quite plainly that much of what may seem fateful at first is not that fateful after all. Whether or not one is aware of these cybernetic phenomena, just as people are aware of the natural laws of physics, makes a fundamental difference.

Long before these natural laws were discovered and described by scientists, man has intuitively used them. He did not have to wait for Newton to discover gravity in the 17th century, to find out that apples fall from trees to the ground and not upward. Everyone knew it, just like everyone knows the problems caused by complexity because we permanently experience them. Before Newton, however, what people did not know is *why* it is that way. Likewise, before the achievements of the founders of cybernetics, nobody knew what causes desired and undesired innate dynamics, even if they have probably always existed. So what is the logical consequence of it all?

The Consequence

The technical revolution, and thus the industrial age, occurred as a result of the increasing exploration and conscious application of the natural laws of physics. The cybernetic ᴿEvolution, and thus the much-cited *information age*, is a result of the increasing exploration and conscious application of the natural laws of cybernetics and of system theory about information, systems, and complexity. From it evolved our current information, communication, and automation technology, which characterizes our present-day, digitally controlled world and leads to an explosive expansion of complexity.

It goes without saying that in management it has to be the Master Controls of corporate policy that I am presenting here, which enable society's social systems to follow that evolution, which is doubtlessly inexorable. Without the control, regulating, and steering systems I am presenting in this book series, the complex systems that have spontaneously emerged cannot be shaped and directed effectively. In the long run, there is no other way to control complex systems. This is a fact because the nature of things is as it is. Even if they are being burnt at the modern-day stake, as it were, it will not change anything.

Chapter 3

Mastering the Master Controls – Source of Leadership

As I previously pointed out, having established the right policy is probably the most important way to leadership, albeit hardly ever mentioned, even though it is really obvious. *Corporate policy* as such is complemented by its proper handling, as I will explain using the other two top management tasks mentioned before: the ability to determine the system's *modus operandi* and to choose the right *corporate issues*. This triad is what the term *corporate governance* should really have been reserved for, supplemented by those tasks of top management bodies which serve that purpose. *Corporate governance* would then have been the ideal term for the top-level responsibility for the overall functioning of that complex system, the corporation.

Master Control through Corporate Policy

With regard to corporate policy, there is no need to say more at this point. Just as a summary, in figure 45 I will once again show the model that has accompanied and enabled navigation through the whole book. It shows, in a clear and comprehensive structure, the essence of what is needed for the management and exploitation of complexity in the age of complexification. The sub*systems*, each of them highly complex, are captured in three specific *models*, in such a way that three *concepts* with the following content follow from them: *"...the entirety of all basic decisions which are to stipulate, over the longer term, the baselines of everything that is going to happen in a company in the future."* As you may remember, this is the definition of corporate policy by which I started my remarks *on corporate policy*.

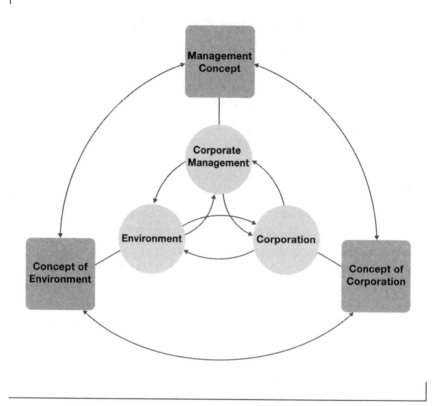

Figure 45: Navigation for cybernetic corporate policy – Master Control

The corporate policy, as I understand it and configure it in this book, comprises all the factors required for the categorical change described under "Frame of Reference". They enable top managers to not only manage change but also to take the lead, and thus be a *change leader.*

The models as such do not replace or make any decisions. That should always be the responsibility of individuals and groups in top management. What they are is navigation tools which, in the dynamic labyrinths of complex systems, help to define and understand one's particular situation and to determine the right approach for dealing with the particular complexity one is facing.

The Master Controls of corporate systems policy absorb complexity and provide points of orientation and bases for action. They are capable of evolution, and elements of order suitable for evolution, in the uncertainty of such decision situations.

That does not mean, however, that one can *always* adhere to the policies defined – indeed unforeseen situations can trigger fundamental changes of policy. But they are the platform from which the policies have to be adjusted, and from which new policies can emerge, without having to reinvent the wheel every single time.

Leadership largely consists in having the right policy, as mentioned earlier in this book. It is put to the test even more when it comes to applying policy and mustering the flexibility required for that. Pragmatism, understood correctly, is not acting without policy but acting based on policy – but in a way that is appropriate for the particular situation. This is what characterizes a true master of system control. The following section explains how Master Controls support top management, through self-organization, in quickly bringing about the necessary changes of direction.

Master Control through Corporate Modes

The more complex a system is, the greater are its potential dynamics and susceptibility to malfunction. Complex organizations therefore have to be capable not only of devising new responses within a very short time, but of changing their entire *mode of behavior.*

The classical case is the mode commonly referred to as a *state of alert.* In order to realize it in due time, and broadly enough, the required programs and triggers must be defined in advance long before. Using them as a standard procedure must come so natural that they can be applied without thinking.

At this point, an element comes into play which in commercial organizations is perfectly common for operating systems, such as manufacturing, but not at the senior management levels. In other fields the alert mode has long been part of everyday practice at the top level, and is constantly dealt with and trained for – e.g. in the security and healthcare sectors.

Getting the organization into the situation-specific mode of behavior every time, and quickly enough, is part of the top management task. All activities at the organization must then be subordinated to one overriding priority.

The autodynamics which lead to the switching of behavior modes within seconds can be observed in animals, when they switch from resting mode to escape mode. Both modes are mutually exclusive. An animal cannot flee and eat at the same time, or fight and drink. It can only do one or the other. For higher organisms there are about 15 modes of this kind. They belong to the most powerful controls for the mastering of complexity. Warren McCulloch, the pioneer of neuro-cybernetics. has referred to the neuronal mode switching as *redundancy of potential command.*[113]

A modal control step consists in announcing a predefined general state, to which all other activities have to be subordinated. As a result, the organism's undivided attention and the use of all forces are focused onto one specific mode.

Depending on the type of organization, there are widely differing behavioral modes as Master Controls. Most executives know controls of this kind only intuitively. Outside cybernetics, these questions are hardly ever dealt with.

Modes of Organization

The following seven modes can be distinguished in organizations:

1. business as usual,
2. explicit pursuit of growth,
3. change mode,
4. special-case mode,
5. explicit retreat,
6. crisis, and
7. emergency.

Mode 1 – business as usual – is not a problem because it is the normal state of things.

Mode 2 – the explicit pursuit of growth – is usually well accepted by management bodies, investors, unions, and the general public. It is, however, usually more difficult to implement effectively and visibly, as natural inertia tends to get in the way. Among other things, it depends on how growth

---

113 Mc Culloch, Warren, *Embodiments of Mind*, Cambridge, 1965.

is to be accomplished. Growth based on one's own resources requires a different management focus than growth by acquisition.

Mode 3 – fundamental change – may be en vogue semantically, but most organizations have severe difficulties accomplishing it. Causes lie in a wrong understanding of management, and in wrong management training.

Mode 4 – the special-case mode – is a highly effective variety of *Master Control* for those who master that mode, as it provides plenty of flexibility. It is closely connected to issue management, which we will discuss shortly. The art consists in deciding, for each situation, whether an issue is to be tackled inside or outside the usual problem-solving structures. Companies with a sophisticated project management in place will not have a problem with this mode.

Mode 5 – explicit retreat – is usually difficult; how much, however, depends on whether the retreat will be partial or affecting the whole organization. Investors' responses will be different from those of employees and the unions. Often, a retreat will collide with managers' self-image and the expectations put on them inside and outside the organization. Even partial retreats are often initiated very hesitantly. Military organizations are a totally different story: retreat is part of the standard repertoire of every commander, and the troops are trained accordingly.

Mode 6 – the mastering of a crisis – and *mode 7* – the emergency – are regularly activated much too late. They often hit the organization unexpectedly because people lack the courage to face up to the situation in due time. Decisions are often difficult to get through the decision-making bodies. This, however, is precisely where leadership is required and where it can be demonstrated.

Dealing with Behavioral Modes

Dealing with such situations for a switch of behavioral modes requires, throughout the organization, as follows:

1. opinion-building in order to recognize the situation,
2. a decision about the triggering moment,
3. communication about the decision on the mode required.

It is about initiating a totally new behavioral program – one could speak of a *master switch* – which inherently involves all the known difficulties of human and organizational persistence.

Master Control through Corporate Issues

Issues are particular subjects of temporary significance, that require fundamental thinking from an overall perspective, as well as the authority of top management.

They can be subjects of importance to every institution and its top management. Those I consider important for the foreseeable future will be dealt with in the following section. Issues can also be subjects that are only relevant for one particular organization.

Issue management helps the organization be more flexible, thus providing a counterbalance to policy stipulations. As outlined above, corporate policy defines the organization in its basic features and over the long term. It therefore increases complexity to the extent that is needed for the organization to function, for basically any number of employees, in order to enable them to work in a self-organizing manner. At the same time, however, it also *stipulates* and thus reduces complexity. Both are necessary.

In developing a corporate policy, one can only take into account the information available at the time. However, as the organization and its environment never stand still, top management must permanently check new developments as to their relevance for their current policy. The selection filter is part of the policy itself. It determines the relevance for selecting issues to be dealt with.

Designed to increase flexibility and variety, issue management is the conscious interruption or circumvention of established organizational and personal approaches and responsibilities, so that a given matter can rigorously be dealt with according to its *importance* to the greater whole.

Issue management is more than what is usually meant when we say *a matter for the boss*. It means dealing with a challenge outside the established organizational patterns. It therefore often has negative and even alarming connotations for employees. After all, it requires that executives forego some of the responsibilities they have been given at an earlier point, and that is usually misunderstood as a symptom of, and response to, utter failure. That, in turn, makes the task of top managers even more difficult because now they have to deal with employee conflict instead of the current issue.

Because of the Master Control effect of good corporate policy, in particular if based on a sophisticated management system, management capacity is freed up for things that would otherwise be subordinated to the operational business, or have to be decided upon when they come up, and which usually get much too little attention. They are ignored. Ignoring them might be a good thing – but only when unimportant matters are at stake.

Chapter 4

A Look Forward –
Current Top Management Issues

For the foreseeable future, I think it is important that top executives have the following issues on their agendas – not only to clarify them for their own organization but, even more, to communicate with the public, the media, shareholders, and politicians.

Informing and "Educating" Shareholders and Representatives of the Financial Sector

This topic has been dealt with in the chapter on business purpose. The essential messages and arguments can be found there. As a result of the stock market bias that has followed from the shareholder value debate, doing business and making money are usually equated with one another in the world of finance.

Given the highly specialized nature of their knowledge, experts on finance live in a world of their own, where vital aspects of the far more complex events that are happening in the economy at large can be, and have to be, ignored. It is not necessary to go so far as Peter F. Drucker – who once said that bankers know all about money but nothing about business – to acknowledge the importance of the question as to how people can be given an understanding of what doing business in the real economy is all about. Today, via investment and pension funds, shareholders come from all sections of the population. We cannot expect them to have any knowledge of the complicated interlinkages existing in business. The top executives of the business world will personally have to take on the task of explaining, from their point of view, the basics and underlying interconnections of doing business to investors, their clientele, their representatives, and to the media as well as the public. Trust and credibility in these questions depend on the personal commitment they bring, and on their explaining these complex things in a way that is generally comprehensible, and via media that actually get through to people. The internet plays an increasingly significant role in this.

What is Profit? What is Wealth?

In close connection with the first issue, profit and wealth have to be explained from the point of view of corporate leaders. There are more than enough theories from the relevant specialist sciences. To non-specialists, however, they are incomprehensible. The perspective of management is almost entirely ignored. To date, business itself, with the few exceptions cited here – Maucher, Wiedeking – has remained silent about itself and about how it works. It has left it to others to explain these things, often to people who lack real business experience.

Outside management cybernetics, there is no theory of corporate management to this date. Management does not feature in economic theories. So far, the Austrian economist and Harvard professor Joseph Schumpeter has basically been the only economist to have taken any serious and fruitful interest in the figure of the entrepreneur and in the function that the institution fulfills for the economy. From the explicit perspective of management, the crucial contributions have been made by Peter F. Drucker

It takes experience from active corporate management to create a credible alternative to the views of outsiders, including the specialized scientific ones. And it does not suffice to have functionaries of business associations appear on the occasional talk-show – they do not carry enough weight. At this point it may be worth mentioning that management cybernetics originated in business itself, not at some university. I advise the reader to study the biography of and the books written by its pioneer, Stafford Beer, who was active in international top management much of his life – at first in the steel industry, then in a media company.[114]

---

114 Please visit www.managementcybernetics.com

Entrepreneurship and Top Management

Top managers are constantly faced with the unfortunate distinction between *managers* and *entrepreneurs* and are implicitly under pressure to justify what they do. The meanings of both terms have been shaped by misconceptions, prejudices and clichés that all originate from the world of business itself. If business is to be understood, this division has to be overcome. This is why the topic is on my proposed list.

Due to the orientation to shareholders and finance, doing business has acquired another negative meaning. Management can be successful only if it is *entrepreneurial*. It was for this reason that I created the term EME, the "entrepreneurially managed enterprise". Anything other than this ought not even to be called *management*. True entrepreneurial thinking has nothing to do with lust for profits or greed, which is how it is perceived due to the most unfortunate state of communication; rather, it is *making a sustainable, productive contribution to society by creating satisfied customers*, as I keep pointing out.

A top manager who did not think entrepreneurially would be incapable of managing a company for even a short length of time. Conversely, an entrepreneur who did not take the questions of management seriously would not be successful for long. Sooner or later – and especially if he is successful – the entrepreneur changes into the corporate *manager*. The two terms have to be integrated.

The Importance of Knowledge

The whole complex of questions relating to the so-called *knowledge society* also has to be discussed at the top level as an issue, and clarified for the institution. Knowledge as a new productive resource, the productivity of knowledge, the importance of knowledge in global competition, and the emergence of the knowledge worker and knowledge work are things that will bring fundamental changes to every institution, as pointed out before. The importance of knowledge differs by industry and type of institution. The views that a media company will have on it will obviously differ from those held by an automobile manufacturer. But all companies are radically affected by knowledge and knowledge work. It is all the more important that top management in each individual company have clear ideas on this matter.

Thinking through the Strengths

Dealing with the strengths of the institution has been discussed in the section on business mission. It is a permanent task of corporate management to think through what the particular strengths of the organization are, and where it threatens to lose key strengths. The process by which strengths come into being and are lost is usually a gradual one and therefore difficult to detect. It is therefore all the more important for it to be a regular concern of top management.

Unlike strengths, it is relatively easy to see where the institution has weaknesses. Eliminating weaknesses is certainly necessary, but only seldom does it lead to resounding success. All it does is remove the obstacles to success. Entrepreneurial successes are always the result of the exploitation of strengths, which is why these need to be an item on the top management agenda at all times.

Developing Top Performers

Regardless of all their other human resources principles, one task of top managers is to look after the top performers. They have to identify and support them, particularly when the organization has a highly developed human resources function. This has to be accurately directed to ensure that *high potentials* become *high performers*. The following key questions must be on the top management agenda:

1. By what standards should we measure high performers?
2. What do we have to look out for to recognize them?
3. For what abilities do we have to test them?
4. What tests do we have to give them, in order to enable them to prove themselves?
5. How do we get them ready for the really big tasks?

It must absolutely be avoided that the above tasks are drowned in a flood of departmental procedures and administrative systems. Steps must also be taken to prevent them from turning into fashionable topics, such as the nonsensical "war for talent". It is a matter of performance, not talents. The future of the organization depends on the high performers. This demands the attention of top management. It includes, amongst other things, dealing with what is known as *elites*. A functioning society does need elites, but elites who can do without any pretentious behavior.

What is a Functioning Society?

People in top management must not and should not become social philosophers. Yet there is an inseparable relationship between functioning business and a functioning society. Business can only function in a healthy society.

Thinking through the mutual relations between business and society must not be left to the specialist disciplines of science and to intellectual zeitgeist commentators, because they, too, focus on the particular points of view of each science. It is one of the main problems of the scientific system that the advantages of specialization usually have to be traded off against the lack of practice-orientation and problem focus.[115] The perspective of the experienced practitioner at the top level is crucial to the forming of a public opinion. Making it known to people is his very specific task, because it will bring another weight into the discussion, and is the only thing at all that can provide some balance. It is at least as important as the point of view of scientists, politicians or the media.

What Is the Meaning of Responsibility?

Managers carry responsibility. But what does it mean in practice? All through history, entrepreneurs have been forced to accept *personal liability*. In this way, responsibility has been discharged in a clear and inescapable way that serves as a direct corrective. With the modern legal forms of companies, the matter of liability has taken a back seat, but it has lost none of its significance.

A society that does not solve the problem of responsibility in top management cannot function in the long term. Who could be more competent

---

115 This is visualized in by figure 4 in the chapter on the corporate environment.

for thinking through this question from a practical point of view and introducing it into the debate than the corporate managers themselves? Philosophical contributions to this question abound. Often they are of little practical relevance.

Top Managers' Compensation

Hardly anything has caused more misunderstandings lately than the way in which top management compensation is determined. Consequences have included aggressive behavior towards managers, bitterness, agony, demotivation, und fresh social divides. The subject is not going to go away.

For one's own company it is clear that questions of compensation are a matter for top management. However, they are also a matter with much potential for conflict, in both politics and society as a whole, particularly in times of economic downturn.

The key point is not the absolute level of earnings, but how they are determined and justified to the outside world. It is quite possible that the compensation of really capable top managers ought to be even higher than what it is now. However, they should be compensated for doing the *right* things, not the *wrong* ones.

Long-term strategic action is a mere illusion as long as incomes are primarily tied to short-term financial operating results – no matter whether these are share prices or internal financial figures reflecting added value. I say this without restraint. The more top managers are rewarded for their operating results, the more will they pay lip service to strategy, actually referring to little more than the extrapolation of operating figures.

Not only must incomes cease to be tied to financial parameters; there must also be no mathematical-mechanical link to any other indicators. Peter F. Drucker said long ago that there are only two kinds of income systems for top management: bad and miserable ones, or something to that effect. There is little that the shareholder approach has proved more effectively.[116]

---

116 These subjects will be elaborated on in Volumes 5 and 6.

Chapter 5

The Crisis of Top Executive Bodies and Their ᴿEvolution

Top management is presently undergoing its severest crisis since the emergence of modern-day forms of enterprise. At the same time, this is the greatest opportunity for those ready to face up to ᴿEvolutionary change, and to use it to lift their systems to a higher level of functioning. Change will happen in any case; it is an inevitable consequence of complexification. It will, however, be impossible to solve the crisis with the same means that provoked it – which is one of the overriding hypotheses of this book.

Lack of Theory for Top Management Structures

The organization structure of top management is a matter of experimenting and improvisation. To this day there is no theoretical foundation for the structures found in practice. Current organization structures are essentially based on the requirements of corporate law, lately complemented by the recommendations of corporate governance codes.

Existing legal provisions, however, are mostly misaligned with the actual top management function – the task of *managing*. They are becoming ever more irrelevant to its requirements in today's highly complex situation. Legal provisions are dominated by other criteria, such as those of *creditor protection* and the – supposed – *shareholder interests*. The responsibility of senior managers is oriented by the *commercial due diligence* which has little importance for the fulfilling of the purpose of an institution. Even someone exerting a maximum degree of diligence can steer a company into bankruptcy.

The corporate governance debate has changed the function of senior corporate management bodies to the extent that corporate supervision has considerably gained importance and major obstacles have been eliminated. These changes, however, have been effected within the old structural paradigm. It originated at a time when two key things were different from today: the environment was clearly less turbulent, and the supervisory boards of companies consisted of their *owners*. While the Carnegies, Morgans, Krupps, and so on, retired from the operational business as their companies got bigger, they did not retire from the companies as such. They were full-time members of supervisory or administrative boards, and over long periods of time knew the business better than their management boards did, for they had built the companies themselves.

Will Formation Works Differently Today

This kind of top management structure has long been outdated. This is evident from the fact that the true processes in which opinions are formed and decisions made do not at all work as one might expect, based on what is found in the stock corporation law, company bylaws, and relevant literature. Anyone with personal experience in such decision-making bodies knows that.

That does not mean these bodies do not conform to legal provisions; it means that the quasi-official modes of function are far from sufficient to cope with the complexity at hand, and even less so to aggressively exploit it.

In the formal meetings of such decision-making bodies, decisions may be approved and announced, but they are hardly ever *made* in the true sense of the word. Resolutions are made, and decisions are recorded and afterwards announced, and thus put into force. The procedures, however, by which decisions are *brought about,* which requires the formation of opinions and commitments in often highly complex processes, is an entirely different matter.

Top management decisions are much too complex for what traditional decision-making bodies are able to accomplish. Ignorant people tend to assume that top-level decisions are generated by power-hungry, scheming conspirators of the alpha-leader type in a continually reconfigured process.

Indeed, the exploration and formation of a joint opinion and will, as required for major meetings, takes place long before: in the corridors, dozens of bilateral telephone conversations and multilateral telephone conferences. The required coordination – further complicated by time differences – takes up all of the time of the respective mangers' personal assistants. Such interactions are also made at business lunches and, depending on the regional culture, on the golf course or in the sauna. The processes involve people far beyond the inner circle of formal members of the decision-making bodies, because the latter typically have plenty of knowledge but lack the necessary information.

This refers to foreseeable decision-making situations. In exceptional cases, such as sudden problems or opportunities, the phenomena described are exponentiated, sometimes to the extent of a functional collapse. This is how corporate emergencies happen – in particular those that catch the attention of the media, which must constantly be reckoned with these days.

Breeding Ground for Conspiracy Theories

Conspiracies occur. But they hardly matter here, except if one wishes to view decision-making processes as conspiracies, which would provide little insight into the way organizations really work. The main problem is the enormous amount of information required, and which all those involved have to process, far beyond the document stacks sent around beforehand and the formal presentations given at meetings. You need to have experienced it in order to believe it.

So-called scientific studies, usually carried out with questionnaires and interviews, do not give even the remotest idea of the actual complexity and the communication processes needed to cope with it. The actual processes are nothing but self-organization – and it is only through the organizing, controlling and regulating effect of policies and experienced protagonists that they produce good decisions as an output.

Media workers reporting and commenting in terms of conspiracy and hunger for power cause gross misunderstandings in the general public, as well as prejudices with regard to the way societal institutions work, what the personalities involved are like, and what executives do. Since the media often have no legitimate access to information, but depend on contacts with selfish, media-addicted and scheming members of decision-making bodies or organizations, media reports tend to gain particular importance and dubious real content by way of so-called *insider information*, because members of the decision-making bodies are often unable to really understand what is going on. Metaphorically speaking, they fail to realize that the circular shape they see is the shadow cast by a sphere. There is no way around it: complex circumstances are impossible to comprehend in conventional ways.

Legal provisions and corporate governance codes define the minimal limits which have to be observed in decision-making processes in order to ensure validity and prevent legal liability consequences. They do not help to asses whether the decisions made are right and good, and will enable the company to take the competitive lead.

Laws, codes, and due diligence are the bases. The goal, however, must be success for the institution. This is exactly where there is a gap between corporate governance and corporate policy: good governance must be complied with; success, however, is achieved with good corporate policy and right management.

Why Traditional Corporate Governance Is Not Enough

The legal situation is not going to change in the near future. There is no need for it to change. But there is a need for clarity on what decision-making bodies can and cannot accomplish. The requirements of the law are doubtlessly met, but the requirements of the management of highly complex system are not. The standards of responsibility, diligence, and factual thoroughness are not the same as legal provisions. The latter have to fulfill other functions.

The evolution of corporate governance has brought some improvements with regard to the way decision-making bodies work, but it has also resulted in deteriorations. Beginning at the start of this book, I have mentioned several times that the common understanding of entrepreneurial work and top management tasks is currently too confined to financial questions, financial performance aids, and the short-term perspective. Also, the behavior of the members of such bodies is increasingly characterized by risk avoidance and the attempt to protect themselves from potential legal consequences. The changes required to master complexity will therefore have to happen within the framework of the given decision-making bodies, but they will still have to be radical. The instruments and methods of complexity-compatible corporate management are basically unaffected by the structures of the institution's organs. What does need to change, however, is the way decisions are prepared in the phases of the decision-making process; preferably also the way the bodies themselves work, but not their responsibility according to the law and the company bylaws.

A new method of operation, as the one made possible by using cybernetic tools, will partly be perceived as unusual. It will also have many advocates, in particular among those personalities who have long been dissatisfied with traditional approaches but have not been able to find alternatives.

The situation for managing bodies at highly complex organizations in the public sector differ from those in the private sector with regard to legal and economic standards, but not regarding the requirements to effective management. It begins with peer-like management structures and their bodies, and goes on to those of governments, which more and more often have to be newly formed as a result of elections. The demands on these hyper-sensitive scopes of activity for a society are and will be higher than ever, too, because the recipients of their services depend on them for their existence. In the absence of monopolies, a severe disturbance in business, including even the bankruptcy of customers, is usually coped with reasonably well because there are alternatives. A severe disturbance in the public sector is a disaster not only for those directly involved but for society at large. It can only be avoided by means of a high-precision management of mastering complexity, in particular with the *Master Controls* of the corresponding policy.

Chapter 6

ᴿEvolution: From Chief Executive Officer to Master Control Function

So far we know but one way to organize the chief executive *function*. We concentrate it in *one* person, and thus one brain – that of the chief executive officer. At least this is how general perception and theory put it.

The mastering of complexity depends on a complete overview, syntegrative thinking, and coherent control at the top level. It is therefore necessary to create, throughout the system, what in human beings would be called *integral self-awareness*, the *being aware of oneself*, or in other words, organic and personal identity and unity. The chief executive officer can hardly be the only solution to achieve that, at least not alone, which is why in practice he is not. The *chief executive function* does not suffice either – rather, in line with the system, it has to be the *Master Control function*.

Supercontrol instead of Superperson

The word "executive" comprises the key elements of *acting, putting in effect,* and *carrying out*. But "executive authority" alone is not enough. Right management needs more.

Executive action must have a *purpose* and a *direction*, and it needs *goals* – so, to remain within the political-philosophical terminology, it needs a legislative authority in addition to the executive one. Furthermore, acting needs *regulation* and *correction* – which is the analogy of the judicial authority. After all, the executive branch also needs its legitimation, that is, *meaning* and *responsibility*. Political-philosophical terminology, however, is too loaded to be of any use. Today we have the cybernetics terminology, which is better by far and lends itself to generalization. It goes without saying that a chief executive function, understood in a wholistic sense, is much more indeed: it is the *Master Control* function.

The task of top management as a whole, and specifically of the CEO, is much more complex today than anyone could have imagined ten years ago. The only constellation where it is indeed the best solution to have a CE officer, or the principle of concentrating Master Control in one person, is the rare situation when a *exceptionally* capable person is at the top of the organization – a superperson, so to speak. With this solution, it is understandable and unavoidable for the charisma discussion to arise, because such people have that effect generally referred to as charisma – and they need it to master a *superhuman* task.

The CEO principle is the worst of all conceivable solutions whenever a poorly skilled person is at the top. Much as the CEO position's wealth of power enables a true leader to achieve absolute top performance, it is just as inevitable that with irresponsible and incapable people at the top the CEO principle will lead to disaster.

Total System Master Control Function

The mere fact that it takes such personalities – bordering on genius – to manage a complex institution is evidence enough that top management is actually in a deep crisis, and that no generalizable solutions have so far been found. And while there are people who are – still – up to the task, there are not nearly enough of them. And we are still far from having reached the end of complexification; actually, it is only just beginning. Hence, the ingenious CEO cannot be the solution for future institutions.

Obviously, the best CEOs do not manage with their immediate skills and their charisma alone – they manage by policies, as I am proposing here, and they have well-functioning teams in which there is competition but no power struggle. Alfred P. Sloan was one of the first to realize this. Then, as some tentative first approaches, he implemented it at General Motors – and he had resounding success.

Anyone looking beyond the *surface structure* to the cybernetic *deep structure* will realize – in what equates to a Copernican shift – that in well-functioning organizations the task of the chief executive is not fulfilled by a person at all but, as important as that person may be, consists of a *function*. In cybernetics this is referred to as a *distributed function*. In other words, the chief executive task is carried out by a *system* in which tasks are shared. Truly outstanding CEOs – although mentioning examples in this area is a sensitive issue, some (no longer active) references include Helmut Maucher of Nestlé, Jack Welch of GE, and Sandorf Weill of Citigroup – have understood, and fulfilled, their task much more comprehensively than their position titles would suggest. They were the visible representatives of the *total system Master Control function* in the best sense of the word, and to a substantial degree also the m*aster minds* of their systems.

To master complexity where the problem has been recognized, solutions are currently being tested; others are materializing in the cybernetics context. Each of these solutions requires comprehensive policies in the sense of the three corporate policy concepts outlined in Part III. There is a series of possibilities. I am going to mention three of them here; some more will be outlined in Volume 4, where particular emphasis will be on top management structures and processes. Further alternatives are necessary in particular for the management of federalistic structures, alliances, cooperations, and of all those kinds of networks where Master Control is necessary and possible but where there is no way of establishing command.

Alternative 1: Master Control Function by Expanding Classical Divisional Structures

Whatever way top executive responsibilities are structured – by function, region, or line of business – and even if every top manager is in charge of *several* of those dimensions at a time, the actual Master Control tasks of general management cannot be reflected in this structure. There must be some kind of superstructure to bring about the integrating Master Control effect.

The general management tasks are not identical to the standard dimensions of an organization mentioned above. In any case, the latter cannot be applied to other kinds of organizations, for hospitals, universities, and government departments have different responsibility structures.

And while these standard dimensions are clearly *top* management tasks, they are top *special* management tasks by nature, rather than top *general* management tasks. The tasks pertaining to *general* management stretch across all top-level divisions, as shown in figure 46.

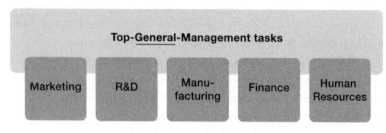

Figure 46: Interaction of top special and top general tasks

As could not be expected otherwise, these top *general* tasks cover the essential subjects of corporate policy, below slightly rephrased:

1. Determining the corporate policy, as pointed out here, including the corporate purpose, mission, performance controls, and strategy.
2. Designing the institution's overall structure.
3. Shaping the corporate culture by defining values and standards and providing a visible role model.
4. Developing and educating the human resources for top-level key positions.
5. Maintaining the institution's key relationships to outside parties.
6. Taking care of the institution's representation to the outside world.
7. Being prepared for exceptional situations, including both crises and opportunities.

Alternative 2: Master Control Function Through Central Performance Control Structure

Another design variant for the chief executive function is the concept of *Central Performance Control*, which has been introduced in the chapter on company performance. What, if not the Essential Variables, should be the focus of general management, based on the policy? As the corporate policy itself comprises the Essential Variables as *Central Performance Controls*, this effectively leads to unity, wholeness, and identity.

In part, the ongoing evolution of the division of tasks at the top of the company is pointing to this direction: in the form of the *finance* and the *human resources functions*. Contrary to what these functions commonly comprise, however, the CPC variables – and this is of essential importance – in part cover very different things than the conventional understanding of these areas of responsibilities and their designations would suggest.

Hence, under this solution there would be one integrated chief executive responsibility each for market position, innovation performance, productivities, attractiveness to the right people, liquidity, and profitability. Instead of having six people, as would be the case in larger corporations, the tasks could also be concentrated on fewer persons. Figure 47 shows the resulting personal structure.

Jack Welch chose this approach for GE. Next to him, at an almost equal level, there were the *Chief Financial Officer* and the *Chief Human Resources Officer*. Remarkably, both were explicitly excluded from the succession to the CEO position, which helped prevent potential struggles for

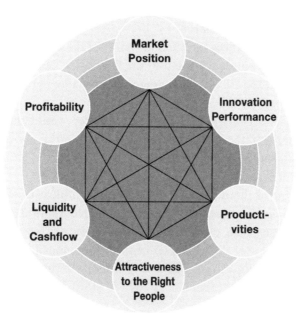

Figure 47: CPC as top management structure

rank and power. Another way to avoid power struggles has been practiced by the Catholic Church for centuries: the Popes stay in office until death.

One variant consists in uniting the heads of major business units in a *Master Control committee* and putting each of them in charge of one of the Essential Variables. The disadvantage of this model is that the *Master Control function* depends on the business success achieved by the individuals. It will hardly be possible for someone to achieve the necessary authority for the general management tasks if his unit performs poorly. It was not without reasons that A.P. Sloan, so many years ago, insisted on a strict separation between divisional management and corporate management.

Alternative 3: Master Control Function By Establishing Change Leaders

Figure 48 once more calls to mind the basic problem of top general management, and the three resulting top management tasks: operational, strategic, and normative corporate management. In this context, the current Chief Operating Officer (COO) is in charge of all activities represented by the S-curve of *present* existence.

A Chief *Change* Officer (CCO) is in charge of the *future* existence. Some companies have a similar position in the Corporate Development Officer, a solution where the CEO is simultaneously in charge of the Chief Change Officer function.

What today is called Chief Executive Officer would then become a Chief Normative Officer, focusing his attention on the *normative* corporate management. A similar solution exists in one of the globally leading financial institutions.

This variant of the three part structure (which must be strictly distinguished from the three organs of current German corporation law!) will be crucial for coping with categorical change. Physically separating the new from the old is one of the principles of successful innovation – even in the case of ordinary innovations at the object level. Without this solution, it will hardly be possible to fundamentally transform the entire organization in the manner presumed here.

To develop a sufficient degree of transformatory power and concentration, this approach to the top management structure will have to be combined with the CPC approach. After all, the mutated organization will

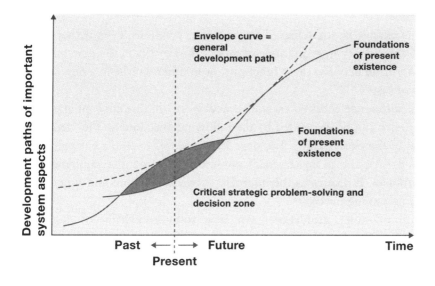

Figure 48: Categorical change in the top management structure

have the same Essential Variables but their content will be new and different. Consequently, the organization will have to render performance in these six areas in totally new ways.

Functioning instead of Personifying

In all the alternative solutions outlined here, complexity can be mastered only if the system is designed to be *self*-organizing and *self-steering* (by means of the tools and methods of a syntegral corporate policy). The terms used here, such as Chief Change Officer or CEO, etc., are functional designations because they represent task clusters, but they are also names of positions. This always involves the risk of seeing the old in the new, and of mentally falling back into old categories, in particular into the habit of associating things with people. Important as it may be to establish the right positions, what is crucial are the processes of exploring opinions, forming opinions, and forming wills. Top general management, or Master Control, is a process that needs structure but will unfold and take effect on its own over time.

True change is not achieved by renaming positions, even if they stand for ^REvolutionary new divisions of tasks. The key lies in the new forms of *collaboration* between these functions, or in other words, in a new way of *functioning*.[117]

The difference between *creating* a new work-sharing concept and making it *work* can be illustrated by the following anecdote on the "reorganization of the chess game". For over 20 years, this example has helped all of the participants in my seminars and workshops to understand and solve the problem. It illustrates the interplay between structure and function of decision-making processes.

I am assuming, dear reader, you have some knowledge of chess. On each side of the board, we have one player who plays chess in an integral manner – that is, based on a sound knowledge of the underlying rules and maintaining an overview of the current state and course of the game at all times – in other words, with real-time control in the best sense of the word.

A young business economist watches a game of chess. He notices the players' tension, nervousness, and stress, and also, how long it takes until each of them makes a move – obviously, he concludes, it is an inefficient and inhuman thing, and thus a case for reorganization. According to conventional wisdom, organizing means pooling what is equal, and getting a capable person to be the boss. In other words, all things to do with money belong in the finance department, all things to do with people belong in the human resources department, all things to do with computers are IT, and all things to do with customers are marketing, and so on.

So what are "equal things" in chess? All pawns are pooled and given a head of pawns. The same goes for castles; they may be a small department only but they seem to be important, so we need a head of castles. When it comes to the knights, the organizer hesitates – they seem to have very complex tasks and considerable importance. Put both under one management?

---

117 How this interaction can be organized in an effective and ^REvolutionary manner will be explained in Volume 4, which is dedicated to the subject of organization structure.

Or each of them separately? Due to cost considerations, place both under one management for the time being, and rethink it later. Now what about the bishops? They can make linear moves only – so they need only one boss. The king and queen, of course, need one manager each: both are so important that no costs are to be spared and the CEO personally manages the king.

A wonderful solution: less stress, more efficiency, although not right away, but as soon as the new solution sorts itself out and the specialization takes hold... Now the management team... well, it seems a little big. Seven people! Let's solve that problem by forming a management board of three, in charge of the king, the queen, and the knights. In addition, we will have four authorized signatories for the rest, which is fair enough in view of the complexity of the "business". As a result, we have an expanded management board staffed with seven people all in all. The signatories will attend the meetings flexibly, as needed.

At this point, however, a new problem arises: the problem of coordination. No problem – for there are proven, pragmatic solutions for that: every Monday we will hold board meetings – with or without the signatories attending, but usually including them, as otherwise there will be a lack of information. First, the head of pawns will hold a presentation on where he moved the pawns in the past weeks, and which of the opponent's pieces he has captured that way. He knows that the bishop manager is angry with him because he wanted to move a bishop exactly where he has placed a pawn. The head of bishops presents his situation and brings forward a motion to have the head of pawns remove his pawn by coming Wednesday at the latest, because he needs to move his bishop to that square to threaten the opponent's queen. There is strong objection from the head of knights, who sees a possibility to give check to the opponent's king within three moves, but for that he will need the castle and two pawns to support him... The discussion heats up, there are accusations and shouting.

The boss of the king proposes – on grounds of it being impossible to work like this – that there is an urgent need for training in conflict management and communication. In the course of the same meeting, the CEO delegates his tasks to the boss of the queen and announces that he will concentrate on strategy and public relations in the future...

For any 15-year-old playing on the opposing side of the same game, it will be a piece of cake to beat that team – even though or particularly if it consists of several grand masters – since it is impossible for the management team to collaborate successfully in this way. For this team would not only have to be structured as one – it would also have to work as one single brain to beat the 15-year-old.

Chess is a small "firm", 16 employees, one competitor of the same size; the player has a complete overview at all times, everyone knows what the competitor is currently doing. Chess has a complexity of only 10^{155} moves – a 10 with 155 zeros. Corporate management is by far more complex. Whatever approach we choose to organizing and reorganizing within the traditional paradigm, the complexity of the real, global, complexifying world will not manageable this way. That is only possible if we use the tools and methods of corporate and systems policy described in this book, namely, by achieving a joint understanding and communication by means of the models of the management system presented here – through the physical or virtual control or operations room as a coherent environment for decisions, and through the Master Controls of the three system-political concepts presented here. These are indispensable prerequisites for any well-functioning, complexity-compatible division of tasks at the top.

Chapter 7

Top Management Teams

It takes team work for top management to work out. The tasks at the top – whether in business or in the public sector – are so complex that individuals cannot by themselves perform them comprehensively and competently in the long run. The one-person top management either represents a risk to the organization, or it is a fiction.

To all appearances, there may be a person at the top, an impression which is additionally promoted by the term CEO. On closer inspection, however, it often turns out that - particularly in organizations where CEOs operate successfully - the work is actually done by a team. It is part of the core skills of truly outstanding CEOs that they are team builders, particularly under the difficult conditions prevailing at the top of the company.

Team is a word that is used quickly. Forming a team and making it work is difficult, though. This is particularly true for top management. Top managers are usually strong and hard-edged personalities, and nearly always distinct *individualists*. Therefore, in order for top teams to work out, it takes *three prerequisites* and *six rules*.

Three Prerequisites

The first prerequisite is obvious and generally finds consensus. The second is only partly accepted; the third is rejected by most, due to a widespread misconception. The three prerequisites are:

1. complete discipline,
2. putting personal relationships aside, and
3. absolutely disregarding the "chemistry" factor.

Firm adherence to agreed policies and principles is important for any team, not only in top management. There, however, teams must meet the absolute highest standards in terms of discipline. There is a clear *criterion* for the transition from a *group* to a *team*: it is the conscious renunciation of *group-dynamic* scuffles, which are replaced by an appropriate degree of (self-)discipline. There is generally consensus on this prerequisite.

The *second* prerequisite, *putting personal relationships aside,* is accepted not generally but by a majority of experienced executives. Personal relations, sympathies, friendships, and, in extreme cases, budding are not acceptable in the top team. Its work must be dominated by *fact-based relations*. It is therefore always advisable to members of top management bodies to keep an equal distance to all other members, for appearances can easily be clouded. Of course, it is not always possible (nor desirable) to avoid friendships. Incidentally, they often arise from collaboration that is so rigorously dominated by fact-based relationships that there arises a kind of mutual reliability that one might refer to as a safe support, or *friendship*. By contrast, what I am talking about here is, obviously, to steer clear of potential advantages through personal, informal relationships.

The *third* prerequisite – disregarding "chemistry" – regularly meets with much resistance. The reason lies in a misunderstanding that is easy to eliminate. Of course, the "chemistry" between people should be right. That makes things easier. However, the members of top teams usually cannot choose their team colleagues. Executive board members are nominated by the supervisory board, which, in turn, is elected by shareholders. And there are many other situations in which one is forced to work with people with whom is connected through organization relations but not through personal sympathy.

The prerequisite I am talking about here refers to cases where, for one reason or another, the chemistry is not right. It refers to such cases, and only those. A top management team must be capable of working together *nevertheless*. A top team must not function *because* of the "chemistry" but it has to be capable of constructive, fact-based collaboration *in spite of* the chemistry. If that is no longer possible, a replacement of team members is inevitable.

Six Rules

The foundations for the effective functioning of a top management team are simple, and just another example of Master Controls in the sense of cybernetic policy principles. These rules are independent of the actual organization structure, and they are independent of what kind of responsibility is required legally. For instance, the collective responsibility stipulated under German law does not say anything about how a management board actually works, which may not be the function of a law but is very important in practice.

Of course, observing six team rules in top management cannot guarantee the institution's success. It would be naïve to expect that; success requires much more. Disregarding the six rules, however, involves risks and is almost a guarantee of failure, because difficulties will then be hard to avoid.

To be functional and effective, a team must observe the following rules:[118]

1. Every member of a top management team has the last say in his or her sphere of responsibility. He speaks on behalf of the whole team, and his words create a commitment for it.

Each individual team member represents, in his area of responsibility, the authority of the entire executive body. This means that it is not admissible for members to refer to another member of the managing team, when an employee protests again his decision or that of another member of the top team. Everyone must abide by his own and the group's collective decisions. Otherwise, authority and trust would be at risk. For very special cases, the possibility of recourse to the overall body or its chairman may be established.

2. Nobody takes a decision in another area of responsibility.

Rule No. 2 is the counterpart to the first. The sphere of responsibility of each team member must be respected by all. Any violation of these first two rules creates confusion, paralyzes the ability to act, and leads to power struggles.

3. Outside the team there is no qualification of any one team member above others.

---

118 See also Drucker, Peter F., *Management*, London, 1973.

The members of a management team actually do not have to like each other. Notwithstanding, they must refrain from mutual judgment, both inside and outside the team, and above all, there must not be any kind of agitation.

4. A team is not a committee; it therefore needs a team leader with the right to a deciding vote.

Contrary to widespread opinion, a team is not a group of equals. Teams are about effectiveness, not democracy. Everyone is a member of the team because he or she has to make a distinct contribution. That is why functioning teams have an inner structure and a management.

The leader of a team must ensure that the team performs its tasks and obeys the rules for the team's functionality. In addition, he or she is the key person in situations where the team is paralyzing itself. For such cases the team leader needs to have the authority to overcome a stalemate situation.

In an ideal case, the team leader will never use his right to the deciding vote. If he has to use it often, it is a symptom of fundamental problems within the team.

In order for decisions to be taken, several formulas are possible and customary; for instance, decisions by simple majority, by qualified majority, or the principle of unanimity. For the top executive body *unanimity* seems preferable, although it has its disadvantages. In a case of crisis, however, the *decision-making ability* is most important.

Polling should be an exception in teamwork. The team leader must manage the team in such a way that there will be *consensus*. Consensus does not mean ostensible harmony, but true mutual consent based on insight and conviction. Decisions by general acclamation are always risky. The team manager therefore needs to be able to deal with *systematic dissent*. Sustainable consensus – the kind that will hold even through difficult phases of implementation – only arises from disagreement openly voiced.

If polling is necessary, however, because consensus cannot be reached, it is indispensable that the minority will back the majority decision and act loyally. Neither active nor passive opposition is admissible. Misbehavior of that kind, even if subtle and only insinuated, undermines the executive body's authority and effectiveness, If someone is definitely unable to back a decision, there is no other option than for that person to leave the organization.

5. Certain decisions must be left to the team as a whole.

The first rule says that every member of the team has the last say in his or her sphere of responsibility, that he speaks on behalf of the whole team, and that his words create a commitment for the team. This is an important rule for powerful and quick action. Taken alone, this rule could lead to abuse. It therefore requires corrective measures. Certain decisions must *not* be taken *alone by anyone*. They require *everybody's* consent. Typical cases include acquisitions or alliances, large-scale innovations, the establishing or closing down of whole lines of business, or staffing decisions for key positions.

These cases, which are reserved to team decisions, must be stipulated in the company bylaws. At the same time, there must be a general clause according to which *in cases of doubt* the team, not an individual member, has to make a decision. The supervisory body's rights of approval, or co-decision, remain unaffected in any case.

6. Each team member is obliged to keep the other members informed about what is going on in his or her area of responsibility.

This rule, too, is a corrective of rule No. 1. If there are *autonomous decisions* in each sphere of responsibility, there must also be *comprehensive information* to all other team members. The tools by which these things are regulated are the business assignment plan and the bylaws.

Chapter 8

Master Controls for Leadership

The subject of leadership has to be dealt with in several volumes of this book series, for it is just as important to *corporate policy* as it is to *corporate culture* and *executives*, albeit with different accents and from different perspectives. This is a result of the network nature of a management system that works. Such a system is not a lexicographic classifier of subjects, but an organizer of solution-oriented knowledge.

In this volume, the subject of leadership must be covered because it is what the expansion of *Master Controls* in an evolving system depends on. In short: the more true leaders a system has, the better its self-organization will work. In chapter 2 I have pointed out that corporate policy enables a new and much-neglected approach to leadership. At this point I want to come back to this thought. The rationale is that, contrary to what is often said, leadership is mainly, or even exclusively, owed to *personal* qualities. There are *four other reasons* why a person is considered a leader, and has the effect that we call leadership. Before I list them, let me repeat that I clearly distinguish between the so-called *great* and the *true* leaders.

1. The first reason for true leadership is the ability to practice the *right policy*, for wrong policies lead to mis-leadership, in particular if paired with the much-demanded charisma.
2. The second reason is the ability to put the organization into the operational mode that is right at the time. This requires clear perspective and assessment of the situation, as well as personal courage.
3. The third reason is the ability to select the *right* issues and make sure they are tackled in the right way. That is issue leadership, and this is where what we call *having a nose for things* truly shows.
4. The fourth reason is rules or principles which guide the person's actions, and thus the implementation of policies.

What Distinguishes Leaders

The effect ascribed to leadership is desirable for any key position, not only at the top of the company. Armies have realized this early on, and tried to teach leadership qualities in their educational facilities for senior staff. The mission statement of the West Point Military Academy is: "*We educate leaders who deserve trust*".

My approach to leadership deviates from the current mainstream thinking which I have commented on critically in various publications. According to general perception, leadership is tied to an *outstanding, charismatic personality*. There is no denying that there are people with charisma who make a great impression on others. But first of all, they do not exist in sufficient numbers; secondly, the outcome of their actions is not always desirable; thirdly, this type of personality is not required for leadership, as we know from numerous historical examples. In those instances, however, where charisma meets with the necessary skills and responsibility, the outcome will doubtlessly be truly great works and deeds.

Leadership is also a matter of the right rules, not only the personality. Leadership in an organization, in the sense of Master Control, can be activated and cultivated by establishing the right rules. Of equal importance are clarity on leadership and a knowledge of its rules, thus preventing misunderstandings arising from the general discussion.

In actual fact, there are *no* commonalities in the *characteristics* of people typically considered to be leaders. A closer look at the relevant biographies will clearly reveal this. Some leaders are highly intelligent, others rather average. Some are "nice people", easy-going and open-minded; others are inaccessible, reserved, and awkward people, characterized by strict discipline and even asceticism. Some are daredevils and "macho" types; others are cultivated, noble and low-key. Some love luxury and show, others cannot stand it. Some are rather impulsive and spontaneous; others tend to study everything thoroughly, and have to go through periods of brooding and serious doubt in order to reach a decision. Some seek contact with people and keep an open office or house, while others do not feel at ease in a group, preferring solitude and privacy.

As individuals, leaders are as different as human beings can be. What they have in common is a *certain kind of behavior*. It can be studied, and certain *Master Controls of leadership* can be derived from it.

Leadership Arises – From a Situation

Leadership is not absolute but relative, depending on the *situation*, and it can only be understood and explained based on a given situation. The same person can prove to be an outstanding leader in one situation, and a rather poor one in the next. Leadership does not spring from the person alone, possibly even to a very small extent. For instance, it was the special situation of World War II that turned Winston Churchill and Franklin Dr. Roosevelt into leaders, which they were according to most experts. Churchill was well aware of it, due to his historical knowledge.

It is the situation and the specific action in this situation that generates leadership. Without the situation, the action referred to as *leadership* would be neither necessary nor possible, nor would it make any sense. It is the situation – usually a crisis – which separates mere show from substance.

Without the test of a special situation, any judgment with regard to people's leadership capabilities ought to be withheld. The risk of misjudgments is substantial, as is the risk of wrong human resource decisions.

In order to find the secret of leadership, one needs to ask: what was it, of or in that special situation the person was in, that made him a leader – or better even: that let him become one?

Master Controls for True Leadership

The foundation of good management is *craftsmanship* – that is, *skills* that can be taught and learnt. The basis of that is *knowledge and experience*. Even leaders cannot do without the practical basis for right management, and there is no organization that works without that basis.

True leaders, however, do *not stand still*. They go a few small but important steps *further*. They have outstanding command of some things – not because of innate abilities (although that can be the case, which enables them to deal with things much more easily than other people) but because they know and sense that, as the ordinary human beings that they ultimately are, have limited ways of mobilizing human strengths. They therefore concentrate on the essential things, and consistently work on the crucial elements of effective management. From their actions we can learn the principles and rules that guide them. These rules can be learnt, they can provide an orientation, and they can be applied.

For the following, let me again emphasize the distinction between *great* and *true* leaders, in order to prevent misunderstandings. There are people considered *great* leaders who, upon closer inspection, cannot be referred to as true leaders. On the other hand there are people whom nobody would consider *great*, but who were or are *true* leaders nevertheless. Wars, natural disasters, and traffic jams provide more than enough examples for how people demonstrate true leadership without being celebrated as "historically great leaders".

True Leaders Focus on the Task

True leaders do not go by their personal needs. The key question they ask is not: *what do I want, what convenient for me?* Rather, it is: *what has to be done in this situation, for the best of everyone involved?* The immediate return usually does not matter to them. They do not pay much attention to the reward, least of all a monetary one. They feel an obligation to do what needs to be done.

This obligation can even come to the point of obsession, and blocking out all other things. The driving force, however, is the *task* at hand, rather than the fulfillment of personal needs. In other words, these people's most urgent need is their task. Quite often they will put aside their personal needs, and take on substantial sacrifices and surrender – which often meets with a lack of comprehension by those around them.

They are not interested in the usual motivators, least of all in the constant talk about motivation. Their motivation and their strength result from the task and the achievements involved. *They are working for a cause...* A task solved well is enough satisfaction to them, at very least – often it is the ultimate satisfaction.

True Leaders Force Themselves to Listen

The emphasis is on "forcing themselves" because nobody will find that easy to do at all times. Many leaders are impatient because they know the importance of being fast, and because they are deeply convinced they are acting the right way.

Above all, however, they know how important the information is that they can only obtain from *others*, in particular from the roots of their organization. Over and over again, they muster the will and self-discipline to listen – not least because they know that otherwise they would lose their people's *trust*. That does not necessarily mean they listen for *long*. They usually have little time available, but during that time they listen attentively, as those around them will notice.

True Leaders Tirelessly Work on Making Themselves Understood

They are aware of the fact that what is clear to *them* – their views, *their own* imagination – is *not necessarily evident* to others, and often cannot be. This is why they *repeat* the messages they consider important, again and again, with patience and persistence.

In their endeavor to make themselves understood, they make sure they use simple, comprehensible language and the terminology of their target groups. They also use metaphors. Occasionally they oversimplify, because they know that complicated things cannot be understood, and thus cannot become effective, or will even become counterproductive.

To be understood, they use the best means of communication wherever possible: *they demonstrate how things are done*. They act in the way they expect others to act. Every leader has learnt from experience, one way or another, that he can ultimately only lead *by setting a personal example*. Leaders must follow the rules they want to see implemented. They may take privileges in other areas, but they must observe the basic rules, as otherwise they lose *credibility*. Once they violate this principle, it will be the start of the erosion of their leadership position.

True Leaders Do Without Alibis and Excuses

A true leader is interested in *results*. When they are not achieved he will not resort to lame excuses. This is a good point for establishing where persons in history have failed. Their leadership positions started showing the first cracks when they began to operate with alibis and excuses, or with scapegoats and conspiracy theories.

That may work for a while, but it carries the seed of failure, of losing credibility and power of conviction. In concrete situations it may have taken longer until the failure was fully evident. Still, it usually begins when the leader is *no longer authentic* and *no longer honest* in that respect. Many kinds of gamesmanship may be tolerated, or even admired as a sign of particular intelligence and smartness – but not if someone tricks with regard to results.

True Leaders Accept Their Own Meaninglessness Relative to the Task

Note that this rule says "relative to the task" – not "relative to other people". This is a point of frequent misunderstandings. Leaders are well aware of their importance, and they let others feel it, too.

Even though there may be *personality cults* around good leaders, often demanded by those around them and against their will, they *subordinate* themselves to the task, which they always consider greater and more important than themselves. This is the only way to maintain sufficient *objectivity* for a clear assessment of the situation, despite and because of the uniqueness of a leadership situation. They *accept* the task in all its significance, but they do not *identify* with it. The task always remains something to be distinguished from themselves; they always separate it clearly from themselves as individuals. This is a point where many historical leaders have failed. Once the „*L' état c'est moi*" attitude took center stage, this may have initiated a particularly *glamorous period for the* person in question, but in most cases it was also the *beginning of the end of leadership*.

There is yet another point that is more important than the aspect previously outlined: the acceptance of meaninglessness of one's own person, relative to the task, enables true leaders to muster *courage and stand up for their convictions* where it matters – in those moments when they have to choose between the significance of their task *on the one hand*, and their own career on *the other*. In case of doubt they will sacrifice their careers for the cause. That is what gets them the *respect* of others. It is one substantial source of their *power of conviction*. Those around them see that they are not primarily interested in their own concerns but in the good of the cause – and to such an extent that they risk their own personal failure to serve that cause. There is not much more that a person can put at stake. When he does that, it is a very clear signal to others that he *means* what he says. Hence it is the ultimate proof of *personal integrity*.

True Leaders Do Not Steal Their People's Achievements

Despite all the achievements they may have, and all their conviction that they could do many things better than others, true leaders do not adorn themselves with borrowed plumes. They think in terms of "we" rather than "I". They know what their people and their organization accomplish, and they *acknowledge* it. Success in a *matter* is more important to them than *their* success as an individual.

True Leaders Are Not Afraid of Strong People

This applies in both directions: vis-à-vis superiors and subordinates. True leaders know that it takes the *best people* to fulfill the great tasks of the organization. Hence they do anything to *attract and develop* the best people and *bring them to good use*. They may counter any attempts to question their *authority* with rigor and even brutality. But they will not eliminate strong people out of fear for their own position.

Anyone gathering *weaklings, minions, and yes-men* around him displays *poor* leadership, and it usually shows at an early stage. True and strong leaders are allergic to sycophants. They want honest and controversial opinions, although they might respond with annoyance and gruffness. The point is that they consider differing views and criticism as valuable information.

Not that leaders *like* to hear criticism. Quite the opposite is usually the case, as with most people. It is therefore quite probable that a leader will respond gruffly to criticism. Still – and this is what matters – a *weak* leader will ignore criticism, and even suppress it by muzzling those who uttered it. *True* leaders, however, make sure they learn about critical opinions – no matter how they feel about them. They *take notice*, which does not mean they always accept it.

True Leaders Do Not Have to Be Inspiring Individuals

A consistent demand in literature and discussion is that leaders must be *inspiring* people, people instilling *enthusiasm* in others. In my opinion this is more than a fallacy – in truly critical leadership situations, enthusiasm is actually an *obstacle*.

Anyone demanding of leaders the ability to enthuse others obviously has in mind the *positive* and *easy* leadership situations. True leadership is only necessary and called for when it comes to dealing with *difficult* situations requiring serious sacrifices – sacrifices which, although they are clearly right, meet with resistance – or in other words, when far-reaching and unpopular decisions have to be made. Anything that people *can* be excited about does not require true leadership; usually, rhetoric and showmanship will suffice.

Leaders may have to take *tough* decisions, and demand superhuman commitment of people. In situations like those, they need to be *convincing* – but enthusiasm would nearly always be counterproductive. Churchill knew that.

Typical cases in point are military retreat orders after lost combats when troops have been decimated, or situations where corporate managements are forced to lay off tens of thousands of people. Only cynics and sadists could muster enthusiasm for such measures, or attempt to enthuse others. It is the most depressing things in an organization that require truly difficult leadership decisions. Nobody takes such decisions with enthusiasm, and if he did, he would immediately lose the trust and loyalty of his people. They might bow to his factual power – but not follow his "leadership".

True Leaders Are Not Dreamers

They may have a vision – or better even, a *mission* – but they are not out to create heaven on earth. Rather, they concentrate on avoiding hell. True leaders are *realists* with regard to *human nature* and they make an effort to learn from history.

They know that, despite all the fascinating, utopian philosophies, it is impossible to create the New Man – all we can do is alleviate the misery in the world, step by step and very moderately. In their public relations work, they might operate with a *touch of utopia*, as they know about people's fascination with such concepts. In their *actions*, however, they go by what they know about the risks of each intervention in a complex social structure, and about the unintentional side-effects of even the most well-meant changes. They know it is *impossible* to make utopia come true.

True Leaders Are Neither Born Nor Made That Way

If they are neither born nor made to be leaders, what are they? They are nearly always *self*-made, and the way to do that is always the same: there are *four* elements that are important:

- It starts with the situation a person is in. It may be a historically significant situation which historiography will point out later. It may also be an everyday situation that will never be mentioned by historians. It is a matter of coincidence, for hardly anyone can choose the situation that provides a chance – or liability – to prove true leadership.
- It is in such a situation that they recognize the crucial task that is critical for changing the situation. It can be a crisis that is coped with, or an opportunity that is exploited. That is where the much-cited vision may be relevant. In the majority of cases, however, it is not a transcendental or creative spark that brings a vision to life, but simple - though careful and conscientious - thinking through the options and priorities.
- They face up to the task without hesitation. The situation and the task may be as significant historically as those that Churchill faced after years of leading an insignificant back-bench existence as a member of parliament. It may be as mundane as the task of a mother who cares for her sick child night after night until the crisis is overcome. In both case we have all elements of true leadership. The value that historians attribute to both situations may be different. Their valuation by those involved is always the same, as we know from Viktor Frankl.
- They take responsibility for a crucial task. It reminds me of a very expressive statement by the American post-war president Harry S. Truman. *"I am president now, and the buck stops here..."* What he wanted to express was that it was up to him to fulfill the task and take the decision – and he could not delegate it to anyone.

Charisma?

The term *charisma* has become an ordinary, much-used word, and charisma trainings are offered everywhere. But what does charisma really mean? Here is what the encyclopedias tell us:

"sociological term: natural gift for a specific service, in particular for taking over a leadership role and a resulting irrational dominance." "Translated from *Meyers Handlexikon*"

"Charismatic leadership based on the belief in the extraordinary qualities of a personality ('leader and follower' type)"

"Greek: God-given gift, an uncommon, presumably supernatural quality of a person, based on which that person is considered superhuman, God-sent, exemplary, and therefore an authority or leadership personality."

»Charisma, the special quality attributed to persons due to skills or strengths assumed to be uncommon, outstanding, and inaccessible to other people, or due to presumed connections to supernatural, possibly even destiny-shaping forces, and due to which they are perceived to be exceptionally gifted and predestined in particular for leadership roles. Research findings from modern social psychology are not able to prove, however, that there are "natural born" leaders who, independently of a given group structure and of the expectations of those being led, can take their positions in a group, clan, or people." (These three quotes have been translated from: Brockhaus, multimedial, 2006).

Field Marshal Montgomery was one of the most outstanding and charismatic military leaders of the Second World War, and it was due to this very charisma that Churchill did *not* choose him over General Eisenhower, although this decision cost Churchill his reelection. As a young lieutenant in British India, Montgomery had gotten the following evaluation from his superior: *„People will follow Lieutenant Montgomery wherever he will go. But I suspect it will be out of curiosity and not out of confidence."*

Montgomery was a daredevil, a hero, who would storm ahead of his troops "with his sabre drawn". Something like that has an effect on people, it interests them – and they will follow like lemmings. But they do it reflexively and out of curiosity, not because they trust him. Leaders like that have a *crowd of followers* because "something is happening there". True leaders have a *following* because people trust them. They lead by self-discipline and by example, not by grand slogans and shouts of hurrah. Their capital is not charisma but trust.

The crucial point is not *whether* we are led, but *where*. It is not the departure that matters but the arrival, not the intention but the outcome. Charismatic leaders are a risk when they do not carry true leadership within themselves. They are incalculable. They pursue utopias they believe in. Historically, charismatic people often were not *leaders* but *misleaders*.

Chapter 9

Heuristics for Winners:
The Logic of Succeeding

The Bamberg psychologist Dietrich Dörner has done unrivalled research into the *logic of failure,* and pointed the way to a *logic of succeeding* – an expression I first encountered in the writings of Maria Pruckner.

It was not under that nice-sounding title but referring to the same content that, in the years from 1976 to 1978, I assembled for my habilitation treatise a collection of classical principles and rules for mastering complexity. Over hundreds and thousands of years they had proved their worth for orientation, decision-making and management in conditions of great uncertainty. Here, now, is a small selection that is relevant for this book and the top management level. For more information in greater detail, I refer readers to my book *Strategie des Managements komplexer Systems* ["Strategy of the Management of Complex Systems"].

In the technical terminology, these rules are referred to as *heuristics.* They are rules of a particular kind that have to be distinguished from rules of another type that are called *algorithms.* In games, for example, there are the rules of the game that have to be observed if the game is going to be played at all. This kind of rules includes algorithms. They define the game as such; for instance, chess is defined by the rules of chess. These are algorithms because it is precisely specified what further moves are permitted at any given point in time, i.e. what moves are *legitimate in chess.* And while it is possible to *play* chess with rules of this kind, they are no guarantee for winning. Clearly, professional chess players master the chess algorithms, but apart from these, they also know some entirely different rules: those that enable them most certainly to *win.* Rules that are followed to master a situation and to influence the likelihood of winning are *heuristics.*

At the beginning of this book, in the context of distinguishing between the subject and the system level, I mentioned Mihail Botvinnik, the Russian world champion of chess from 1948 to 1963, and his studies about the system rules of winning in chess. One of his findings is the rule: "Keep the knights concentrated in the center" – for what purpose and what reason is impossible to predict. Doing so is the only thing that is rational in a situation where it is not possible to have more information. Is it naïve? Is it trite? Only to a person who assumes a situation where he can know more than that, given the complexity of chess, some 10^{155} moves are possible. Corporate management in the global economy is far more complex than chess...

The principles that are presented below are classic strategic principles for mastering complex situations. Many of them are as old as the hills. They are often misunderstood as strategies for acquiring and retaining power. But in fact, they do not have very much to do with power. Their actual nature is to provide direction and orientation in complex circumstances, about which not enough is or can be known, but in which one has to prove oneself nevertheless.[119]

Power is not the precondition but the result of a professional approach to dealing with complexity. On the basis of these heuristics, one may well reflect that where great power appears to hold sway is often the very place where there is great impotence, and vice versa. If one is not aware of this fact, many of the principles given here seem to be horribly wrong. However, precisely in the case of the principles mentioned above it will show that, along with their ethical implications, they are also the most important ones. Only they are not sufficient, unfortunately, because mankind does not consist solely of saints.

The following principles have not originated from cybernetics, although some are identical to cybernetic ones in substance. As was mentioned before, these principles are much older than cybernetics as a science, but they are cybernetic because they provide control even where other means fail.

---

119 See, inter alia, Feldmann, Josef, „Nachrichten – wie man sie gebraucht und missbraucht" in: Krieg, Walter/Galler, Klaus/Stadelmann, Peter (Hrsg.), *Richtiges und gutes Management: vom System zur Praxis*, Berne/Stuttgart/Vienna, 2004.

Principles for Assessing the Situation

Principle of Meta-Systemic Assessment of the Situation

This principle relates to what has been discussed in the introduction to this book: the careful and conscious distinction between subject and system matters. Otherwise there is a risk of inconsiderately diverting to the object level when assessing situations for system-related matters. The consequences have been outlined. One will end up in the midst of a wealth of details, and lose one's bearings. Anyone losing track of coherences will find it hard to find simple and effective solutions for self-control.

Typical problems that arise when system-related issues are confused with subject-related ones, or the former turn into the latter, include those associated with the leadership and technical qualifications required. Will the best scientist of a university also be the most capable candidate for president? Even if that is the case: will it be good for the university to appoint him president? Questions like these cannot be resolved at the object level, but only at the system level. How many highly qualified scientists will this professor attract to the university? What funds can he acquire based on his reputation? What would be the consequence if his presidency affected the level and quality of performance at his institute? These are the relevant system-related considerations. What and how many papers this scientist has published, how highly his international reputation must be valued, how often and by whom he is quoted and how often he appears in the media--all these are subject-related questions which could be discussed without end, but would not help to find out whether he is a good candidate for the president's position.

Principle of Making a Rounded Assessment of the Situation

The principle of making a rounded assessment of the situation relates to the problem of the selective nature of perception, and is closely connected to the first principle. When systems are hyper-complex, the nature of what is being dealt with implies that it is never possible to have complete knowledge of them. This is the very reason why this principle is important.

On the one hand, it serves as a constant reminder of the fact of our inevitable not-knowing. Even more importantly, the principle of making a rounded assessment of the situation particularly calls for a situation to be assessed *not only from one's own point of view* but also from the perspective of other parties that are involved or affected. It is not enough just to consider how one assesses a situation oneself. Thought must also be given to how others might view, appraise and deal with the circumstances. It is, therefore, necessary to reflect on all the parties to a relationship, as well as on the relationships themselves. This includes how one is seen by the other parties and what they think of one. *How do we think the competitor/opponent might view the actions we take? How do we think the competitor might think that we see him? How do we think that the competitor might think that we think that he sees us?* These are the typical questions that are posed in this case. Their relevance to winning in the competitive struggle is obvious. Rounded information about a situation needs to be gathered, but if this requirement is abandoned and the situation is seen only from a self-centered point of view, this will cause blindness to reality.

Because their conception of the world is outdated, many people tend to think in terms of *causal relationships*. No matter what happens, their first reaction, and often their only one, is to look for a *cause*. In social relationships, this generally means looking for a *culprit*. However, in complex circumstances, events can hardly ever be understood or explained by thinking in terms of single causes. There are always entire complexes of factors that act. This is something that has to be remembered whenever a situation is being assessed. Otherwise, one runs the risk of making totally incorrect appraisals.

This is seen particularly in the cases where simple cause-and-effect thinking leads to the different various types of usual suspects and conspiracy theories. It reassures many people to have just any explanation, no matter what it may be, for something; the main thing is they have one. This attitude, however, makes it impossible for situations to be assessed correctly, especially when it is manifested en masse by groups, thus leading to the phenomenon of "group think", a phenomenon that has been thoroughly researched but is, nevertheless, repeatedly and noticeably apparent at the highest levels and then leads to disaster.[120]

---

120 Historical cases have been described by Barbara Tuchman in *The March of Folly. From Troy to Vietnam.* What inevitably comes to mind is 9/11, Al Quaida, the War against Terror, Iraq, and numerous further examples of a similar kind. People will have to learn to appreciate the heuristics dealt with here.

Principle of the Open System

The principle of the open system calls attention to the fact that is must be considered that unpredictable developments must always be reckoned with in complex and thus dynamic systems. This fact must be part of every situation assessment.

The openness of a system, in system theory, means that systems being imbedded in larger systems, or their environment, are in a constant exchange of matter, energy, and information, and that the relevant variables of a system change. Here, steady change is at work, bringing new, unexpected and unimaginable developments. In clinics, for instance, people have long been prepared for this – but not in business.

Principle of Strengths Against Weaknesses

The principle of strengths against weaknesses requires that any assessment of a situation must be based on the relative strengths and weaknesses of the respective parties in relationships. Any actions taken to influence the situation must likewise follow this principle. Here, too, it is a question of making a realistic estimate of relative strengths.

One important principle is, amongst others, never to think of the other side as being more stupid than one's own side or oneself. The effect of any such disdain is all the more significant the more difficult it is to appraise the other side. It is all the more helpful, however, to be viewed by the other side as being more stupid, or weaker in some other way, than one actually is. On the one hand, it is an invitation to check whether one does in fact have such deficiencies of strength, on the other it provides information as to what possibilities the other side has of assessing the situation realistically and where the limits are. This circumstance is just as helpful in competitive situations as it is in cooperative ones. In the former case it is necessary to arm oneself accordingly; in the latter case one knows where it is necessary to provide information.

Principle of Selecting Ambiguous Goals

The principle of selecting ambiguous goals implies that, when selecting interventions, the actions selected need be those that – like a missile with multiple warheads, as it were – have the potential to aim at several goals or targets at the same time. It increases the diversity of the effect by exploiting complexity. When multiple goals are selected, it becomes difficult for the other side to get a clear picture of one's own strategy.

Principle of Avoiding Being Influenced by Biased Information

This principle reminds one to protect oneself against misleading hints when assessing a situation. It guards against the risks posed by naive staff work done by inexperienced people who, though they may collect data meticulously using what appear to be scientific methods, give no thought to the nature or source of the data.

Under this principle the assessment of the situation should be as realistic as possible, which requires taking into account that, both in everyday human relationships and in competitive relationships, all kinds of deceptive tactics and smoke-screening and camouflaging maneuvers – even extending to all the sorts of disinformation put about by secret services – are among the facts of life of and in complex systems. At the same time, the principle also relates to protecting oneself against being influenced by false doctrines and outdated and unsuitable theories; that is to say, against "flat-world" thinking in a "spherical world" reality.

Principles for the Ability to Direct and Relate

The Principle of Flexibility

The principle of flexibility requires that one avoid making hard and fast stipulations and firm commitments when these are *not necessary*, or *are not necessary yet*. In brief, the principle goes like this: keep your freedom of action and do not commit yourself until you absolutely have to. Its purpose is to allow one to leave room for future developments and to enable one to react as flexibly as possible to unforeseeable events and to ones that prove unfavorable as things develop. By tying oneself down at the outset, this flexibility is needlessly lost. This must be avoided.

The Principle of Providing for the Future

This principle refers to the necessity of checking strategic actions for their potential future impact, and of ascertaining whether the necessary resources exist, or could be created, for the scenarios that might occur. An important fixed point is to take on risks only to the extent that, even in the case of severe losses, one retains the possibility to master any situation.

From a practical standpoint, this principle means, for instance, that it is not enough to develop annual budgets but that the actual budget development has to not only be monitored but to be realistically anticipated as far as possible. That, in turn, means that the objective cannot be to spend the entire amounts budgeted, as is often done especially in the public sector, because public annual budgets are usually based on the previous year's figures. The goal must be to use up no more than what is required, because it is never entirely certain what resources will be available and gained in the future.

Principle of Reversibility

The principle of reversibility demands, in all cases, considering whether and under what conditions a decision or a step can be reversed and what the result of doing so will be.

It is clear that it is not always possible to avoid making irreversible decisions. Strategically speaking, however, it is important to get a clear picture of the context in which it is possible to make irreversible decisions, and the context in which it is possible to make reversible ones. Reversible decisions can be made differently and, above all, more quickly than irreversible ones, for which one should take enough time to think them through carefully and reflect on them in advance.

Principle of Taking Small Steps

The principle of taking small steps implies that thought be given at each step as to what intermediate results resulting from that step can be achieved. These intermediate results should be taken into account before the next strategic step is taken. The more complex a situation is, the more important is this principle.

In simple terms, the principle could be: "Do not take the next step until you have seen the effect of the previous one." It is only then that you can judge whether the second step that is planned is in fact the right one. The more far-reaching a step is – and new policies, for example, are far-reaching steps – the more helpful is this principle.

Making the next step only after the effect of the first has been seen, and carefully assessing the results obtained, provides information on system compatibilities that are necessary in order to make the right second step.

This is why major reforms, for instance, cannot be carried out all in one go, but only after having evaluated the small steps, which have to be based on a careful, systemic-cybernetic layout. Hence, this is not about the steps being small, but about their having a system-regulating effect which permits and facilitates the subsequent step. This way, misguided developments can be avoided, which may not be reversible after the fact.

Many reforms and change projects fail because this principle is not heeded. There is often a lack of any deliberate point-of-*return* management. When this is the case, it is often found, to everyone's surprise, that the point of *no return* has long been passed and nobody noticed.

Principle of Keeping the Initiative

The principle of keeping the initiative means that the attempt should always be made to determine, or at least to play a part in determining, the course of action oneself, in order not to find one's hand being forced. This means always staying on the offensive as far as possible, and not losing the prerogative of acting.

It is precisely in unclear and impenetrable situations that there is always an opportunity to go on the offensive, if one asks oneself: "What can I do to find out what I am facing here?" This will often reveal a way that protects one from being on the defensive. It is important to distinguish between whether one *cannot* do anything, or one *deliberately* does not do anything obvious.

Principle of Occupying Sanction Centers

Sanctions, in the sense of reward or punishment, or approval or rejection, are known and distinctive approaches to control. This principle means that one has to try occupying existing or recognizable centers of potential sanctions, in order to maximise the number of one's control options.

Principle of Reward Motivation

This principle aims at establishing relationships which are significant for the *self*-control of complex systems. Providing rewards are clearly more effective for self-regulation than are punishments, as the unit to be controlled willingly renders the required performance out of an interest in the reward, while the prospect of punishment will tend to motivate people to avoid necessary but risky action.

Principle of Monitoring All Options

This principle refers to the fact that the optimal way of dealing with complexity requires achieving and constantly maintaining an overview all available options for decision and behavior. That means that one must constantly look out for new options that exist, or may exist, in addition to those already known.

In complex systems, it easily happens that seemingly paradoxical situations and hopeless dilemmas occur – in particular if one's perspective is restricted to the level of individual subject matters. One of the most frequent phenomena, for instance, is a communication failure referred to as *double bind*. It means that someone receives two conflicting messages with regard to the same matter, along the lines of "washing the fur without wetting it". At the object level, demands like this cannot be fulfilled. The only possibility is to choose between the two wrong options – washing the fur or leaving it dry.

This double bind is a typical symptom in the *complexity trap*.[121] In situations of stress, performance pressure or burden of responsibility, double

---

121 Pruckner, Maria, *Die Komplexitätsfalle. Wie sich Komplexität auf den Men-*

binds occur with particular frequency and concentration. That includes people who have difficulties making decisions and who dread responsibility. Often, double bind messages are uttered not intentionally but driven by fear, in an effort to avoid the responsibility of an unambiguous decision. In other cases, they occur due to sheer bad luck – as a result of rushed replies, decisions, or "solutions" which are taken without due consideration to get a matter off the table.

The rules and regulations of corporate policies that are non-systematic, and which have not been developed according to systemic-cybernetic principles, often lead to numerous double binds – stipulations that contradict each other to the extent that neither one can be met without violating the other.

Double binds are perceived as particularly straining by the weaker parts in asymmetric dependency relationships, because that part is forced to comply with the stronger part's demands for existential reasons – such as employees vis-à-vis their superiors, children vis-à-vis their parents and teachers, citizens vis-à-vis the state, and so on. In these constellations, double blinds are often perceived as a state of being hopelessly exposed to the others' arbitrariness. It is as though one had the choice between jumping off the roof of a burning high-rise building or dying in the fire.

Dilemmas of this kind can only be solved form a meta-systemic point of view. People have to look from an eagle's perspective, so to speak, surveying the overall situation in the system, in order to look for further options from that vantage. In the case of the fur that is supposed to be washed without wetting it, a possible alternative could be brushing it clean.

A perfect imperative for pursuing this principle in a sensible way has been formulated by the great cybernetics pioneer Heinz von Foerster: *always act so as to increase the number of choices.*

Principle of the Golden Bridge

The principle of the golden bridge means that influencing measures should never be designed in such a way that the unit to be directed is maneuvered into a hopeless situation. When dealing with individuals, for instance, this

---

schen auswirkt – vom Informationsmangel bis zum Zusammenbruch. Norderstedt, 2005.

is about avoiding any loss of face, maintaining at least an ultimate basis for discussion, and the like, so as to be able, sooner or later, to reestablish a relationship suitable for effective control. The imperative *always make sure a possibility for discussion is maintained*, which is also by Heinz von Foerster, expresses this principle.

Principle of Proximity to Information

Principles for Influencing the Supply of Information

This principle requires making all information paths as short and direct as possible and keeping them that way, in order to avoid distortions, unintentional and uncontrolled filter effects and things like that. It is one of the fundamental principles of applied cybernetics.

The basic rule is: the closer the transfer of relevant information is to real time, the better the possibilities to steer and regulate in a complex system. With his method of Syntegration and his Viable System Model, both integral parts of the *Malik Management System*, Stafford Beer has fulfilled this principle with mathematical precision.

This principle also demonstrates the enormous importance of system-compatible corporate policy. Policies along these lines fulfill the requirements for necessary real-time information everywhere and any time, no matter where management bodies are at the moment in question and whether they can or cannot be reached.

Principle of Explaining One's Actions

This principle contains a warning to keep thinking, in all strategic actions, about how they could be (mis-) understood and (mis-) interpreted by other parties or systems not directly involved.

For the widely known problem of communication alone, there will always have to be strategic situations in which one needs to take care to avoid misunderstandings and misinterpretations. It is done by declaring one's intentions in an unambiguous way. The aim is to build trust by making situations that are incalculable by nature predictable and calculable through declarations of intention; for instance, by stating something along the lines of "*When such and such happens, I will…*". The precondition is that such declarations are complied with afterwards. Otherwise, the results are a loss of authority, and the creation or increase of distrust.

Principle of Concealing

A polar opposite of the principle above, this one refers to all those situations in which it is more advisable to keep certain actions concealed, in order to retain information which is thought of as leading to counterproductive responses and unwanted dynamics. For instance, if the risk of misunderstanding is too high or the matter requires too much explaining.

Principle of Evaluation

The principle of evaluation means considering in advance what information can be used to test the effectiveness of actions of control and regulation, and how to create situations where an evaluation is possible.

In particular when it comes to normative and strategic management, it is likely that the levels below will lack insight into the dimensions of thinking and decision-making that prevail at the senior or management level. For instance, the formulation of a policy is no guarantee for its being understood and complied with correctly. This is why training courses are required. But even these do not guarantee that policies will be complied with. When people distrust them, and doubt that they make any sense, they will not adhere to them unquestioningly, and may even try to undermine them. Evaluation helps ascertain whether sensible policies are being formulated in a sensible way, and communicated and implemented effectively.

In highway traffic, there are median and side strips and traffic signs indicating to motorists whether they are on the right track and heading in the right direction. No matter whether we deal with social or technical systems, this principle is about providing the landmarks that will enable people to perceive early on, and at all times, whether the steps being taken will serve the intended purpose and lead to the goal pursued, and what will be the likely outcome.

Principles for the Power of Conviction

Principle of Reliability

The principle of reliability requires that obligations, once accepted, are actually met. It is the key condition for safeguarding one's power of conviction, future credibility, reputation, and personal authority. This, in turn, reinforces the system's security since its directing unit is perceived to be reliable.

Principle of Constancy

The principle of constancy relates to the consistency with which one adheres to one's own strategies, plans and principles. There are few things that undermine one's personal credibility more quickly and effectively than renouncing intentions that have previously been announced. Something to be borne in mind here, however, is that one may be pinned down to principles by people who have not understood them, do not want to understand them, or are interpreting them in their favor.

This principle has nothing to do with pedantry or stubbornness. What it means is that one should only announce intentions that one is in fact willing and able to carry out. Announcing things that *cannot* be implemented is ineffective and counterproductive.

It makes perfect sense, however, to refrain from making decisions or adopting attitudes where there is not yet compelling evidence or logic. In that case, however, one should always give appropriate reasons, so as not to lose any of one's potential for direction and control.

Principle of the Rare Bluff

This principle refers to situations in which it is unavoidable to take covert action. It requires, if at all, operating with a very cleverly devised bluff and using it only in rare cases where there is no alternative. The last principle below explains why.

Principle of the Concealed Avenue of Retreat

The purpose of the principle of the concealed avenue of retreat is to take precautions so as to be able to retreat without any damage or loss of face, as far as this is possible, in case anything goes wrong. Note, however, that if you decide to use that tool you must be aware that there is nothing more detrimental or embarrassing than having one's bluff called. Consequently, under this principle you need to think in advance about how you are going to get out of such a situation while saving face.

As a general rule, in complex systems it is always necessary to be prepared for surprises. You should never assume that things will develop as planned and expected. It is therefore important to give some general thought as to how you will get out of a situation while limiting the damage or even creating advantages. Hence, it should be part of any strategic action to consider what is happening and what might happen, and what to do if the situation develops differently from what was expected.

As mentioned at the beginning, the principles laid out here are a selection. They help managers maintain an overview where others have long gone astray in the maze of complex systems.[122]

---

122 A larger collection of heuristics can be found in my habilitation treatise *Strategie des Managements komplexer Systeme*.

Epilogue

To conclude my remarks on corporate policy and governance for the age of complexity based on the laws of nature, may I once again remind the reader of Hans Ulrich's definition of corporate policy: *Corporate policy is*

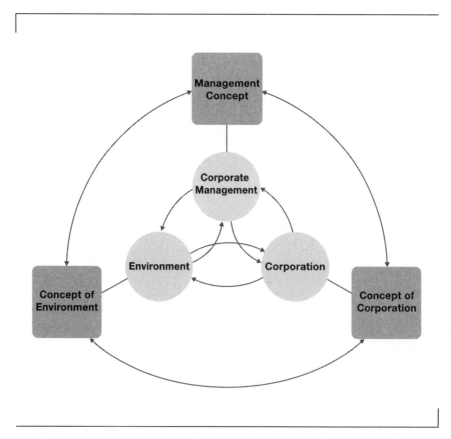

Figure 49: The three-concept system of corporate policy

the entirety of all basic decisions which are to stipulate, over the longer term, the baselines of everything that is going to happen in a company in the future.

In this book, these *fundamental* stipulations, and what they refer to, have been captured and defined as Master Controls in the three concepts of corporate policy: in the Concept of Corporation, the Concept of Environment, and the Management Concept – as indicated in the navigation chart guiding through the book.

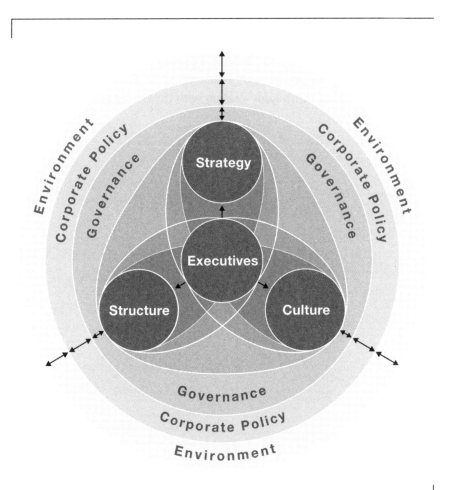

Figure 50: The General Management Model

The Master Controls derive their system-wide effectiveness from the sub-systems of my general management system – strategy, culture, and culture – and the actions of executives guided by them. These are the subjects dealt with in the following volumes of the series *Management: Mastering Complexity.*

Master Controls are translated into performance and results if the right strategy, structure, and culture are implemented. They also help to master complexity in a dynamic system ecology of the global society – that is to say, by its institutions, be they located in business or other sectors of society.

Strategy, structure, culture, and executives are the topics of the remaining four volumes of the series *Management: Mastering Complexity*. Compelling as the potential of the Master Controls may seem for triggering self-organization, the professional manager in the age of complexity will not be able to avoid thoroughly dealing with these four aspects.

Appendix

The Malik Management System
And Its Users

The first impulses for the development of my management system go back as far as the 1970s, when both the *System-Oriented Management Theory* and the *St. Gallen Management Model* were created under the guidance of my former academic mentor and superior, Prof. Dr. Hans Ulrich, and my friend and colleague Prof. Dr. Walter Krieg. There were even earlier origins in General Cybernetics, strongly influenced by my first contacts with its main creators, above all Heinz von Foerster, Francesco Varela, Gordon Pask, Hermann Haken, Gotthardt Günther, Stafford Beer, and Frederic Vester, the strategy pioneer Aloys Gälweiler, the evolutionary theoretician and biologist Rupert Riedl, and the art historian Ernst Gombrich. Other major influences were my encounters with Karl R. Popper, Friedrich von Hayek, Hans Albert, Cesare Marchetti at the legendary Alpach University Weeks and, above all, with Peter F. Drucker .

With my habilitation treatise, the title of which translates as "Strategy for the Management of Complex Systems"[123], I developed my own theoretical concept, based on which an open, networked, dynamic system of cybernetic principles emerged through an ongoing pursuit of both theory and practice – the *Malik Management System*. As such, it refers to wholistic management in all three meanings of the word:

1. Management as a societal function,
2. Management in the sense of institutional organs, and
3. Management in the sense of what managers do.

---

123 Malik, Fredmund, *Strategie des Managements komplexer Systeme*, Berne/Stuttgart/Vienna, 1984, 9th edition 2006.

Designations and Identities

The official and probably clearest name for my overall system is *Malik Management System*. It corresponds to *Malik Management*, the name of the organization that I founded and whose purpose is to develop, disseminate and apply my management system.

When studying and describing complex systems, one does not know at first what the outcome will be. In their early stages the systems usually carry working titles, and it often takes a while until they are given their final names or brands. This is what happened with my overall system and its subsystems as well. There is a host of different names for them, for the most part improvised during different development stages, projects, publications, seminars, programs and the like, often even by readers and customers. Examples include *The Integrated Management System, Right and Good Management, Managerial Effectiveness, Effective Management, The General Management Model, The Standard Model, the "Management Wheel", The Malik Model, Malik on Management,* and several others.

Experienced users are aware that the actual identity of systems is never defined by their names but always by the systems themselves, their contents and versions. From the very beginning I have tried to make this transparent in my publications for reasons of accuracy and trustworthiness, in so far as straightforward descriptions were possible at all.

History of Development

It has been over 30 years since I started developing my Management System, and I have been dedicating all my time and resources to it ever since. The extraordinary turning point from the industrial era to the era of complexity was clearly in sight back then, but it was equally clear that the general awareness in both society and the market of the resulting complexity-driven problems and opportunities would be a long time in coming.

Hence, securing the elaborate research and development work in my company required much persistence and it has been a difficult balancing act over all these years. From the very start we had to meet the requirements of our customers, while at the same time striving to develop a General Management System independent of time, culture, industry, and company function. On the one hand, we needed to address the tasks, questions, and issues that were entering into society's awareness at any given point; on the other hand, we had to think and work ahead as far and as comprehensively as was possible.

The time is right now for the more sophisticated development of the cybernetic backgrounds of the overall concept, which were the first to be developed as they constitute the basic prerequisites for my management system's ability to function. The technical conditions for their practical application were created just recently; by now there is a sufficient number of practitioners who have gathered enough experience with complexity to develop an interest in it.

Thus, after several decades my strategy and policy of dedicating all my resources to the requirements of management in the era of complexity – which was a rather daring step back then – has finally been confirmed.

Applications and Effects

The *Malik Management System* has been designed for the life situation of man in the hybrid system world of the age of complexity. Such systems for management and self-management need to become the new civilizing and cultural techniques which have become necessary in this still-young world. Without them, existing and potential resources can neither be recognized nor transformed into results. The latter requires the kind of information and knowledge which, in the *Malik Management System*, I have organized as navigation systems, models, sets of rules and tools.

While our world is complex, and we face numerous highly complex issues, it does not follow that the solutions need to be complicated, too. On the contrary – they can be very simple, provided they contain the potential for unfolding the necessary complexity. The fact that the *Malik Management System* meets these requirements is owed to decades of persistence and focus.

Anyone will understand that there is information which, while being brief, clear, and simple, triggers exactly the kind of actions within a system that it requires at the time. One example is the fire siren: it mobilizes all the forces required for safety because everyone can hear it, everyone knows what the alarm means and what to do when it sounds. Thanks to its modular structure, my management system meets this requirement of providing that kind of relatively simple but highly effective signal-effect information, which will support and maintain a system, as well as configure, activate and vitalize it as necessary.

The modules of the *Malik Management System* have been designed for maximum effectiveness, efficiency, and viability, based on the forces of the information-driven coherences that typically exist in systems. As such, they can be *combined, configured,* and *applied* without limits. Depending on the configuration and combination, it is a management system for entire organizations, their subsystems and for the self-management of the individual, both including their environments.

Hence, for any conceivable purpose, for any size and kind of organization in any development phase, for any area of activity and for any order of magnitude, the *Malik Management System* provides a system-logical basis that is capable of evolving. It is suitable for both nature and mind, and is certain to help focus on the essential. It is the evolutionable "operating system" for complex institutions.

The *Malik Management System* grows with an organization or person. It interacts with them. It ensures that they both keep developing in a mutual evolutionary process. The interface between them is the human brain and mind.

Autonomy for Management and Managers

From the *Malik Management System,* every person and every organization can configure their *"Our/My Own Management System"*, provided they observe certain rules; just like it is possible to configure one's own computer according to one's individual requirements. This is crucial because managers in the age of complexity need a degree of intellectual autonomy that they can only achieve and maintain, without major time losses, by resorting to general management systems that are organized to the last detail – systems that are generally valid but adjustable to their individual requirements.

Hence, the challenge in creating my management system was to provide a basis for management that does not conform to a certain period of time, a region, or even a fashion, but only to those principles that are generally and permanently valid. Just as technicians create systems that obey the natural laws of physics, I had to create a system that obeyed the natural laws of information, communication, systems, and complexity. The key foundation for that is the science of cybernetics, the laws of which govern the nature of complex systems.

Consequently, the systemic structure of the *Malik Management System* is based on applied cybernetics; and the system itself *is* applied cybernetics. It follows the cybernetic principle to *design a system in such a way that the greatest possible number of applications can arise from the smallest possible number of modules*. This principle renders the user autonomous. It depends on him, and him alone, to what degree he will mentally conquer such a system. He will not be dependent on the developer.

Modularity and Interfaces

The *Malik Management System* has a *modular* structure. Its modules are compatible with each other and with the user's world and can be combined in any way. Their interfaces are:

1. All the cybernetic management models that provide the necessary insight in crucial active elements and connections.
2. All the tools required for generating and applying the required information.
3. All the methods required for solving tasks.
4. All the concepts helping to reflect on things.
5. All the rules of application by which every system can be brought to maximum performance.

Users can apply either the whole *Malik Management System* or its modules in different forms and across different languages. They are available in books, numerous essays and articles, training courses, entire training programs, DVDs, CDs, MP3 format files, e-management learning programs, and, as far as sensible and system-supported, also as digital tools and software.

Above all, however, the *Malik Management System* must be a program for the brain, because a good executive must be able to identify current themes and respond to them faster than they could be fed into and processed by a computer. As far as is sensible and helpful, however, modules can be randomly combined and configured by information-technological tools, due to their evolutionary structure. Moreover, when it comes to transferring knowledge and information and complex problem solutions from one brain to another, there are experts available in my organization whom I have trained myself.

A Management System for Self-Thinkers

Anyone working on organizational solutions for maximum effectiveness and efficiency is essentially working on becoming superfluous. Accordingly, one of the major goals of my management system is to render managers independent of management consultants. In the 20th century there were certainly good reasons why management consultants played a major role, as the discipline of management was only just emerging.

In the 21th century and beyond, however, the world needs executives who are aware why in management there can be no simple, fail-safe formula for success, and why no one can spare them from making their own observations and deliberations. They will have to master their profession comprehensively enough to know that, particularly under complex circumstances, it is much more important to ask the *right questions* than to have the right answers. The reason is that under complex conditions, it is impossible in many respects to know for sure whether one's answers are correct. This is exactly what the *Malik Management System* has been designed for, in order to prevent any potential malfunctions or aberrations.

Potential for Success Increasing With Qualification

One of the typical effects of the development history of my management system was that, for a long time, only the simplest and most plausible-seeming models would meet with broad acceptance and even become standard. The much more sophisticated cybernetic functional backgrounds preceding them have largely remained unknown to this date.

Anyone interested in making full use of my management system should know, however, that his autonomy will grow along with his command of not only the simplest functions but also the deeper grounding. Everything required for that is available to him – the management system in everyday user language, the cybernetic models, and pure cybernetics itself. The latter, above all, will help him solve individual management or factual issues without making unnecessary deviations.

At the same time, users should know that the use of even one single principle from the entire management system can and will have enormous systemic effects. The manager's own effectiveness, however, is maximized by his ability to combine all the relevant contents of the system quickly and correctly; the more so as others can communicate and cooperate with him on this basis.

Self-Motivation for Self-Developers

A manager making use of the *Malik Management System*, and in particular developing his own solutions on this basis, also needs to know that he lives in a time when he is increasingly given more credit for what others can understand of him than for what he actually accomplishes.

For the most part, his motivation to shape and handle systems in the way they require by nature will not come from outside – he will have to find it in himself. After all, users and other parties concerned will naturally assess the performance and value of a system by what they can get out of it, irrespective of what and how much is actually in it. The developer, by contrast, most values the intricate backgrounds of this system because he knows that everything depends on them. Therefore, good developers will inevitably get much more credit for achievements they themselves do not value so much, while those that they are really proud of are often disregarded and hardly ever appreciated. That, however, should neither hurt nor discourage them: proper acknowledgment will come from the system itself, because it only really functions when people allow themselves to be guided by its "needs", that is to say, its inner laws and regularities.

Care versus Kudos

It is the fate of responsible executives and experts in the age of complexity that, to the majority of those around them, they can do things either the *right and good* way or the *popular and desired* way. Reconciling both is getting increasingly impossible. It will continue that way as long as common thinking and knowledge have not sufficiently adjusted to the requirements of the age of complexity.

More than ever, the true professionals and pioneers will face problems created by self- or media-acclaimed gurus, dilettantes and dazzlers in pursuit of fast but short-lived successes, who attract not only plenty of attention but, lamentably, also a host of misconceptions difficult to dispel. In the age of complexity, such superficiality will become more than dangerous. We therefore need a solid fact basis for management enabling people to distinguish the real experts from *gurus, spin doctors,* and *pseudo-enlightened* individuals. This is what I work for. This is what my management system stands for, this is what my motto *right and good management* is meant to express.

Hence, here is one final practical piece of advice to the self-thinkers and self-developers among my readers: the motto *easier said than done* may be true for many situations, but it does not apply for dealing with complex systems and cybernetics. Quite the opposite is true here: *easier done than said.* It is much easier and, above all, takes much less time to *show* what the matter is and to *do something about* it than to describe it.

Anyone working with the *Malik Management System* will find that it will help them solve many tasks quickly. They will, however, need a lot of time to describe their *own* developments to others in a comprehensive, correct, and comprehensible manner. For classical management practice, the latter is not really necessary anyway. It becomes relevant once people use my system to develop their own, intending to provide a reliable help to others.

In the age of complexity, more than ever before, managers and experts will be alone with their really great achievements. They will meet with less appreciation than ever, and often get no encouragement. They will also find that they are admired for trivial things while their true accomplishments are ignored. They will feel like Albert Einstein would have, if he had been celebrated for his ability to explain gravitation. The recognition they deserve for their successful brain work and system work will come from the systems themselves, which they shape, direct, and regulate based on solid foundations.

Authors and Acknowledgments

To my knowledge, the *Malik Management System* is currently the only comprehensive, wholistic, integrated general management system consistently based on cybernetics as a science of regulation, explicitly geared toward the coping with complexity, and designed specifically for the management of complex systems. The majority of the related concepts were developed by me. My greatest contribution, however, has been the development of the overall system itself. After all, the *Malik Management System* is ultimately owed to long-standing, close cooperation and friendships with the best minds of the areas of management, cybernetics, and management cybernetics, as well as system sciences. All rights for all modules have been reserved by me. They predominantly follow from the copyright; rights for other authors' developments have been contractually acquired.[124]

In my publications I also refer to numerous leading authors of management theory, in particular Peter F. Drucker, Hans Ulrich, Walter Krieg, my former colleagues at the St. Gallen University's Institute of Business Economics, Stafford Beer, and many others in other areas. My sincere thanks go to all authors and customers, all discussion partners and friends, and the people in my organization.

---

124 The work, including all its parts, is copyright-protected. Also subject to copyright protection are all modules, terms, models, depictions, etc., referred to here. Any exploitation, application, or use, etc. outside the narrow defines of the copyright is not permissible, without the prior written approval of the publishers, and is liable for prosecution That is true, in particular, for duplications, disseminations, reproductions , translations, micro-fiches, the storing and processing by electronic systems, as well as any form of commercial distribution.

About the Author

Hardly anyone has managed to do what Fredmund Malik has been doing for several decades: make the necessary concessions to traditional, everyday understanding and, at the same time, work for a new era. It has polarized managers into adversaries and advocates, as inevitably happens with pioneers.

After graduating from high school, with a focus on economics, and gathering several years of industry practice, Fredmund Malik studied economics, business administration and social sciences as well as the philosophy of logic and epistemology at the universities of Innsbruck and St. Gallen. In 1971 he wrote his master thesis on *Cybernetic Models and Management Concepts*. In 1975, he took his doctoral degree with his PhD-thesis on "System Methodology – Foundations of a Methodology for Exploring and Shaping Complex Sociotechnical Systems"; in 1978 he submitted his post doctoral thesis and received his Venia Legendi for corporate management theory. This thesis was entitled *Strategie des Managements komplexer Systeme* ["Strategy of the Management of Complex Systems"].

In 1977, Fredmund Malik became Managing Director of the Management Zentrum St. Gallen, from 1979 to 1984 he also was a member of the board of directors of the Institute for Business Administration at St. Gallen University, in charge of its management consulting. In 1984, he took over the Management Zentrum St. Gallen in a friendly buy-out and established what is today Malik Management. Since that day, he has been the chairman of the Board of Directors of MZ Holding AG and its subsidiaries, now with offices in St. Gallen, Zürich, Vienna, Berlin, London, Shanghai and Toronto, which employ some 250 consultants specially trained on his management systems.

Fredmund Malik owns several companies and holds seats in several Corporate Governance boards, and administrative, supervisory, and advisory (foundation) councils. As a management consultant and educator, he has been working for numerous renowned companies of all sizes, sectors, and industries in Switzerland and elsewhere, as well as with executives at all levels, for over 30 years. From 1978 to 2004 he also taught at the University of St. Gallen and he was a visiting lecturer at the University of Innsbruck from 1981 – 1982 and a visiting professor at the Vienna University of Economics and Business between 1992 and 1997.

Fredmund Malik is the author and publisher of the monthly management letter Malik on Management (M.o.M.); the list of his publications comprises over 300 items. As a columnist, Malik writes for several newspapers and magazines including *Trend, Cash, Basler Zeitung, Handelsblatt, Die Welt, Manager Magazin online, Süddeutsche Zeitung*, and *Junior Consult* (a magazine for students at St. Gallen University).

Fredmund Malik is married and has two children. His main interests are philosophy, in particular philosophy of science, as well as history with a special focus on the history of ideas and of art, spanning all epochs and cultures. He dedicates his leisure time to literature and music, sports, and his passion for mountaineering.

Malik Management
Geltenwilenstraße 18
9001 St. Gallen
Switzerland

Telephone: +41 (0) 71 274 34 00

info@malik-mzsg.ch
www.malik-mzsg.ch

Literature

Albert, Hans, *Freiheit und Ordnung*, Tübingen 1986
- *Traktat über kritische Vernunft*, Tübingen 1991
- *Traktat über rationale Praxis*, Tübingen 1978
Ashby, W. Ross, *An Introduction to Cybernetics*, London 1956, 5th edition 1970
- *Mechanisms of Intelligence: Ross Ashby's Writings on Cybernetics* / Edited by Roger Conant, Seaside/California 1981
- *Design for a Brain – The Origin of Adaptive Behaviour*, 3rd ed., London 1970

Barthlott, Wilhelm/Neinhuis, Christoph, "Purity of the sacred lotus or escape from contamination in biological surfaces", in: *Planta*, Ausgabe 202, 1997
Beer, Stafford, *Beyond Dispute, The Invention of Team Syntegrity*, Chichester 1994
- *Decision and Control*, London 1966, 2nd edition 1994
- *The Heart of Enterprise*, London 1979, 1994
- *Platform for Change*, London 1975
- *Brain of the Firm. The Managerial Cybernetics of Organization*, Chichester 1972, 1994
- "Towards the Cybernetic Factory", in: Foerster, Heinz von/Zopf, G.W., *Principles of Self-Organization*, Oxford 1962, wiederveröffentlicht in: Harnden, R./Leonhard A., *How many Grapes went into the Wine. Stafford Beer on the Art and Science of Holistic Management*, Chichester 1994
Bionik und Management, *Proceedings (DVD) des 1. Internationalen Bionik-Kongresses für das Top-Management, Der Quantensprung im Top-Management: Mit Kybernetik, Systemik und Bio-Logik die Zukunft sichern*, Malik Management, Interlaken, März 2006
Bionik und Management, *Proceedings (DVD) des 2. Internationalen Bionik-Kongresses für das Top-Management, Strategie der Evolution: Phantastische Lösungspotentiale für komplexe Probleme*, Malik Management, Interlaken, März 2007
Birg, Hedwig, *Die ausgefallene Generation. Was die Demographie über unsere Zukunft sagt*, München 2005
- *Die Weltbevölkerung. Dynamik und Gefahren*, September 2004
Blüchel, Kurt G., *Bionik. Wie wir die geheimen Baupläne der Natur nutzen können*, München 2005

Blüchel, Kurt G./Malik, Fredmund, *Faszination Bionik: Die Intelligenz der Schöpfung*, München 2006

Buzzell, Robert D./Gale, Bradley, T., *The PIMS Principles. Linking Strategy to Performance*, New York 1987

Clausewitz, Carl von, *Kriegstheorie und Kriegsgeschichte: Vom Kriege, Erstdruck*: Berlin 1832/34, Frankfurt am Main 1993, Neuauflage 2005

Clavell, James, *The Art of War Sun Tzu*, New York 1983

Dörner, Dietrich, *Logik des Misslingens. Strategisches Denken in komplexen Situationen*, Reinbek bei Hamburg 1989, 2004

Drucker, Peter F./Paschek, Peter (Hrsg.), *Kardinaltugenden effektiver Führung*, Frankfurt am Main 2004

Drucker, Peter F., *Management*, London 1973

– *Management Challenges for the 21st Century*, New York 1999

– "We need Middle-Economics", in: Krieg, Walter/Galler, Klaus/Stadelmann, Peter (Hrsg.), *Richtiges und gutes Management: vom System zur Praxis*, Festschrift für Fredmund Malik, Bern/Stuttgart/Wien 2004

Eggler, Andreas, *Diffusions- und Substitutionsprozesse – Struktur, Ablauf und ihre Bedeutung für die strategische Unternehmensführung*, Dissertation Universität St. Gallen 1991

Ferguson, Adam, *An Essay on the History of Civil Society*, London 1767

Foerster, Heinz von, *KybernEthik*, Berlin 1993

Foerster, Heinz von/Zopf, G.W., *Principles of Self-Organization*, Oxford 1962

Forrester, Jay, *Industrial Dynamics*, Cambridge Mass., 1969

Frankl, Viktor, *Der Mensch vor der Frage nach dem Sinn*, München 1979, 3. Auflage 1982

Gale, Bradley T., *Managing Customer Value. Creating Quality & Service That Customers Can See*, New York 1994

Gälweiler, Aloys, *Strategische Unternehmensführung*, Frankfurt/New York 1990, 3. Auflage 2005

Gigerenzer, Gerd, *Das Einmaleins der Skepsis. Über den richtigen Umgang mit Zahlen und Risiken*, Berlin 2002

Gomez, Peter/Malik, Fredmund/Oeller, Karl-Heinz, *Systemmethodik: Grundlagen einer Methodik zur Erforschung und Gestaltung kompexer soziotechnischer Systeme*, Band 1 u. 2, Bern/Stuttgart 1978

Gorn, Saul, "The Individual and Political Life of Information Systems", in: E. B. Heilprin et al. (Eds), Warrington Va 1965

Gross, Peter, *Die Multioptionsgesellschaft*, Frankfurt am Main 1994

– *Jenseits der Erlösung*, Bielefeld 2007

Grübler, Arnulf, *Technology and Global Change*, Cambridge 1998

Haken, Hermann, "Synergetik: Von der Laser-Metaphorik zum Selbstorganisations-konzept im Management", in: Krieg, Walter/Galler, Klaus/Stadelmann Peter (Hrsg.), *Richtiges und gutes Management: vom System zur Praxis*, Festschrift für Fredmund Malik, Bern/Stuttgart/Wien 2005
Harnden, Roger/Leonhard Allenna, *How many Grapes went into the Wine. Stafford Beer on the Art and Science of Holistic Management*, Chichester 1994
Hayek, Friedrich A. von, *Law, Legislation and Liberty*, Band 1-3, Chicago 1976
– *The Sensory Order. An Inquiry into the foundations of theoretical psychology*, London 1952
Heinsohn, Gunnar, *Söhne und Weltmacht*, Zürich 2006
– "Warum gibt es Märkte?", in: Krieg, Walter/Galler, Klaus/Stadelmann, Peter (Hrsg.), *Richtiges und gutes Management: vom System zur Praxis*, Festschrift für Fredmund Malik, Bern/Stuttgart/Wien 2004
Heinsohn, Gunnar/Steiger, Otto, *Eigentumsökonomik*, Marburg 2006
Hill, Bernd, *Erfinden mit der Natur. Funktionen und Strukturen biologischer Konst-ruktionen als Innovationspotentiale für die Technik*, Aachen 1998

Krämer, Walter, *So lügt man mit Statistik*, München 2000
– *Statistik verstehen. Eine Gebrauchsanweisung*, München 2001
Krieg, Walter; *Kybernetische Grundlagen der Unternehmensgestaltung*, Bern/Stutt-gart 1971
Krieg, Walter/Galler, Klaus/Stadelmann Peter (Hrsg.), *Richtiges und gutes Manage-ment: vom System zur Praxis*, Festschrift für Fredmund Malik, Bern/Stuttgart/Wien 2005

Lorenz, Konrad, *Die Rückseite des Spiegels. Versuch einer Naturgeschichte mensch-lichen Erkennens*, München/Zürich 1973
– *Das Wirkungsgefüge der Natur und das Schicksal des Menschen*, München/Zü-rich 1978

Malik, Constantin, *Anticipatory Legislation. How Crowd Psychology and Manage-rial Cybernetics Combine to Transform Legislative Action*, Dissertation Univer-sität Klagenfurt, 2006
Malik, Fredmund, *Führen Leisten Leben. Wirksames Management für eine neue Zeit*, Frankfurt/New York 2006
– *Management. Das A und O des Handwerks*, Band 1 der Reihe *Management: Komplexität meistern*, Frankfurt/New York 2007
– *Strategie des Managements komplexer Systeme – Ein Beitrag zur Management-Kybernetik evolutionärer Systeme*, Bern/Stuttgart 1984, 9. Auflage 2006
– *Die Neue Corporate Governance. Richtiges Top-Management – Wirksame Unter-nehmensaufsicht*, Frankfurt am Main 1997, 3. Auflage 2002

– *Systemmethodik. Grundlagen einer Methodik zur Erforschung und Gestaltung komplexer soziotechnischer Systeme*, Band 1 u. 2, gemeinsam mit Peter Gomez und Karl-Heinz Oeller, Bern/Stuttgart 1978

Marchetti, Cesare, "Fifty-Year Pulsations in Human Affairs", in: *Futures* 17(3): 376 – 388

– *Intelligence at Work, Life Cycles for Painters, Writers and Criminals, Conference on the Evolutionary Biology of Intelligence*, Poppi, Italien 1986

– *On Time and Crime*, Working Paper IIASA 85-84, IIASA Laxenburg

– "Modeling Innovation Diffusion", in: Henry, B. (Ed.), Forecasting Technological Innovation, Brüssel/Luxemburg 1991

– "Society as a Learning System, Discovery, Invention and Innovation Cycles Revisited", in: *Technological Forecasting and Social Change*, S. 18-267

Martin, Paul C., "Heulen und Zähneklappern. Historische Versuche, Manager zu sanktionieren", in: Krieg, Walter/Galler, Klaus/Stadelmann Peter (Hrsg.), *Richtiges und gutes Management: vom System zur Praxis*, Festschrift für Fredmund Malik, Bern/Stuttgart/Wien 2005

Maucher, Helmut, *Management-Brevier. Ein Leitfaden für unternehmerischen Erfolg*, Frankfurt/New York 2007

Mensch, Gerhard, *Das technologische Patt. Innovationen überwinden die Depression*, Frankfurt/New York 1975

– engl. Ausgabe: *Stalemate in Technology. Innovations Overcome the Depression*, 1979

McCulloch, Warren, *Embodiments of Mind*, Cambridge 1965

Modis, Theodore, *Predictions. Societies Telltale Signature Reveals The Past and Forecasts the Future*, New York 1992

Nachtigall, Werner, *Bionik. Grundlagen und Beispiele für Ingenieure und Naturwissenschaftler*, Berlin/Heidelberg 1998, 2002

Nakicenovich, Nebojsa/Grübler, Arnulf (Eds), *Diffusion of Technologies and Social Behavior*, Berlin/Heidelberg 1990

Pelzmann, Linda, "Im Sog der Masse. Die Marktmacht der Psychologie", in: *Die Bank*, 02/2006, S. 54-58

– "Massenpsychologie von Wirtschaftsprozessen", in: Pelzmann, Linda, *Wirtschaftspsychologie*, Wien/New York 2006, S. XVII-XLII

– "Wo Tauben sind, da fliegen Tauben zu. Das Gesetz der Wirkungsfortpflanzung", in: *Malik on Management*, 13. Jahrgang, 2005, 164-175

Pelzmann, Linda/Malik, Constantin/Miklautz Michaela, "The Critical Mass of Preferences for Customization", in: Blecker, Th./ Friedrich G., (Eds), *Mass Customization: Concepts, Tools, Realization*, Berlin 2005

Pelzmann, Linda/Hudnik, Urska/Miklautz, Michaela, "Reasoning or reacting to others? How consumers use the rationality of other consumers", in: *Brain Research Bulletin*, 67 (5), 2004, S. 341-442

Pengg, Hermann, *Marktchancen erkennen. Erfolgreiche Marktprognosen mit Hilfe der S-Kurven-Methode*, Bern 2003

PIMS-Letters:
- Chussil Mark/Roberts, Keith, *The meaning and value of customer value*, London 2007
- Stöger, R./Mispagel, J./Herse, R., *Richtige Qualität zum richtigen Preis*, St. Gallen 2006

Pohl, Friedrich-Wilhelm, *Die Geschichte der Navigation*, Hamburg 2004

Popper, Karl R., "Why are the Calculi of Logic and Arithmetic applicable to Reality?", in: *Conjectures and Refutations. The Growth of Scientific Knowledge*, London 1963
- *Objective Knowledge, An Evolutionary Approach*, Oxford 1972
- *Eine Welt der Propensitäten*, Tübingen 1995

Prechter, Robert, Jr., *The Wave Principle of Human Social Behavior and the New Science of Socionomics*, 1999
- *Pioneering Studies in Socionomics*, 2003

Probst, Gilbert/Raisch, Sebastian, "Das Unternehmen im Gleichgewicht", in: Krieg, Walter/Galler, Klaus/Stadelmann, Peter (Hrsg.), *Richtiges und gutes Management: vom System zur Praxis*, Festschrift für Fredmund Malik, Bern/Stuttgart/Wien 2004

Pruckner, Maria, *Die Komplexitätsfalle. Wie sich Komplexität auf den Menschen auswirkt – vom Informationsmangel bis zum Zusammenbruch*, Norderstedt 2005

Rechenberg, Ingo, *Evolutionsstrategie '94*, Band 1 der Reihe *Werkstatt Bionik und Evolutionstechnik*, Stuttgart 1994

Reither, Franz, *Komplexitätsmanagement: Denken und Handeln in komplexen Situationen*, München 1997

Riedl, Rupert, *Die Ordnung des Lebendigen, Systembedingungen der Evolution*, Hamburg/Berlin 1975
- *Die Strategie der Genesis, Naturgeschichte der realen Welt*, München/Zürich 1976
- *Strukturen der Komplexität. Eine Morphologie des Erkennens und Erklärens*, Berlin/Heidelberg 2000
- *Verlust der Morphologie*, Wien 2006

Roberts, Keith/Chussil, Mark, *The meaning and value of customer value*, Malik Management, PIMS-OnlineBlatt 2/2007

Rossmann, Torsten/Tropea, Cameron (Hrsg.), "Bionik. Aktuelle Forschungsergebnisse", in: *Natur – Ingenieur – und Geisteswissenschaft*, Berlin/Heidelberg 2004

Simon, Hermann, *Hidden Champions des 21. Jahrhunderts. Erfolgsstrategien der Weltmarktführer*, Frankfurt/New York 2007

Sloan, Alfred P., *My Years with General Motors*, New York 1964, 1999

Sobel, Dava/Andrews, William J. H., *Längengrad. Die wahre Geschichte eines einsa-*

men Genies, welches das größte wissenschaftliche Problem seiner Zeit löste, Berlin 1999, illustrierte Ausgabe

Steiger, Otto, "Eigentum und Recht und Freiheit", in: Krieg, Walter/Galler, Klaus/ Stadelmann, Peter (Hrsg.), *Richtiges und gutes Management: vom System zur Praxis,* Festschrift für Fredmund Malik, Bern/Stuttgart/Wien 2005

Sterman, J. D., *Business Dynamics, Systems Thinking and Modeling for a Complex World,* Boston 2000

Stöger, Roman/Mispagel, Jan/Herse, Ronald, *Kundennutzen: Richtige Qualität zum richtigen Preis,* Malik Management, OnlineBlatt 5/2005

Tolstoi, Leo, *Anna Karenina,* München 1997

Tuchman, Barbara, *Torheit der Regierenden. Von Troja bis Vietnam,* Frankfurt am Main 2001

Ulrich, Hans/Krieg, Walter, *Das St. Galler Management-Modell,* 1972; wiederveröffentlicht in: Ulrich, Hans, *Gesammelte Schriften,* Band 2, Bern/Stuttgart/ Wien 2001

Ulrich, Hans, *Unternehmungspolitik,* Bern/Stuttgart 1978

Ulrich, Peter, *Ethik in Wirtschaft und Gesellschaft,* Bern/Stuttgart 1996

Ulrich, Probst, *Self-Organization and Management of Social Systems,* Berlin/Heidelberg 1984

Varela, Franzisco, "Two Principles for Self-Organization", in: Ulrich/Probst, *Self-Organization and management of Social Systems,* Berlin/Heidelberg 1984

– "A Calculus for Self-Reference", in: *Intern. Journal of General Systems,* 2, 1975, No 1: S. 1-25

Venohr, Bernd, *Wachsen wie Würth. Das Geheimnis des Welterfolgs,* Frankfurt/New York 2006

Vester, Frederic, *Die Kunst vernetzt zu denken,* München 2007

Watzlawick, Paul/Beavin, Janet, H./Jackson, Don D., *Menschliche Kommunikation, Formen, Störungen, Paradoxien,* Bern 1969

Wiedeking, Wendelin, *Anders ist besser,* München 2006

Wiener, Norbert, *Cybernetics or control and communication in the animal and the machine,* Cambridge 1948

– *Ich und die Kybernetik. Der Lebensweg eines Genies,* Düsseldorf 1971

Zweig, Stefan, *Amerigo,* Stockholm 1944, Frankfurt am Main 1995

Index

performance 50, 64f., 69, 73, 81, 84, 108, 135, 143, 149, 151f., 154- 156, 162f., 167-173, 175-186, 190, 192, 196f., 199, 207, 214, 223, 225f., 228f., 230-233, 238, 246, 250, 256, 277, 283, 286, 288f., 291, 312, 318, 326, 333, 335

perspective 26, 34, 36, 38, 40f., 45, 59, 70, 75, 91, 111, 144, 148, 150, 175, 196f., 272, 275, 278, 283, 300, 313, 318f.

physics 34, 117, 266, 33

PIMS 150, 173, 176f., 214

PIMS research 149, 167, 171

policy 13f., 17-20, 28, 30, 37-55, 63, 65, 67, 69, 71-74, 82, 85, 88, 93-111, 113f., 123-125, 129, 132-134, 139, 145f., 151, 166, 169, 172, 175f., 180, 184, 189, 192, 197, 202, 204f., 211, 214, 216, 218f., 221, 224-227, 230f., 233f., 237-240, 243f., 250, 253-255, 261, 263, 266-269, 272f., 283f., 287f., 291, 294, 297, 300, 320f., 324f., 331

Popper, Carl 87, 90, 132, 208, 329

power 13, 30, 39, 54, 65f., 69-73, 76, 92f., 97, 104, 106, 111, 129, 131, 152- 154, 156, 164, 168, 185f., 192, 199, 207, 219, 260, 282, 286, 290, 297, 305, 307, 311, 322

Pragmatism 96f., 269

pride 135, 162f., 165, 186

principal agent problem 141

principles 17, 29, 40-43, 46, 48, 50f., 58, 63-66, 68-71, 81, 86f., 96-100, 102, 104, 107f., 141f., 149, 166, 189f., 201, 215, 217, 220, 222, 224-226, 228-231, 234, 237f., 244, 246, 255, 261, 277, 290, 296f., 300, 303, 310, 311f., 315, 319f., 322f., 329, 333

private banks 85

productivity 173, 178, 192, 206

productivity of knowledge 173, 175, 219, 276

professionalism 108, 228f., 235, 243, 260, 265

profit 38, 42, 46, 50, 93, 109, 143, 146-148, 157f., 169, 174f., 179, 184, 192, 214, 232, 241, 275f.

profit maximization 157f., 169, 262

profit minimum 175

profitability 135, 143, 167, 170, 174-176, 178, 180, 183f., 197, 289

property economics 205

Pruckner, Maria 14, 81, 210, 256, 310

Psycho-logic 262-264

purpose 20, 22, 29f., 34, 45f., 50, 55f., 58f., 63, 68, 72, 82, 95f., 99, 107-110, 113f., 117, 119, 122-124, 127, 132, 139f., 143-147, 149-153, 156-160, 163, 166-168, 170, 172, 185f., 190, 192, 197, 201f., 206, 213, 224, 230, 232, 236f., 267, 274, 280, 285, 288, 311, 315, 321, 232, 330, 332

real economy 45, 153, 274

real-time control 113, 121, 292

real-time navigator 112

Rechenberg, Ingo 87

recursion principle 131

recursive 125, 129, 131, 184, 195f., 225, 249

reductionism 90, 131

Redundancy 19f., 197, 270

regulation 24, 27, 39-41, 43, 46, 58, 60, 65-68, 70, 74, 76f., 83, 86, 92, 95f., 100, 102, 105-107, 110, 115-117, 121, 146, 149, 166, 176, 185, 198, 221, 241, 243, 285, 319, 321, 337

relations 18-20, 118, 125f., 128, 131, 191, 278, 293, 296, 307

relevance 42, 143, 177, 186, 189, 191, 239, 272, 279, 313

religion 75, 98, 130

subject knowledge 141
subject level 41-43, 69, 74, 107, 159
Sun Tzu 65, 99
Swiss tax system 83
Switzerland 83, 339
symphony orchestra 84, 228
synergy 91, 193
Syntegration 91, 104, 166, 178, 193 f.,
    200, 320
synthesizer 112
system architect 43, 128, 132
system level 42, 107, 140, 159, 178,
    230, 243, 310, 312
system model 20, 124, 215 f., 320
systems policy 13, 37 f., 40, 42 f., 65,
    71, 73, 93, 108, 139, 146, 254, 268,
    294
system regulation 40 f., 43, 100
system rule 41, 311
system sciences 162, 337
system theory 43, 69, 266, 314
systematic 28 f., 71, 76, 83, 98, 193,
    226, 229, 235, 238, 243, 246, 298
systemic evolution 83
systemic wholeness 118, 130
system-immanent 44, 46, 65, 256
systems governance 36

takeover, hostile 149, 489
taking advantage of complexity 28, 30
taxes 25, 82 f., 157, 218
Team Syntegrity theory 104
technomorph 79
Ten Commandments 104
the information on how it functions 65
thinking 14, 17, 19, 22-24, 29, 34,
    36 f., 39, 64, 67 f., 74, 76, 78-80, 82,
    91, 99, 101, 104, 111, 114-116,
    122, 126, 130, 132, 134, 140, 144,
    161, 174, 189 f., 192, 201-204, 211,
    215, 231, 237, 241, 256, 260, 269,
    272, 276-279, 285, 301, 308, 313,
    315, 320 f., 336

top management 15, 33, 35, 38, 43, 48,
    52 f., 57, 60, 64, 68, 96, 113, 119,
    150-152, 161, 167, 183, 187-189,
    193, 217, 238, 241, 244, 253-255,
    259-261, 263-265, 267-269, 272,
    274-281, 283, 286 f., 289-291,
    295 f., 310
top management team 94, 120, 295-
    297
traffic circle 91-93
transformation 22, 33, 48, 145 f., 148,
    230, 256
trend research 192, 209
trivial machines 29
trust 231, 275, 297, 301, 304, 307,
    309, 320, 330
turnover rate 172
type of question 91

Ulrich, Hans 22, 39, 94 f., 221, 324,
    329, 337
universal validity 105
unlimited organizational expansion 81,
    234
unmanageable systems 77
USA 199, 206 f., 213

value for the customer 150
value-based theories 206
variety 29, 58, 73, 76, 83 f., 127 f., 152,
    156, 185, 199, 223, 239, 254, 271 f.
Vester, Frederic 117, 176, 191, 216,
    329
viability 23, 39, 55, 73, 116, 169, 171,
    176, 332
Viable System Model (VSM) 124, 215,
    320
Vietnam 72
vision 159, 307 f.

Wall Street scandals 141
warfare 99
weaknesses 161, 206 f., 231, 277, 314